A PROFESSION AT A CROSSROAD

AHMED RIAHI-BELKAOUI

Preface

The accounting profession and discipline face fundamental problems that need to be addressed and corrected to avert potential crises. These problems relate to the following:

- New developments that shape a new conflictual order in the accounting environment failure to properly situate itself as a profession, its heavy reliance on credentialism, its role in fragmentation of knowledge and services in the certified public accounting (CPA) firm, its tenuous positions in court, and its failure to be adequately regulated
- The increase of fraudulent cases in accounting and auditing that shake the credibility of the profession and the field as guarantors of the integrity of the financial reporting system
- The decline of the work process in accounting as a result of a phenomena of proletarianization, alienation, and de-skilling
- Problems in the organizational climate of a CPA firms, mainly with regard to job dissatisfaction and high turnover
- Problems in the production of knowledge in accounting because of a contamination of the research process at the hands of academics and distorted transformation of the accounting knowledge at the hands of the profession

Accordingly, the book consists of the following six chapters:
1. The Context of the Contemporary Accounting Profession
2. The Accounting Profession at a Crossroad
3. Fraud in the Accounting Environment
4. The Decline of the Work Process in Accounting
5. The Organizational Climate in Accounting Firms
6. The Problematics of the Production of Knowledge in Accounting

The book will be of interest to practicing accountants, academics, businessmen, students, legislators, social scientists, and others interested in averting the coming crisis in accounting and in correcting some of the problems experienced by the profession and the discipline.

A special note of appreciation is extended to my research assistant Elizabeth Alvarez for her cheerful and intelligent assistance.

THE CONTEXT OF THE CONTEMPORARY CONTEMPORARY ACCOUNTING PROFESSION
1

Standard setting, the practice of the auditing and accounting craft and accounting research, in order to be successful needs to be congruent with the underlying environmental conditions. If the environmental conditions change, these professional activities characterizing the field of accounting need to adapt and accept these new conditions as part of their fundamental assumptions. This chapter argues that the environmental conditions have changed as the result of the emergence of four new structural variables: (1) the technical and ideological proletarianization of accountants in public and private practices, (2) the manufactured consciousness of users of accounting information, (3) the institutional capitalism of the new governing class, and (4) the academic accountants as part of a flawed universal class.

TECHNICAL AND IDEOLOGICAL PROLETARIANIZATION OF ACCOUNTANTS

Accountants as professional employees in accounting or nonaccounting organizations are considered members of a new class of salaried professionals. They are identified by Daniel Bell (1973) and other "post-industrial" theorists as the major protagonists of the coming post-industrial society, the "new working class" or "professional-managerial class" as identified by Marxist theorists as a major new actor in contemporary capitalism.[1-3] A Marxist definition includes in this professional-managerial class "salaried mental workers who do not own the means of production and whose major function in the social division of labor may be described broadly as the reproduction of capitalists culture and capitalist class relations."[4] As a profession, there has also been a tremendous growth of accountants in the labor force from 22,916 in 1900 (0.08% of the labor force) to 1,047,000 in 1980 (1.08% of the labor force), a percentage increase from 1900-80 of 4,468.86%.[5] It had the highest increase of salaries in the class of professionals, including physicians (224.01%), lawyers (408.27%), architects (750.58%), dentists (371.94%), engineers (3,717.26%), and natural scientists (2,399.17%). These data are taken from the Bureau of Labor

Statistics and the Bureau of the Census. The Bureau of Labor Statistics reports that in 1986 there were 1.3 million accountants and auditors, up from 1.1 million in 1983.[6]

This growth of accountants followed the need for more advanced accounting technologies to deal with the requirements of a more sophisticated production apparatus. The use of these advanced technologies required accountants to pool their efforts in small and/or large certified public accounting (CPA) firms, leading to a decline in opportunities for self-employment in the field and to their dependence on the financial and institutional resources of corporations and the state, a phenomenon also observed for other types of salaried professionals.[7]

The accountants, like other salaried professionals constrained to abandon the idea of an independent economic position, joined accounting and nonaccounting firms, small and large, in corporate or state bureaucracies, and in the process became the subject to the authority and control of heteronomous management, and a slow degradation of work and reward. The starting salaries of accounting undergraduates joining the big CPA firms have declined in real terms in the 1980s, hovering in 1987 around $22,000. What really resulted from these developments is a *proletarianization of accountants*, working according to a division of labor conceived and monitored by management, according to procedural rules and repertories created by administrative processes and/or fiat. Although they maintain exclusive control over their own knowledge base, which gives them some negotiating powers, their contractual employment subjects them to a total subordination to a heteronomous management who had appropriated the power over the total labor process, including those of accountants.

With the proletarianization of accountants came a shift of control toward employers or management and a loss of the creative freedom they used to enjoy as self-employed. Thus the change in accounting technology forced a change in the structure of the accounting labor process and put the accountants in a new form of "proletarian class," subordinated, as the craftsmen before them, to the structure of capitalist management. In the process, as theorized by Marx, they lost control of both the *means* and *ends* of labor, a phenomenon labeled *technical proletarianization*.[8,9] The change has been speeded up and made easier by the higher degree of specialization and fragmentation generally imposed on accounting works, a process of *"de-skilling*," that is, of rationalizing previously professional tasks into a number of completely routine functions that require little training. An American Institute of Certified Public Accountants task force developed a list of 41 activities that describe the six general work categories performed by CPAs in public accounting practice: engagement management and administration, auditing, tax practice, management advisory services, other professional services, and office and firm administration. A big challenge facing accounting firms over the coming decade will be the need for even more *specialization* in auditing, tax practice, and consulting.

In addition to technical proletarianization, the emergence of the new working class led also to an *ideological proletarianization*, which refers to the appropriation of control by management over the goals and social purposes to which work is put.[10] The degree of ideological proletarianization is more pronounced in accounting, given the general inability of accountants to shape or control broad organizational policy and the specific goals and purposes of their work, unless they are part of the managerial strata. Accountants, bound by the specialized tasks, have lost control of the nature of the total product and may be indifferent to the outcome of the activities they were involved in. It is this loss of vision of the total product, its use and disposition, that allows the direct management of labor (i.e., the technical proletarianization). Therefore, technical and ideological proletarianization feed on each other in the case of accountants as salaried professionals and members of the new proletarian class. The separation between the old and the new proletarian class is made by drawing a distinction between labor necessary for production of commodities and labor necessary for the reproduction of capitalist social relations,[11] or a distinction between productive and nonproductive labor.[12]

The technical proletarianization of the accountant will lead next to a state in which the accountant could also lose the knowledge base as management and clients restructure the specification of the product and management restructures the organization of work. The growth of Management Advisory Services (MAS) activities, the increased specialization in the profession, the emerging conflict between professionalism and commercialism in accounting, and the call for non-CPA associate membership for non-CPAs serving on the professional skills of CPA firms are a good example.[13] Deprived of their beliefs in their capacity to organize their own work, the accountants could gradually lose the negotiating and other counterveiling power they used to have vis-à-vis management.

The proletarianization reduces the accountant to a mere technician of functionaries, separate from the major social, moral, and technological issues of the profession as he or she becomes aware of the nature and disposition of the total product. The end and social use of the accountant's labor is institutionally channeled with no links made to his or her interest as a professional and to the interest of the clients. The Report of the National Commission on Fraudulent Financial Reporting noticed a breakdown in the financial reporting system and revealed that fraudulent financial reporting usually occurs as the result of certain environmental, institutional, or individual forces and opportunities. These forces and opportunities and the ensuing pressures encourage some people to engage in financial reporting fraud.[14] Accountants faithfully serve organizational interests, sometimes at the expense of professional interests when the interests of clients are sacrificed. The managing partner of the Grant Thronton accounting firm, who had a crucial role in the fraud at E.S.M. Government Securities, Inc., gave this account of the same conflict:

I often wondered what I would do if somebody walked in and said, "Look what I've found." But it never happened. I gave them (his team of auditors) the same baloney answer that I had been given back in '78. It never dawned on them that it just didn't make sense.[15]

They do so because that is the new reality of power and expected behavior in accounting and nonaccounting organizations.

This practice may have led to the decrease in the number and quality of people entering accounting programs. The accounting profession is viewed as lacking "glamour." Survey results suggest that accountants come from poorer socioeconomic backgrounds than attorneys and physicians.[16] The director of personnel at one of the Big Eight explains: "Part of it is that a number of people find investment banking sexier, more exciting. You can make a big buck a lot quicker."[17] The lack of glamour, a direct result of the ideological and technical proletarianization, is leading the profession to offer high entry-level salaries. Late in 1987 Price Waterhouse boosted entry-level pay for top accounting graduates from 20% to 35% but eliminated overtime pay, which has long been a tradition for starting accountants, particularly during the busy tax season. The boost isn't as big as it seems and is expected to cost Price's partners $15,000 a year.[18] The chairman and senior partner of Price Waterhouse, at the time, rationalized the move as follows:

Even those of us who supported the move aren't happy about taking money out of our own pockets. . . . But we have a trusteeship to hand to the next generation running this firm a better share so that they make a longer term commitment to public accounting.[19]

For now, in answer to the technical and ideological proletarianization, the accountant, as well as other members of the new working class, may respond by either *ideological desensitization*, a denial or separation of the self from the ideological control of the job, disclaiming both interest and responsibility for the social issues to which their work is put, or *ideological cooperation*, a redefinition of one's goal to make them consistent with institutional imperatives.[20] In either case, ideological desensitization or ideological cooperation, there is a high likelihood of alienation of the accountant from his work and conditions, as evidenced by the high level of turnover. About 85% of the accounting graduates who join big CPA firms will leave them within ten years for positions in government, industry, education, or smaller CPA firms.[21] Benke and Rhode (1984) estimate the replacement cost of each entry-level staff accountant to exceed $20,000; this means that for one large CPA firm with a turnover of

10,000 employees over a recent ten-year period[22] replacement costs would run about $200,000,000. Other studies report an increase in the level of turnover.[23,23] Variables that explain this high turnover were found to be (a) the work environment in the audit department, (b) the co-workers and uncompensated overtime (in the tax department), and (c) professional challenge in the management services department.[25]

The situation is serious, as alienation in the work domain has a fourfold aspect: Man is alienated from the object he produces, from the process of production, from himself, and from the community of his fellows. As Marx stated:

The object produced by labor, its product, now stands opposed to it as an alien being, as a power independent of the producer. . . . The more the worker extends himself in work the more powerful becomes the world of objects which he creates in face of himself, the poorer he becomes in his inner life, and the less he belongs to himself. . . .

However, alienation appears not merely in the result but also in the process of production, within productive activity itself. . . . If the product of labor is alienation, production itself must be active alienation. . . . The alienation of the object of labor merely summarizes the alienation in the work activity itself.[26]

In their alienated condition the whole mind-set of accountants, their consciousness, is, to a large extent, only the reflection of the conditions in which they find themselves and of the position in the process of production in which they are variously placed. This situation is particularly serious for female accountants. The percentage of female accounting graduates with bachelor's and master's degrees has increased from 28% in 1976-77 to 49% in 1985-86. Yet they believe that they don't have the same chance for promotion as men[27] and they don't earn as much.[28]

INSTITUTIONAL CAPITALISM AND CLASSWIDE RATIONALITY

The social organization of the corporate community is composed of enduring formal and informal networks among large corporations, senior managers and directors of these companies, and the associations that represent them to the public. The policies espoused by business are the product of this social organization. Although the results are not conclusive, there is still the generally accepted notion that the corporate community is socially unified, cognizant of its classwide interests, and politically active. It is characterized by a socially cohesive national upper class, chiefly composed of corporate executives, primary owners, and their descendants that constitute "the governing class of America."[29] The same conclusion is drawn for Britain with the argument that

elite pluralism does not. . . . prevent elites in capitalist society from constituting a dominant economic class, possessed of a high degree of cohesion and solidarity, with common interests and common purposes which far transcend their specific differences and disagreements.[30]

This governing class is composed of

those who own and those who control capital on a larger scale: whether top business executives or renters makes no difference in this context. Whatever divergences of interests there may be among them on this score and others, latent as well as manifest, they have a common stake in one overriding cause: to keep the working rule of the society capitalist.[31]

From this common cause stemmed the need for the governing class to have common background and patterns of socialization, generally articulated in a new class awareness.[32] This new class entered the political arena with an unusual force and coherence, ensuring the success of the likes of Ronald Reagan and Margaret Thatcher and influencing their policies.[33] This situation precipitated the shift from "managerial capitalism" to "institutional capitalism." With managerial capitalism replacing family capitalism, managers and professionals management found themselves in charge. Institutional capitalism, spurred by the rise of the new governing class, emerged to give to corporations a new power and class orientation. As stated by Useem:

Company management is now less than fully in charge, classwide issues intrude into company decisions; and competition is less pitched. Management decisions to underwrite political candidates, devote company resources to charitable causes, give advertising space to matters of public movement, and assume more socially responsible attitudes derive in part from company calculus, but also from a classwide calculus.[34]

A *classwide rationality*, replacing the former assumption of *corporate rationality*, assumes that the corporate elite is largely capable of identifying and promoting its common political objectives. The decisive political significance of the governing class is pointed out in Miliband's Marxist-informed study of class politics (1969) and rejected by Bell's non-Marxist essay on the breakup of family capitalism (1961).

This classwide principle, replacing both the *upper-class principle* and its successor, the corporate principle, and asserting that membership in the corporate elite is primarily determined in a set of interrelated networks transecting virtually all corporations, is also present in the accounting firms. Although corporate rationality still characterizes much of the internal organization of accounting firms, classwide rationality now characterizes its highest circles. Old school ties and kindred signs of proper breeding facilitate the access to the highest circles of the CPA firms. Following Marx's analysis in the *Eighteenth Brumaire* because both corporations and accounting firms live under economic conditions of existence that separate their mode of life, their interests, and their culture from those of other classes, and that put them in hostile opposition to the latter, they form a class.

The classwide principle espoused by the managerial elite of the CPA firms leads them to espouse the broader need of big business, and to oppose public regulation of their trade.[35-39] While tenuous assumptions underlying the calculations dictate careful interpretation, Arthur Andersen & Co., basing its computations on company- supplied data, estimated the annual cost of governmental regulation (1977 impact of six general regulatory agencies and programs on 48 large companies, all members of the Business Roundtable) at $2.6 billion. Throughout the report Arthur Andersen did not bother to provide an estimate of the benefits of regulation.[40-44] This view is not limited to the elite accounting firms: the political interests of the new corporate elite has been shown to transcend individual firms and to possess an internal cohesion that facilitates expression of those interests in the political process.[45] In fact, challenges to the position of accounting firms, whether from

Congress or from the Securities and Exchange Commission (SEC), have further consolidated the political capacities of the new corporate elite of accounting firms as they were able to weather the storms of various congressional investigations, the findings of special task forces, and SEC interventions. The classwide rationality of the high circles of the CPA firms, the social cohesion of its members, and their commitment to special interests have proven to be formidable weapons to any attempts to regulate them.

For example, in 1986 a bill introduced in the House of Representatives required auditors to report immediately to federal authorities any suspicions of fraud that they detected in auditing a company's books. The bill also called for the financial statements to be signed by the individual auditor, not just the firm. Because of the pressures put forth by the accounting profession the bill did not pass.

In addition to their professional role, accountants and other financial specialists are prominently represented in the managerial hierarchies of corporations.[46] In the United Kingdom the company directors with backgrounds in banking or accountancy outnumber those with any form of technical training.[47] An emphasis on financial as against alternative means of control, especially at the higher level, was introduced by the same accountants in key positions.[48] As a result of this trend Peter Armstrong argued that organized professions are competitively engaged in "collective mobility projects"[49] aimed at securing access to key positions of command in management hierarchies.[50] Their goal is seen as complete control by a competitive use of their techniques.

The means of competition is the monopolization of a body of knowledge and expertise which offers, or appears to offer, a solution to a key problem within the functions of capital. The extent that professions succeed by these means in attaining command positions, they are then in a position to sponsor characteristic means of controlling the rest of management hierarchy and, ultimately, the labor process itself (if indeed this was not the crisis which enabled them to achieve dominance in the first place).[51]

THE MANUFACTURED CONSCIOUSNESS OF USERS

Why don't the shareholders and users ask for more and better information? An explanation based on a notion of ideological domination would argue that the socioeconomic hierarchy has been relatively impervious to the information demand because management has managed to keep the shareholders "cajoled" at annual and other meetings. As with the case of any other commodity, the capitalist domination of information can be expressed in three propositions.[52]: (1) the class rule of management is established on the rule that accountants sell their labor and that management appropriates the information product they create; (2) such domination is maintained by the state's enforcement of contractual arrangements, protection of property rights, and maintenance of public order; (3) information tools at the disposition of management, such as annual reports and press releases, allow management to disseminate information useful for the preservation of its interests.[53] The three propositions amount to three forms of domination: market exploitation, legal coercion, and ideological domination. These forms of domination, although analytically separable, are empirically interdependent. They allow management to convey its beliefs to convey its beliefs to the users and, in the process, shape their consciousness about the firm. What the users acquire is a *manufactured consciousness* compatible with the expectations of management.[54] Sometimes, in the process leading to the "manufactured consciousness," management may substitute a "false consciousness" through a process researchers have identified with various labels, from income smoothing[55] to mere fraudulent financial reporting.[56]

In manufacturing the consciousness of users through the selective dissemination of information, management may contribute to class brainwashing and collective hypnosis,[57] or social conditioning.[58]

The concern is, therefore, that the user should be better informed, and thus a democratic norm is upheld. The manufacturing of consciousness is an obstacle to the expansion of data that is relevant to the users. The proper task is to announce the truth, expose the error, and identify all the constraints that can impede inquiring, comprehension, and efficient action. This is the proper task of *Ideologiekritik*.[59] A similar approach, labeled the ethical approach to financial accounting, rests on concepts of fairness, justice, equity, and truth.[60] Fairness, as fair, unbiased, and impartial presentation, implies that the preparers of accounting information have acted in good faith and used ethical business practices and sound accounting judgment.[61,62] After questioning the singular reliance on decision usefulness and its association with serious conceptual problems, Paul Williams presented arguments supporting a concept of fairness as a construct necessary to provide accounting with a lexicon complete enough to discuss accounting problems.[63] A user needs to be informed by normative standards that permit the evaluation of "what is." To be fully informed requires at least minimal competence, not only technical, but also moral and empirical. Failure in any of these competencies exposes the user to ideological dominations that are conveyed in the accounting reports by management, eager to maximize its own interests.

A user needs to be informed of the wide dissemination of accounting reports. The general rationale is that the accounting reports, when disseminated, can have many readers. A better strategy in line with the attribute of better informing the user is to expose the user to various accounting reports from various sources. That is, not only can an accounting report have many users, but also the act of examining accounting reports takes on a new character: from the activities of reading a single "sancrosanct" accounting report (i.e., the annual report) to that of comparing, cross-referencing, combining, and selecting among different reports and different information. The user then assumes a more active role than the relatively passive one of reading a single report, like the annual report. What may result is a shift of the user's expertise: an expansion of the breadth of knowledge that the user may acquire a better sense of what is useful and what is not, and an evaluation of the different preparers of accounting information. Subjecting the preparers to questioning, even if publicly, will be the major result of a better informed user. The level of accounting "informedness" is not necessarily limited to "natural" differences of cognitive ability and motivation, but its acquisition is both a consequence and a cause of the effective exercise of political power. The skills, generated by the information, are the essential part of the political arsenal by which *progressive users* may thwart the simple goals of managers to maximize their own wealth and redirect it to goals of maximizing social welfare.

ACADEMIC ACCOUNTANTS: A FLAWED UNIVERSAL CLASS

The proletariat as a universal class was best expressed by Marx and Engels' theory of the "universal class of the proletariat" in the *Holy Family* (1844), refuting Bruno Bauer's criticisms and doubts that the proletariat could develop consciousness that would be necessary to perform its function as a universal class.[64] Gouldner joined the critical group, arguing that the lowliest class never came to power and that throughout the world during the twentieth century, a new class of intellectuals is emerging, looking like the universal class defined by Hegel[65,66] but not representing a universal class.[67] *The new class is thus a flawed universal class.* Gouldner advanced two major propositions: first, the rise of a new class comprising humanistic intellectuals and technical intelligentsia, whose universalism is badly flawed; and second, the growing dominance of this class as a cultural bourgeoisie having monopoly over cultural capital and professionalism, from which it gains its power.

This new class includes both technical and human intellectuals. It forms one "speech community" that shares a "culture of critical discourse" (CCD). CCD is a concept derived from the different linguistic repertoires identified in sociolinguistics.[68] Its definition is similar. The culture of critical discourse is a historically evolved set of rules, a grammar of discourse, which (1) is conceived to justify its assertions, (2) whose mode of justification does not proceed by involving authorities and (3) prefers to elicit the *voluntary* consent of those addressed solely on the basis of arguments addressed. This is a culture of discourse in which there is nothing that speakers will, on principle, permanently refuse to discuss or make problematic; indeed, they are even willing to talk about the value of talk itself and its possible inferiority to silence or to practice. This grammar is the deep structure of the common ideology shared by the new class.

The shared ideology of the intellectuals and intelligentsia is thus an ideology about discourse. Apart from the underlying technical languages (or sociolects) spoken by specialized professions, intellectuals and intelligentsia are commonly committed to CCD. CCD is the latent but mobilizable infrastructure of modern intellectuals as well as their linguistic culture.

This new class is flawed because it is considered elitist and self-seeking, and uses its special knowledge to advance its own interests and power. Burnam saw the emergence of the new class as necessary to fulfill the basic functional requirements of modern society.[70] It does not represent the universal interest. The new class is a flawed universal class.

The new class is dominant because of its monopolistic access to cultural capital. Borrowing from Pierre Bourdeiu's theory of cultural reproduction,[71] Gouldner suggests that the new class uses cultural reproduction to maintain its interests and power just as economic reproduction is used to serve the interests of the holders of economic capital. Therefore, members of the new class will develop in the process of "cultural capital accumulation" to further their particular interests and the interests of those who share their culture of critical discourse.

The new class relies on credentials in its process of capitalizing culture to monitor the supply of specifically trained labor. "Culture is transmitted through education and socialization. Generally, it is known that those with more formal education have lifetime earnings in excess of those with less. This increased income reflects the capital value of increased education."[72] This gives the new class a privileged position in the labor market and the potential for a new dominant class position. The trend has started with the new class developing a high level of status consciousness to defend their privileges (e.g., academic freedom to publish, to review, to recruit).

Using Gouldner's analysis, the community of academic accountants will appear as part of the flawed universal class.

Whether the supply of accounting research by academic accountants is in response to the demand for value-free knowledge,[73] or to the demands of the markets for excuses,[74] academic accountants are also motivated by self-interest and the pressing need to publish.[75] They have gained a power associated with their monopoly over the cultural accounting capital. The research findings have given them consulting and policymaking powers to advance their own interests rather than the universal interest. For a type of CCD they have developed their linguistic repertoires, which differentiate them from other accounting speech communities.[76-80] As a new class academic accountants also rely on credentials as criteria for membership, including a Ph.D. degree and publications in the "right" journals. They acquire in the process position or authority that they may use to validate claims of knowledge. For some of the accounting paradigms some academic accountants may gain access to power and privilege, not because of the usefulness of their research, but because of the monopoly on some form of cultural capital (e.g., capital market research, positive accounting research). In fact, following Gouldner's analysis, the accounting intellectuals, teachers, academics, and researchers who are involved in one type of "cultural capital accumulation" (e.g., behavioral accounting research) further their own interests through promotion and higher salaries and the interests of all people who share their CCD. Konrad and Szelenyi go one step further by arguing that their knowledge is subordinated to those interests.[81] These same individuals give themselves a professional role. According to Gouldner, "professionalism is one of the public ideologies of the New Class. Professionalism is a tacit claim of the New Class to technical and moral superiority over the old class . . . professionalism tacitly de-authorized the old class. . . . [It] devalues the authority of the old class."[82] Through the new professional role the academic accountants claim their own cultural research domain and in the process receive a higher compensation from the market system for accepting the professional role.[83] "Intellectuals who are willing to behave like professionals are allowed to form a relatively autonomous stratum with particularistic interests. They can use the mechanisms of licensing and the professional associations to establish monopolies with their markets."[84,85] The fragmentation of the American Accounting Association (AAA) with separate "cultural" sections is one evidence of the phenomena.[86]

The same fragmentation orients the accounting researcher more toward immediate political actions (policy) than toward "theoretical" formulations of problems with general significance. This new close relation to the policymaker, whether it is the Financial Accounting Standards Board (FASB), the SEC, the AAA, or any other institution, makes the researcher a "bureaucratic" intellectual who exercises advisory and technical functions within a bureaucracy, as opposed to those intellectuals who elect to stay unattached to the bureaucracy.[87,88] The bureaucratic intellectual is reduced to being an "ideologue" because he subordinates or abandons the search for a universally comprehensive understanding of social, cultural, and physical reality in favor of an immediately instrumental arbitration of competing policies or courses of action.[89] Such a role is unfortunate if one subscribes to the prevailing assumption that a "particularization" of intellectual activity that links or constrains academic inquiry to specific social interests or needs leads to a fall from the "sacred" and a descent into the dishonorable realm of "ideology."[90-92]

In addition, from the role of teachers involved in creating formal knowledge, as opposed to its mere transmission,[93-96] the intellectuals moved to a role of "rationalization." As Shils suggests, in all modern societies (both liberal and totalitarian) "the trend of the present century" has been to increase pressures toward internal homogeneity owing to the "incorporation of intellectuals in organized societies.."[97] The intellectuals were asked to elaborate on the underlying "laws" of national and social organization relevant to the routine development and application of scientific knowledge to economic production and its social organization.[98-101] The call came mostly from the state to assist in reorienting the underlying mass population or in developing policies to ameliorate and prevent disturbances.[102-104] Consequently the legitimacy of contemporary universities is more and more dependent on their ability to adopt national economic and political goals as part of their traditional historical mission.[105] As a result, if not directly members of the upper class, intellectuals have typically labored under the patronage of ruling classes or in institutions controlled by them and inclined toward a new dominant class position.[106,107] The accounting intellectuals fit the described scenarios as they strive to provide the right excuses[108] and create a new, but flawed, universal class.

CONCLUSION

Using a structural perspective this chapter proposes that the new environment of accounting include four new dimensions. First, accountants as members of the new class of salaried professionals have lost control of the labor process, resulting in a technical and ideological proletarianization of the accountants. Second, a new governing class inbred by classwide rationality and internal cohesion has given rise to an institutional capitalism and to espousal of its own interests over those of individual firms. Third, the users, as a result of a capitalist domination of information, acquire either a "manufactured consciousness" or "a false consciousness" of the situation. Finally, the academic accountants, as part of the flawed universal class, are motivated by self-interest and the need to monopolize their special brand of "cultural" capital.

Empirical testing of those propositions will provide a clarification of the exact nature and ramifications of these new environmental conditions of the accounting profession.

NOTES

1. Alan Touraine, *The Post-Industrial Society* (New York: Random House, 1971).

2. Barbara Ehrenreich and John Ehrenreich, "The Professional Managerial Class," *Radical America* 11 (1976): 7-31.

3. Nicos Poulantzas, *Classes in Contemporary Capitalism* (New York: Verso, 1975).

4. Ehrenreich and Ehenreich, "Professional Managerial Class," 13.

5. Charles Derber, "Managing Professionals," *Theory and Society* 12 (1983): 309-41.

6. Carol Kleiman, "Scrutiny Hasn't Put Crimp in Auditing," *Chicago Tribune*, 29 November 1987, sect. 8,1.

7. M. S. Larson, *The Risk of Professionalism: A Sociological Analysis* (Berkeley: University of California Press, 1977).

8. Harry Braverman, *Labor and Monopoly Capital* (New York: Monthly Review Press, 1974).

9. Paul Baran and Paul M. Sweezy, *Monopoly Capital* (New York: Monthly Review Press, 1966).

10. Stephen Marglin, "What Do Bosses Do?" *Review of Radical and Political Economics* 6 (Summer 1975): 60-112; 7 (Spring 1975): 20-37.

11. Poulantzas, *Classes in Contemporary Capitalism*, 27.

12. Andre Gorz, *Strategy for Labor* (Boston: Beacon Press, 1967).

13. A. Belkaoui, *Public Policy and the Practice and Problems of Accounting* (Westport, Conn.: Greenwood Press, Quorum Books, 1985).

14. National Commission on Fraudulent Financial Reporting, *Report of the National Commission on Fraudulent Financial Reporting, Exposure Draft* (Washington, D.C.: National Commission on Fraudulent Financial Reporting, 1987).

15. Martha Brannigan, "Auditor's Downfall Shows a Man Caught in Trap of His Own Making," *Wall Street Journal*, 4 March 1987, 29.

16. Ralph Estes, "An Intergenerational Comparison of Socioeconomic Status Among CPAs, Attorneys, Engineers and Physicians," *Advances in Accounting* 1 (1984): 1-18.

17. Kleinman, "Scrutiny Hasn't Put Crimp in Auditing," 1.

18. Lee Berton, "O'Malley Gets Top Price Waterhouse Post," *Wall Street Journal*, 30 November 1987, 12.

19. Ibid.

20. Derber, "Managing Professionals," 335.

21. F. P. Kollaritsh, "Job Migration Patterns of Accountancy," *Management Accounting* (September 1968): 52-55.

22. J. Healy, "The Drudge is Dead," *MBA* (November 1976): 48-56.

23. C. Konstans and K. Ferris, "Female Turnover in Professional Accounting Firms: Some Preliminary Findings," *Michigan CPA* (Winter 1983): 11-15.

24. R. L. Benke, "A Multivariate Analysis of Job Satisfaction of Professional Employees in Big Eight Public Accounting Firms" (DBA diss., Florida State University, 1978).

25. Ralph L. Benke, Jr., and John Grant Rhode, "Intent to Turnover Among Higher Level Employees in Large CPA Firms," *Advances in Accounting* 1 (1984): 157-74.

26. *Karl Marx: Early Writings*, trans. and ed. T. B. Bottomore (New York: McGraw-Hill, 1964), 122, 124.

27. Susan Jayson and Kathy Williams, "Women in Management Accounting: Moving Up . . . Slowly," *Management Accounting* (July 1986): 20-26.

28. Josephine Olson and Irene Frieze, "Women Accountants-Do They Earn As Much As Men?" *Management Accounting* (July 1986): 20-26.

29. G. William Domhoff, *The Bohemian Grove and Other Retreats* (New York: Harper & Row, 1974), 109.

30. Ralph Miliband, *The State in Capitalist Society* (New York: Basic Books, 1969), 47.

31. John Westergaard and Henrietta Resler, *Class in Capitalist Society* (London: Heineman, 1975), 346.

32. John Scott, *Corporations, Classes and Capitalism* (London: Hutchinson, 1979), 125-26.

33. Michael Useem, "Business and Politics in the United States and United Kingdom," *Theory and Society* 12 (1983): 285.

34. Ibid., 305.

35. Arthur Andersen & Co., *Cost of Government Regulation Study* (New York: Business Roundtable, 1979).

36. Gary John Previts, "The SEC and Its Chief Accountants: Historical Impressions," *Journal of Accountancy* (August 1978): 83-91.

37. Robert K. Elliot and Walter Schuetze, "Regulation of Accounting: Practitioner's Viewpoint," in *Government Regulations of Accounting and Information*, ed. A. Rashad Abdel-Khalik (Gainesville: University Press of Florida, 1979), 142-52.

38. Michael N. Chetkovich, "The Accounting Profession Responds to the Challenge of Regulation," in *Regulation and the Accounting Profession*, ed. J. W. Bruckley and J. F. Weston (Belmont, Calif.: Lifetime Learning Publications, 1980).

39. Eugene H. Flegm, *Accounting: How to Meet the Challenges of Relevance and Regulation* (New York: John Wiley & Sons, 1984).

40. Comptroller General, *Government Regulatory Activity: Justifications, Processes, Impacts, and Alternatives* (Washington, D. C.: General Accounting Office, 1977).

41. Robert Defina, *Public and Private Expenditures for Federal Regulation of Business* (St. Louis: Washington University, Center for the Study of American Business, 1977).

42. Ahmed Belkaoui, *Accounting Theory*, 2nd ed. (San Diego: Harcourt Brace Jovanovich, 1985).

43. Data Resources, *The Macroeconomic Impact of Federal Pollution Control Program, 1978 Assessment* (Washington, D. C.: Council on Environmental Quality, 1979).

44. Mark Green and Norman Waitzman, "Cost, Benefit, and Class," *Working Payers for a New Society* 7 (May/June 1980): 39-51.

45. Michael Useem, "Classwide Rationality in the Politics of Managers and Directors of Large Corporations in the United States and Great Britain," *Administrative Science Quarterly* 27 (1982): 199-226.

46. Peter Armstrong, "The Rise of Accounting Controls in British Capitalist Enterprises," *Accounting, Organizations and Society* (October 1987): 415.

47. BIM, *The Board of Directors: A Survey of Its Structure, Composition, and Role*, Management Survey Report No. 10 (1972).

48. D. Granick, *Managerial Comparisons of Four Developed Countries: France, Britain, the United States and Russia* (Cambridge, Mass.: MIT Press, 1971), 56.

49. Larson, *Risk of Professionalism.*

50. Peter Armstrong, "Changing Management Control Strategies: The Role of Competition Between Accounting and Other Organizational Professions," *Accounting, Organizations and Society*, (May 1985): 129-48.

51. Armstrong, "Rise of Accounting Controls," 416-25.

52. A. P. Simonds, "On Being Informed," *Theory and Society* 11 (1982): 587-616.

53. Stephen Hill and Bryan S. Turner, *The Dominant Ideology Theories* (London: George Allen & Unwin, 1980).

54. Belkaoui, *Accounting Theory.*

55. Joshua Ronen and Sincha Sadan, *Smoothing Income Numbers Objectives, Means and Implications* (Reading, Mass.: Addison Wesley, 1981).

56. National Commission on Fraudulent Financial Reporting, *Report, Exposure Draft.*

57. Goran Therborn, *The Ideology of Power and the Power of Ideology* (New York: Verso, 1980).

58. Tony Tinker, *Paper Prophets: A Social Critique of Accounting* (New York: Praeger, 1985).

59. Simonds, "On Being Informed," 587-616.

60. D. R. Scott, "The Basis for Accounting Principles," *The Accounting Review* (December 1941): 341-49.

61. James W. Patillo, *The Foundations of Financial Accounting* (Baton Rouge: Louisiana State University Press, 1965).

62. Leonard Spacek, *A Search for Fairness in Financial Reporting to the Public* (Chicago: Arthur Andersen & Co., 1965), 38-77, 349-56.

63. Paul F. Williams, "The Legitimate Concern with Fairness," *Accounting Organizations and Society* (March 1987): 169-89.

64. Frederick Engels and Karl Marx, *The Holy Family,*, in Marx and Engels, *Collected Works* (New York: International Publishers, 1975), 4: 86.

65. *Hegel's Philosophy of the Right*, trans. T. M. Knot (Oxford: Clarendon Press, 1942), 131-39.

66. Ibid., 197-200.

67. Alvin W. Gouldner, *The Future of the Intellectuals and the New Class* (New York: Continuum Publishing Corp., 1979).

68. Basil Berstein and Dorothy Hendersen, "Social Class Differences in the Relevance of Language to Socialization," *Sociology* 3 (1969): 1-20.

69. Alvin W. Gouldner, "The New Class Project, I," *Theory and Society* 6 (1978): 176-177.

70. James Burnam, *The Managerial Revolution* (Bloomington: Indiana University Press, 1962).

71. Pierre Bourdeiu, *Reproduction in Education, Society and Culture* (Beverly Hills, Calif.: Sage Publications, 1977).

72. Gouldner, *Future of the Intellectuals*, 26.

73. K. V. Peasnell and D. J. Williams, "Ersatz Academics and Scholar-Saints: The Supply of Financial Accounting Research," *ABACUS* (September 1986): 121-35.

74. R. L. Watts and J. L. Zimmerman, "The Demand for and Supply of Accounting Theories: The Market for Excuses," *The Accounting Review* (April 1979): 273-305.

75. H. Orlans, *The Effects of Federal Programs on Higher Education* (Washington, D. C.: The Brookings Institution, 1962).

76. B. L. Oliver, "The Semantic Differential: A Device for Measuring the Interprofessional Communication of Selected Accounting Concepts," *Journal of Accounting Research* (Fall 1974): 299-316.

77. A. A. Haried, "The Semantic Dimensions of Financial Statements," *Journal of Accounting Research* (August 1969): 330-41.

78. A. A. Haried, "Measurement of Meaning in Financial Reports," *Journal of Accounting Research* (Spring 1973): 117-45.

79. A. Belkaoui, "Linguistic Relativity in Accounting," *Accounting Organizations and Society* (October 1978): 97-100.

80. A. Belkaoui, "The Interprofessional Linguistic Communication of Accounting Concepts: An Experiment in

Sociolinguistics," *Journal of Accounting Research* (Autumn 1980): 362-74.

81. George Konrad and Ivan Szeleyni, *The Intellectuals on the Road to Class Power* (New York: Harcourt Brace Jovanovich, 1979).

82. Gouldner, *Future of the Intellectuals*, 19.

83. Merrill T. Lewis, W. Thomas Lin, and Doyle Z. Williams, "The Economic Status of Accounting Educators: An Empirical Study," *Advances in Accounting* 1 (1984): 127-44.

84. Ivan Szelenyi, "Gouldner's Theory of Intellectuals as a Flawed Universal Class," *Theory and Society* 11 (1982): 779-98.

85. Konrad and Szelenyi, *Intellectuals on the Road to Clan Power*.

86. A. Belkaoui and J. Chan, "Professional Value System of Academic Accountants," *Advances in Public Interest Accounting* (Fall 1987): 1-28.

87. Robert K. Merton, *Social Theory and Social Structure* (New York: Free Press, 1968), 226-65.

88. J. P. Nettl, "Power and the Intellectuals," in *Power and Consciousness*, ed. Conor Cruise O'Brien and William Dean Vanech (New York: New York University Press, 1969), 15-32.

89. Clyde W. Barrow, "Intellectuals in Contemporary Social Theory: A Radical Critique," *Sociological Inquiry* (Fall 1987): 423.

90. Richard Ashcraft, "Political Theory and the Problem of Ideology," *Journal of Politics* (August 1980): 687-705.

91. Karl Mannheim, "The Ideological and Sociological Interpretation of Intellectual Phenomena," in *From Karl Mannheim*, ed. Kurt H. Wolff (New York: Oxford University Press, 1971), 116-31.

92. Karl Mannheim, *Ideology and Utopia* (New York: Harcourt, Brace Jovanovich, 1936), 256-66.

93. Raymond Aron, *The Opinion of the Intellectuals* (New York: W. W. Norton & Co., 1962), 204.

94. Edward Shils, *The Intellectuals and the Powers* (Chicago: University of Chicago press, 1972), 206-9.

95. Seymour Martin Lipset and Richard B. Dobson, "The Intellectual as Critic and Rebel," *Daedalus* 101 (Summer 1972): 137-98.

96. Peter L. Berger, "The Socialist Myth," *Public Interest* 44 (Summer 1976): 5.

97. Edward Shils, *The Constitution of Society* (Chicago: University of Chicago Press, 1972), 191.

98. Fritz Machlup, *The Production and Distribution of Knowledge in the United States* (Princeton, N. J.: Princeton University Press, 1962).

99. Don K. Price, *The Scientific Estate* (Cambridge, Mass.: Harvard University Press, 1965).

100. Daniel Bell, *The Coming of the Post-Industrial Society* (New York: Basic Books, 1973), 165-266.

101. John Kenneth Galbraith, *The New Industrial State* (Boston: Houghton-Mifflin, 1978), 292-306.

102. Jugen Habermas, *Toward a Rational Society* (Boston: Beacon Press, 1970), 62-80.

103. Gouldner, *Future of the Intellectuals*, 24-25.

104. Galbraith, *New Industrial State*, 206-20.

105. Geoffrey Price, " Universities Today: Between the Corporate State and the Market," *Culture, Education and Society* 39 (Winter 1984/85): 43-58.

106. Talcott Parsons, "The Intellectual: A Social Role Category," in *On Intellectuals*, ed. Philip Rieff (Garden City, N.Y.: Doubleday, 1970), 14.

107. Aron, *Opinion of the Intellectuals*, 204.

108. Watts and Zimmerman, "Demand for and Supply of Accounting Theories," 273-305.

REFERENCES

American Institute of Certified Public Accountants. Practice Analysis Task Force. *AICPA Report of the Practice Analysis Task Force.* New York: AICPA, 1983.

Armstrong, Peter. "Changing Management Control Strategies: The Role of Competition Between Accounting and Other

Organizational Professions." *Accounting, Organizations and Society*, May 1985, 129-48.

___. "The Rise of Accounting Controls in British Capitalist Enterprises." *Accounting, Organizations and Society* (October 1987): 415-36.

Aron, Raymond. *The Opinion of the Intellectuals*. New York: W. W. Norton & Co., 1962.

Arthur Andersen & Co. *Cost of Government Regulation Study*. New York: Business Roundtable, 1979.

Ashcraft, Richard. "Political Theory and the Problem of Ideology." *Journal of Politics* (August 1980): 687-705.

Baran, Paul, and Paul M. Sweezy. *Monopoly Capital*. New York: Monthly Review Press, 1966.

Barrow, Clyde W. "Intellectuals in Contemporary Social Theory: A Radical Critique." *Sociological Inquiry* (Fall 1987): 415-30.

Belkaoui, A. "Linguistic Relativity in Accounting." *Accounting Organizations and Society* (October 1978): 97-100.

___. "The Interprofessional Linguistic Communication of Accounting Concepts: An Experiment in Sociolinguistics." *Journal of Accounting Research* (Autumn 1980): 362-74.

___. *Public Policy and the Practice and Problems of Accounting*. Westport, Conn.: Greenwood Press, Quorum Books, 1985.

___. *Accounting Theory*. 2nd ed. New York: Harcourt Brace Jovanovich, 1985.

Belkaoui, A., and J. Chan. "Professional Value System of Academic Accountants." *Advances in Public Interest Accounting* (Fall 1987): 1-28.

Bell, Daniel. *The Coming of the Post-Industrial Society*. New York: Basic Books , 1973.

Bell, David. *The End of Ideology*. New York: Free Press, 1961.

Benke, R. L. "A Multivariate Analysis of Job Satisfaction of Professional Employees in Big Eight Public Accounting Firms." DBA diss., Florida State University, 1978.

Benke, Ralph L., Jr., and John Grant Rhode. "Intent to Turnover Among Higher Level Employees in Large CPA Firms." *Advances in Accounting* 1 (1984): 157-74.

Berger, Peter L. "The Socialist Myth." *Public Interest* 44 (Summer 1976), 3-16.

Berstein, Basil, and Dorothy Hendersen, "Social Class Differences in the Relevance of Language to Socialization." *Sociology* 3 (1969): 1-20.

Berton, Lee. "O'Malley Gets Top Price Waterhouse Post." *Wall Street Journal*, 30 November 1987, 12.

BIM, *The Board of Directors: A Survey of Its Structure, Composition and Role*. Management Survey Report No. 10, 1972.

Bourdieu, Pierre. *Reproduction in Education, Society and Culture*. Beverly Hills, Calif.: Sage Publications, 1977.

Brannigan, Martha. "Auditor's Downfall Shows a Man Caught in Trap of His Own Making.' *Wall Street Journal*, 4 March 1987, 29.

Braverman, Harry. *Labor and Monopoly Capital*. New York: Monthly Review Press, 1966.

Burnam, James. *The Managerial Revolution*. Bloomington: Indian University Press, 1962.

Chetkovich, Michael N. "The Accounting Profession Responds to the Challenge of Regulation." In *Regulation and the Accounting Profession*, edited by J. W. Bruckley and J. F. Weston. Belmont, Calif.: Lifetime Learning Publications, 1980: 142-52.

Comptroller General, *Government Regulatory Activity: Justifications, Processes, Impacts, and Alternatives*. Washington, D.C.: General Accounting Office, 1977.

Data Resources. *The Macroeconomic Impact of Federal Pollution Control Program, 1978 Assessment*. Washington, D.C.: Council on Environmental Quality, 1979.

Defina, Robert. *Public and Private Expenditures for Federal Regulation of Business*. St. Louis: Washington University, Center for the Study of American Business, 1977.

Derber, Charles. "Managing Professionals." *Theory and Society* 12 (1983): 309-41.

Domhoff, G. William. *The Bohemian Grove and Other Retreats.* New York: Harper & Row, 1974.

Ehrenreich, Barbara, and John Ehrenreich. "The Professional Managerial Class." *Radical America* 11 (1976): 7-31.

Elliot, Robert K., and Walter Schuetze. "Regulation of Accounting: Practitioner's Viewpoint." In *Government Regulations of Accounting and Information*, edited by A. Rashad Abdel-Khalik. Gainesville: University Presses of Florida, 1979: 104-32.

Engels, Frederick, and Karl Marx. *The Holy Family.* In Marx and Engels, *Collected Works.* New York: International Publishers, 1975, vol. 4.

Estes, Ralph. "An Intergenerational Comparison of Socioeconomic Status Among CPAs, Attorneys, Engineers and Physicians." *Advances in Accounting* 1 (1984): 1-18.

Flegen, Eugene H. *Accounting: How to Meet the Challenges of Relevance and Regulation.* New York: John Wiley & Sons, 1984.

Galbraith, John Kenneth. *The New Industrial State.* Boston: Houghton-Mifflin, 1978.

Goodin, Robert E. *Manipulatory Politics.* New Haven, Conn.: Yale University Press, 1980.

Gouldner, Alvin W. "The New Class Project, 1." *Theory and Society* 6 (1978): 153-203.

___. *The Future of the Intellectuals and the New Class.* New York: Continuum Publishing Corp., 1979.

Granick, D. *Managerial Comparisons of Four Developed Countries: France, Britain, the United States and Russia.* Cambridge, Mass.: MIT Press, 1971.

Green, Mark, and Norman Waitzman. "Cost, Benefit and Class." *Working Payers for a New Society* 7 (May/June 1980): 39-51.

Habermas, Jurgen. *Toward a Rational Society.* Boston: Beacon Press, 1970.

Haried, A. A. "The Semantic Dimensions of Financial Statements." *Journal of Accounting Research* (Autumn 1969): 330-41.

Healy, J. "The Drudge Is Dead." *MBA* (November 1976): 48-56.

Hegel's Philosophy of the Right. Translated by T. M. Knot. Oxford: Clarendon Press, 1942.

Hill, Stephen, and Bryan S. Turner. *The Dominant Ideology Theories*. London: George Allen & Unwin, 1980.

Jayson, Susan, and Kathy Williams. "Women in Management Accounting: Moving Up . . . Slowly." *Management Accounting* (July 1986): 20-26.

Karl Marx: Early Writings. Translated and edited by T. B. Bottomore. New York: McGraw-Hill, 1964.

Kleiman, Carol. "Scrutiny Hasn't Put Crimp in Auditing." *Chicago Tribune*, 29 November 1987, sect. 8, 1.

Kollaritsh, F. P. "Job Migration Patterns of Accountancy." *Management Accounting* (September 1968): 52-55.

Konrad, George, and Ivan Szelenyi. *The Intellectuals on the Road to Class Power*. New York: Harcourt Brace Jovanovich, 1979.

Konstans, C., and K. Ferris. "Female Turnover in Professional Accounting Firms: Some Preliminary Findings." *Michigan CPA* (Winter 1981): 11-15.

Larson, M. S. *The Risk of Professionalism: A Sociological Analysis*. Berkeley: University of California Press, 1977.

Lewis, Merrill T., W. Thomas Lin, and Doyle Z. Williams. "The Economic Status of Accounting Educators: An Empirical Study." *Advances in Accounting* 1 (1984): 127-44.

Lipset, Seymour Martin, and Richard B. Dobson. "The Intellectual as Critic and Rebel." *Daedalus* 101 (Summer 1972): 137-98.

Machlup, Fritz. *The Production and Distribution of Knowledge in the United States*. Princeton, N.J.: Princeton University Press, 1962.

Mannheim, Karl. *Ideology and Utopia*. New York: Harcourt Brace Jovanovich, 1936.

___. "The Ideological and Sociological Interpretation of Intellectual Phenomena." In *From Karl Mannheim*, edited by Kurt H. Wolff. New York: Oxford University Press, 1971.

Marglin, Stephen. "What Do Bosses Do?" *Review of Radical and Political Economics* 6 (Summer 1975): 60-112; 7 (Spring 1975): 20-37.

Merton, Robert K. *Social Theory and Social Structure*. New York: Free Press, 1968.

Miliband, Ralph. *The State in Capitalist Society*. New York: Basic Books, 1969.

Nettl, J. P. "Power and the Intellectuals." In *Power and Consciousness*, edited by Conor Cruise O'Brien and William Dean Vanech. New York: New York University Press, 1969, 53-124.

Olson, Josephine, and Irene Frieze. "Women Accountants- Do They Earn As Much As Men?" *Management Accounting* (July 1086): 27-31.

Orlans, H. *The Effects of Federal Programs on Higher Education*. Washington, D. C.: The Brookings Institution, 1962.

Parsons, Talcott. "The Intellectual: A Social Role Category." In *On Intellectual,* edited by Philip Rieff. Garden City, N.Y.: Doubleday, 1970.

Patillo, James W. *The Foundations of Financial Accounting*. Baton Rouge: Louisiana State University Press, 1965.

Peasnell, K. V., and D. J. Williams. "Ersatz Academics and Scholar-Saints: The Supply of Financial Accounting Research." *ABACUS* (September 1986): 121-35.

Poulantzas, Nicos. *Classes in Contemporary Capitalism*. New York: Verso, 1975.

Previts, Gary John. "The SEC and Its Chief Accountants: Historical Impressions." *Journal of Accountancy* (August 1978): 83-91.

Price, Don K. *The Scientific Estate*. Cambridge, Mass.: Harvard University Press, 1965.

Price, Geoffrey. "Universities Today: Between the Corporate State and the Market." *Culture, Education and Society* 39 (Winter 1984/85): 43-58.

Ronen, Joshua, and Sincha Sadan. *Smoothing Income Numbers Objectives, Means and Implications.* Reading, Mass.: Addison-Wesley, 1981.

Scott, John. *Corporations, Classes and Capitalism.* London: Hutchinson, 1979.

Scott, D. R. "The Basis for Accounting Principles." *Accounting Review* (December 1941): 341-49.

Simonds, A. P. "On Being Informed." *Theory and Society* 11 (1982): 587-616.

Shils, Edward. *The Intellectuals and the Powers.* Chicago: University of Chicago Press, 1972a.

____. *The Constitution of Society.* Chicago: University of Chicago Press, 1972b.

Spacek, Leonard. *A Search for Fairness in Financial Reporting to the Public.* Chicago: Arthur Andersen & Co., 1965, 38-77, 349-56.

Szelenyi, Ivan. "Gouldner's Theory of Intellectuals as a Flawed Universal Class." *Theory and Society* 11 (1982): 779-98.

Therborn, Goran. *The Ideology of Power and the Power of Ideology.* New York: Verso, 1980.

Useem, Michael. "Classwide Rationality in the Politics of Managers and Directors of Large Corporations in the United States and Great Britain." *Administrative Science Quarterly* 27 (1982): 199-226.

____. "Business and Politics in the United States and United Kingdom." *Theory and Society* 12 (1983): 281-307.

Watts, R. L., and J. L. Zimmerman. "The Demand for and Supply of Accounting Theories: The Market for Excuses." *Accounting Review* (April 1979): 273-305.

Weidenbaum, Murray L. *Business, Government and the Public.* Engelwood Cliffs, N.J.: Prentice-Hall, 1978.

Westergaard, John, and Henrietta Resler. *Class in Capitalist Society.* London: Heineman, 1975.

Williams, Paul F. "The Legitimate Concern with Fairness." *Accounting Organizations and Society* (March 1987): 169-92.

THE ACCOUNTING PROFESSION IN CRISIS
CRISIS
2

The accounting profession is at a crossroad as a result of serious conflict generated by its failure to properly situate itself as a true profession, its heavy reliance on credentialism, its role in the fragmentation of knowledge and services in the certified public accounting (CPA) firm, its tenuous positions in courts, its failure to resist the deprofessionalization drive, and its failure to be adequately regulated. The accounting profession must find effective solutions for these various dilemmas and conflicts.

A DEMYTHOLOGIZATION IS IN ORDER

Over the years the accounting profession has been stereotyped. The stereotype is born of the idea of a commonality of values of accountants. This hypothesized commonality of values has been attributed for all professions to the common training of their students, providing them with a perceptual frame of reference that structures not only their thinking, but also their perceptions, values, and preferences.[1] March and Simon provide their agreement as follows:

In case of professional associations we predict that the greater the degree of professionalization of the individual's job, the greater his identification with a professional group. . . . Professionalization implies specific formal training and thus substantial homogeneity of background. It implies formal regulation of job performance and thus similarity in positions. To the extent that a job is professionalized, techniques and standards of performance are defined by the other members of the profession.[2]

In addition, R. L. Satow argues that the common training of the students precludes an allegiance to an authority system different from the organization that employs the professional, which amounts to an obeisance to an ideology rather than to the norms of the organization.[3]

One could easily assume that these stereotypes are a result of an attribution process.[4] They are, however, an inaccurate picture of the accounting profession, in which (a) membership in the profession does not imply specific formal training and substantial homogeneity of background, and (b) the members of the profession do not adopt an allegiance to the profession and to an ideology. [On the contrary, the members of the accounting profession tend to espouse the goal of their organization and adapt to the requirements of their tasks than to their professional identification. A CPA firm, a big eight firm, will respond to a question about his employment: "I work for XYZ," and not "I am a professional accountant."] The accountant may have adopted a stronger allegiance to the employing organization than to the profession because of his or her awareness of the difficulty of differentiating between a professional and a nonprofessional working in the accounting field. Are bookkeepers not professionals? Is it reserved only for those meeting the criteria of (a) a college education, (b) membership in a professional organization, (c) loyalty to a code of ethics, and (d) possession of necessary skills?

What differentiates an accounting professional from a non-accounting professional, given the various professional accounting degrees offered in the market? Are those who hold CPA certificates necessarily more professional? R. M. Khoury, whose observation can be applied to all professions, claimed that in the absence of empirical evidence, intuition has tended to fill the gap in our understanding.[5] He concluded that occupational professionalization is not synonymous with workers; increases in training time, worker intelligence, and proficiency in skills only explain the professionalization of a minority of occupations.

In short, this study has demonstrated the folly of uncritically accepting common new assumptions and popular belief as statement of fact. A demythologization of the professions is therefore recommended as a logical step in our investigation of this problem area in order to narrow the chasm which currently exists between the imagined and the real.[6]

IS ACCOUNTING A TRUE PROFESSION?

Attributes most mentioned as forming the professional model are (a) a body of expert knowledge, (b) autonomy, (c) group solidarity within a professional community, (d) self-regulation, (e) licensing, (f) authority over clients, and (g) a code of ethics. This attribute approach to professionalization is sometimes replaced by a more historical and process-oriented approach that views professions as self-conscious groups attempting to monopolize their position in the labor force in order to reap social and economic benefits.[7] As stated by Friedson, profession is represented by "that form of occupational organization which has at once gained for its members a labor monopoly and a place in the division of labor that is free of the authority of others over their work."[8]

Whether using the attribute or the historical approach, accounting may appear to the untrained person as a profession. But is it a true profession?

A *true profession* is one whose members exhibit high levels of autonomy from clients and autonomy from employing organizations. Before becoming a true profession the occupational group must go through at least three stages and meet various conditions. In effect, Forsyth and Danisiewing's model of professionalization distinguishes between the three stages of (a) the potential that a particular serving occupation had for establishing a claim to professional status; (b) the public's evaluation of the occupation's claim to professional status and the possible formation of professional autonomy; and (c) the stabilization and maintenance of the profession.[9] In the first, or "potential," stage the profession does not meet two characteristics: (a) the precision of a service deemed essential, exclusive, and complex, and (b) the building of an image through efforts to show that the service is essential, exclusive, and complex. In the second, or formation, stage the public either recognizes or fails to recognize that the occupation performs an essential, exclusive, and complex service. If public recognition does not occur, the profession would just be in the third stage, a *mimic profession*, with no power and whose members lack autonomy. If public recognition is achieved and the members have only secured autonomy from the clients, the profession would be a *client-autonomous semi-profession*. If public recognition is achieved and the members have only secured autonomy from the employing organizations, the profession would be an *organization-autonomous semi-profession*. Only if public recognition is achieved and the members have secured autonomy from both clients and employing organizations can the profession be considered a true profession in the third stage of stabilization.

The accounting profession has met the criteria of the potential stage by offering an essential, exclusive, and complex service to society. It has met the criteria of the formation stage, given the successful public recognition of the utility of the accounting profession on service. It is not a mimic profession. The question remains whether or not it is a true profession. The following options are available for debate.

If the accounting profession can be proven to be only autonomous from the client, it could be considered a client-autonomous semi-profession. The clear evidence, however, seems to suggest a lack of independence in the accounting field in those situations in which the CPA firm provides both auditing and management advisory service to its clients. If the lack of independence continues to be a subject of controversy, the accounting profession could not be considered a client-autonomous semi-profession.

If the accounting profession can be proven to be only autonomous from the employing organization, it could be considered a organization-autonomous semi-profession. The reality of the labor process in accounting is that the accountants are totally dependent on the employing organization for the design and execution of their services as well as their renumeration and promotion. Given that this lack of independence from the employing organization is an important characteristic of the labor process and structure in accounting firms, the accounting profession cannot be considered an organization-autonomous semi-profession. As Braude states, "to the degree that a worker is constrained in the performance of his works by the controls and demands of others, that individual is less professional."[10]

Given that (a) independence from clients continues to be a subject of debate and perhaps a question of necessity and survival for most accounting firms in search of increasing revenues, and (b) that the lack of independence from employing organizations is a permanent characteristic of the labor process, *the accounting profession cannot be considered a true profession.* The solution may reside in educating accounting students about the true nature of the profession and the need to be autonomous of both the client and the employing organization. This is what Merton and Kitt have referred to as *anticipatory socialization*, that is, practicing or taking over the beliefs and values of a group to which one does not belong, but to which one is preparing to belong.[11] If the anticipatory socialization fails because of inadequacies in the accounting education system, and if the accountants remain in the situation of dependence on clients and organizations, they risk the loss of public recognition as an entity providing essential, exclusive, and complex services and the potential to become a mimic profession; like funeral directors, the accounting profession will take the coloration but not the substance of a profession.

Besides not meeting the criteria to be a true profession, the accounting profession shows all the symptoms of an occupation that has taken on some, but not all, of the characteristics commonly ascribed to a profession. Basically, accounting is in a state of incomplete professionalization because of the following situations:

- The accounting profession does not have adequate mechanisms that ensure its continued control over the social object around which it organizes its service and activities. For example, while lawyers have ensured a complete control over the social object of the law, accountants have to share their social object of information with various other professionals, including consultants, operations researchers, and programmers to name a few. Accountants have not been able to gain exclusive control over the social object of information. Hughes has urgently noted that those occupations that have license will, "if they have any sense of self-consciousness and solidarity, also claim a mandate to define what is proper conduct of others toward the matters concerned with their work."[12] The accounting profession has failed to do so because of its loss of control of the concept of information.
- The accounting profession has failed to attract into its institutions truly committed people who will go out and dedicate their lives to altruistic goals and values. In fact, the profession does not have altruistic goals and values that individual members could espouse.
- The accounting profession did not develop any ideology to define the manner in which its members will view information. This in fact has led to a proliferation of sub-expertises within the profession and to the

involvement of non-accountants in the provision of services surrounding the production and dissemination of information. The situation may be blamed on the profession. The current designation of the profession as only made up of CPAs is narrow- out of touch with realities and the future. As Mednick proposes:

> The profession must search for a wider designation to encompass everyone involved in the more comprehensive practice of public accounting today. I have chosen the term *independent information professional*. However, it is not the specific term but rather the concept that is critical to reshaping the future of our profession.[13]

- There is a narrowing of the competence gap in the field of accounting. There may have been an expert accounting professional phenomenon at a time when the general grasp of the accounting discipline by the population was relatively new. This discrepancy, which may be labeled a competence gap, has been eroded by the rising grasp of accounting by various business-oriented disciplines. The rise of the MBA concept, with its exposure to accounting, and the increasing number of MBAs and other business-degree holders have meant a greater sophistication about accounting and auditing activities, some actual sharing of accounting expertise, and greater skepticism about the uncertainties of the accounting practice and craft. In addition, the public is aware of the limitations of the profession and in general felt misled by "audited" information.

- Much of the accounting knowledge, or a considered expert knowledge, is now routinized by the availability of the software and programs and the standardization of some of the knowledge. Many of their tasks now qualify as routine, handled either by subordinates or by the clients themselves. This has been accelerated by the advance in electronic data processing and the availability of computer-generated accounting documents. In fact the same computerization of data and information narrows the scope of the accountants' monopoly by making these data available to all types of users. The SEC Edgar system is a case in point.

- Because not all the knowledge is routinized and standardized, and some of the knowledge has become more complex and more esoteric, an increased internal socialization is taking place in accounting. The specializations have created internal divisions, have begun to threaten the integrity of the profession, and have created internal stratification in the accounting firms based on income, task, and/or type of client. This new stratification is creating favorable conditions for the deprofessionalization of the accounting profession by eroding group solidarity. In effect, not only is group solidarity important in the pursuit of professional status, but it can also be a prerequisite in the mobilization of resources through professional associations in the pursuit of collective goals, such as dealing with sunset reviews and with sunset reviews and with legislatures and public opinions.[14] One general benefit to the public from the break of this solidarity may be the potential of breaking the reluctance of accountants to criticize one another and testify against one another. The reluctance, up to now, has acted as a powerful informal control in sanctioning deviance.[15]

- The rise of corporate fraud, white-collar crimes, fraudulent financial reporting, and audit failures alerted the public to the role of the accountants in these affairs. Lawsuits against accountants and auditors are a fact, as individual investors, investor groups, state legislatures, and the federal government have begun to scrutinize the accounting profession and challenge traditional prerogatives. The frauds are more and more attributed to the failure of the accounting profession to monitor and assure the continuing education and the ethics of its members. The era of self-regulation for the accounting profession is slowly coming to an end as direct external control by concerned parties is viewed more and more as an acceptable alternative to the rising fraud problem.

- The situation may also be blamed on the failure of the profession to attract students that will subscribe more to its professional elements than to the unprofessional qualities of the occupation. One has just to ask accounting students why they joined the field and the answer, if at all coherent, would center on the perception of a quick return on a minimum human capital investment. Basically, accounting students are assured of a career after a rather structured and mechanical four years of undergraduate education. In such a situation the field is not going to attract people who are committed to humanitarian and people-oriented endeavors.

All these developments lead to the conclusion that the accounting profession is either in a state of incomplete professionalization or in a state of gradual deprofessionalization. This is not a situation unique to accounting. Witness the following comment:

Autonomous, monopolistic professions may indeed become an anachronism- a form of social organization rendered obsolete by changing conditions, as were the medieval guilds. Professional dominance may be replaced by a narrower, more clearly circumscribed client-expert relationship that permits the exercise of skill and judgment within a context of accountability to client and public.[16]

THE CREDENTIALISM IN THE ACCOUNTING PROFESSION
Credentialism and Occupational Licensing

To be considered an accountant rather than a mere bookkeeper, a person needs to be certified as a professional accountant. This is possible through the acquisition of a professional degree, like the CPA (certified public accountant), the CMA (certified management accountant), and the CIA (certified internal auditor). These certificates are the credentials needed to convey the message that a homogeneous body of knowledge in accounting has been acquired by holders of the degrees. Credentialism is needed to create the credibility. It acts as a market regional, a message about the capacity and skill of the accountant offering service in the marketplace.[17] Credentialism is at the center of the accountants' power in the marketplace. It allows them to create an occupational cartel that exercises monopolistic control over the supply of accounting services, thereby securing a source of financial rewards to the accountants and protecting them from competition from allied occupations. The accounting cartel works best when it has effective control of the number of people entering the field as well as control of the competitive behavior of its members. To the effect it has to counter the forces of commercialism that may continuously threaten the spirit of professionism necessary for the maintenance of credibility in the marketplace.[18]

Credentialism in accounting takes place in the focus of either occupational licensing or institutional credentialism.[19]

Occupational licensing is the granting by a state board of accountancy permission to work as a professional accountant if the person is at least a holder of a CPA degree in that state. This credentialism puts the profession in an adversary position with all practicing accountants who are also non-CPA holders. A case in point is the National Society of Public Accountants (NSPA), an association of unlicensed accountants who are actively engaged in public practice providing bookkeeping and tax services to clients but who do not perform opinion audits. The NSPA has been understandably pursuing a strong lobbying effort against credentialism in the accounting profession, asking state legislatures to amend the accountancy statutes to provide for the licensing of another class of public accountants who would not be required to pass the CPA examination. CPAs are vehemently opposed to such an amendment, arguing for a "single-class regulatory legislation," that is, a credentialism based on the CPA certificate. The state of the situation is better summarized as follows:

The relations between the NSPA and the AICPA [American Institute of Certified Public Accountants] continued to be adversarial. The struggle for the support of state legislation is likely to continue indefinitely since neither side seems disposed to change its position regarding the licensing of another class of accounting practitioners. It is unfortunate that the issue cannot be satisfactorily resolved to avoid the continuing expenditure of time and money, particularly since it is questionable whether the public interest is served by the ongoing dispute.[20]

The AICPA, however, will have a harder time preventing non-CPAs from compiling and reporting on financial statements, especially given that many engagements do not pretend to offer assurance of reliability of third parties. The NSPA can also argue that the CPA examination as a credential is equivalent to a barrier to entry used to restrict entrance to the profession and thereby restrain the competition. The question of barriers to entry may also come up with the AICPA's refusal to consider the matter of a foreign-language CPA examination in general and a Spanish CPA examination in particular, and its lagging in the licensing of foreign CPAs. It claims a lot of shortsightedness, as explained by Olson:

Clearly, little or no support would be given to the contemplated solution for dealing with foreign applications seeking CPA certificates. Most CPAs were unfamiliar with the international aspects of their profession and have no present interest in practicing across international borders. When the issue of foreign applicants was raised, the domestic problem of dealing with unlicensed practitioners no doubt weighed far more heavily on CPAs' minds than the possibility of their being restricted internationally- an outlook that may prove shortsighted. Increasingly, other countries are attempting to restrict the operations of American CPA firms within their borders; following a hard line in the United States with respect to foreign applicants is likely to accelerate this trend. The risks of foreign retaliation and the domestic danger of inviting the licensing of a second class of practitioner are both difficult to judge; however, they are the factors that must be weighed unless a new solution is devised that avoids a conflict between international and domestic interests.[21]

Credentialism and the Market for Accountants

It is a fact that occupational credentialing can affect the supply of professional accountants. It does not and cannot affect the demand for professional accountants. As Friedson states it:

Obviously taken by itself without implicitly assuming a larger structure of supports, occupational credentialing constitutes only a limited advantage in the mystical market place in which individual sellers freely seek individual buyers and vice versa. In any real market place there are a number of institutions that organize economic relations and prejudice them systematically, as institutional economics have noted. It is not occupational licensing in and of itself that can effectively explain what economic advantages actually accrue to the licensed today. For an adequate explanation we must look to the issue of supportive laws and institutions that control demand.[22]

In the case of accounting security legislation, tax legislation as well as other laws aimed at protecting the public interest require the use of a professional accountant as a prerequisite to some benefit accruing to the corporation using the services of the professional accountant. These are the laws that in fact ensure the survival of the professional accountant in the marketplace: They have a "*gatekeeping*" power, given that the affairs of the corporation would not have credibility or acceptance by the market, the state, or the individual without the services of the professional accountant.[23] Without these laws, even with their credentials, professional accountants would be prepared to convince the marketplace of the need for some of their services.

FRAGMENTATION OF KNOWLEDGE IN THE CPA FIRMS

With the auditing fees declining or stabilizing compared with the management advisory services fees, the role of non-CPAs working in CPA firms has increased to a point where some of them are asking for a non-CPA associate membership. The issue started when, in December 1969, the AICPA board of directors received a letter from a member requesting that the AICPA consider creating an associate membership classification for non-CPAs serving on the professional staff of CPA firms. Should these people be given an associate membership and be brought into a professional relationship with the Institute? To the substantive ranks of CPAs practicing in CPA firms, the answer is no to any form of application for non-CPA specialists.[24] This is a rather awkward situation, as the Institute of Management Consultants, organized by the non-CPA consulting firms, had started a program to accredit "certified management consultants." What may result is a difficulty for the CPA firm to attract and retain high-caliber non-CPA specialists.

In addition, there is definitely a lack of agreement between the CPAs and the members of the other professions who work in the management advisory services of CPA firms. This is part of a general phenomenon that there is more agreement among members within a profession than between members of two professions. Their conflict and, consequently, the lack of interdisciplinary cooperation have been attributed to a "fragmentation of knowledge" resulting from professional jealousy regarding their respective turfs. Langdon Winner postulates that specialists from different disciplines "ride herd on segments of reality" and research them without realizing that they are working on the same subjects and without attempting to investigate the relevance of their own work.[25] This may be attributed to the notion of professionalism espoused by the accountants in CPA firms as they tend to cling to the ideology of their profession rather than to organizational policies and procedures each time they are put in a position of collaboration with nonprofessionals. Basically, only when confronted with the increased role of the nonprofessionals in the CPA firm do the accountants cling to the idea that membership in the accounting profession became the excuse as well as the ultimate refuge when faced with the horde of nonprofessionals invading the CPA firms.

In fact, the happy marriages of accountants and management consultants are on the rocks as top consultants have started to defect, taking business with them.[26] The consulting practices are unhappy with the situation because (a) the balance of power remains with the accountants and (b) there exists a disparity between the revenues that consultants bring in and what they earn. The consultants feel like second-class citizens because most of them aren't CPAs at a time when consulting revenues are surging. In addition, they have, in several cases, been forced to share in paying for the litigation costs of malpractice suits involving alleged faulty audits.[27]

Basically, what is taking place is a conflict that has its works in the divergence of professional values and interests. This conflict has been acknowledged to happen in most professional organizations where more than one profession is involved and to become open and acute in two contexts: (1) the context in which the "work space" of the different groups overlap and (2) the context of the influencing of organizational policy.[28] The conflict in accounting firms is definitely over the issue of the influencing of organizational policy, with the consultants arguing for a greater role, given their role in the revenue generation of the firms. This type of conflict has been explicated as follows:

Undoubtedly the conflicts of greatest import to the organization as well as its professionals, occur over the formulation of policy. With a sizeable collectivity of different kinds of professionals, each of these groupings has its own notions as to what directions the organization should be taking, and where it needs changing. They frequently take differing position on policy matters. There are two organizational contingencies of great importance to how policy conflicts arise and unfold. These contingencies are not peculiar to professional organizations. The first contingency is what are problems for our group may not be problems for other groups. Second, and related, policy decisions are likely to have different consequences for different sectors of the organization.[29]

THE POSITION OF THE ACCOUNTANTS IN THE COURTS

Do the CPAs, because of their credentials as professionals, have special privileges in the legal system? The answer is that both as witness in the conduct of legal inquiry and as defendant in the law of torts the accountants face a difficult and awkward situation.

Loss of Technical Privilege

The court requires of all witnesses that all relevant information be brought to court on pain of a charge of contempt. The best known exception is the lawyer-client privilege. The general rule of privilege of Federal Rule of Evidence 503 reads as follows:

A client has a privilege to refuse to disclose and to prevent any other person from disclosing confidential communications made for the purpose of facilitating the rendition of professional [sic] legal services to the client, (1) between himself or his representative and his lawyer or his lawyer's representative, or (2) between his lawyer and the lawyer's representative, or (3) by him or his lawyer to a lawyer representing another in a matter of common interest, or (4) between representatives of the client or between the client and a representative of the client, or (5) between lawyers representing the client.

The same privilege has also been given to the psychologist-physician [Supreme Court Standard 504] and the clergyman [Supreme Court Standard 506]. How about accountants? Do they function or rate sufficiently high to overweigh the value of requiring them to reveal their secrets to the court? The official decision of the courts is that accountants cannot join the privileged few.

As part of the audit process, accountants review *contingencies* that could affect a company's financial conditions as reflected in its financial statements. They are guided in their analysis by Statement of Financial Accounting Standards (SFAS) No. 5, "Accounting for Contingencies." One of the important contingencies examined is that the Internal Revenue Service (IRS) will audit the company's tax return and make material adjustments to it. The auditor is assumed to estimate the probabilities of such adjustments and their magnitude. In the process the auditor prepares a number of papers, including an audit program, reports to management, and tax accrual work papers. The tax accrual papers, which are the subject of a controversy, usually consist of (a) a summary analysis of the transactions recorded in the taxpayer's income tax accounts, (b) a computation of the tax provision for the current year, and (c) a memorandum that discusses items reflected in the financial statements as income or expense, when the ultimate tax treatment is unclear.

The controversy is that the IRS policy states that its agents may seek access to both audit and tax work papers of independent accountants. Section 7602 of the Internal Revenue Code gives the commissioner of internal revenue sweeping authority to *summons* relevant documents in an investigation of income tax liability. In fact, the section gives the IRS the power to (a) examine any books, papers, records, or other data that may be relevant or material to such inquiry; (b) summon people to produce such books, papers, records, or other data; and (c) give such testimony, under oath, as may be relevant or material to such inquiry.

Would the access of the IRS to the tax accrual papers threaten an accountant's ability to perform an effective audit of a company's financial statements? Most concerned accountants would view the IRS review of their work papers as a fishing expedition and a mind-scam. Most would expect the courts to give them the same treatment as attorneys and reject the mind-scam of accountants. In effect, in Hickman v. Taylor (1947) the Supreme Court rejected a mind-scam of attorneys because it destroys the mental privacy that a professional needs to work effectively. The accountants used the mind-scam argument to argue against the IRS's use of the auditor's work papers. The Court's decisions, for some cases, were favorable to the accounting profession. This was true in United States v. Humble Oil (1974), United States v. Powell (1964), SEC v. Arthur Young & Co. (1979), United States v. Matras (1973), and United States v. Coopers & Lybrand (1977). Not all of the Court's decisions were favorable to accountants. This was true in United States v. Arthur Young & Co. (1981) and United States v. Coopers & Lybrand (1975). In fact, the Supreme Court, in March 1984, overruled the Second Circuit of Appeals and said that the IRS was entitled to see the tax accrual work papers of Arthur Young & Co. in the IRS's probe of Amerada Hess Corp. for 1972 through

1974. The company was accused of setting up a slush fund for political contributions and payments to foreign officials. Arthur Young and Amerada Hess argued that the work papers were irrelevant to any IRS investigation because they were not used in preparing the tax returns. Moreover, they argued that accountants and clients are protected by the same privilege of confidentially as lawyers. Both arguments were rejected. The Court maintained that, first, the papers were relevant and, second, lawyers are "advocates" and "advisers" for their clients, but accountants play as "public watchdog" role as auditors. Chief Justice Burger wrote:

By certifying the public reports that collectively depict a corporation's financial status, the independent auditor assumes a public responsibility transcending any employment relationship with the client. The independent public accountant performing this special function owes ultimate allegiance to the corporations' creditors and stockholders, as well as to the investing public.

The decision is not a cause for joy in the accounting profession despite assurance from the IRS that it will seek work papers only in unusual cases and when it cannot get the information from the taxpayer. But will the IRS stick to the policy in the future? The decision raises many questions:

1. Will the decision lead companies to be less candid with their outside auditors about their tax pictures?
2. Should not the accountants be protected from disclosure by the privilege of confidentiality that applies to work done by accountants in much the same way that it applies to lawyer's work?
3. Are the outside auditors "watchdogs," or "advocates and advisers" to their clients?
4. Will the relationship between the auditors and their clients change toward less communication and more distortion?
5. Will the companies continue to self-disclose if they know that the CPA may have to give the contents of the disclosure of the IRS? Will it lead to less forthright disclosure?
6. Will the discovery of tax accrual work papers provide the IRS with a road map to the corporation's most aggressive interpretations of the Revenue Code?
7. Is the auditor's work-product privilege analogous to the attorney's work-product doctrine?

8. If candid communications between the taxpayer and the auditor are essential to ensure adequate reserves for tax contingencies, would it not be more appropriate that records of communications stating why a tax position was taken by the taxpayer and the settlement posture on that position should seldom, if ever, be discovered by the IRS?
9. Is the full disclosure of questionable positions required for effective revenue collection?
10. Why should corporations provide the IRS with the substance of the case against them?
11. Is the IRS at a disadvantage in its examination of tax returns because the taxpayer, or his or her agent, possesses the sources of information the IRS needs to audit the return?
12. Without client cooperation and self-disclosure, can the auditor review contingencies as required by SFAS No. 5 and be able to give a unqualified opinion, or is the auditor limited now to give only a qualified, or adverse, opinion or a disclaimer?

The Accountant as Defendant in the Law of Torts

The U.S. society is a litigious society. The price tag is enormous, with evidence showing that many civil cases that go to trial- with or without a jury- can easily cost the taxpayers more money than is at stake for any of the litigants. In a speech to the American Bar Association on February 12, 1984, Chief Justice Warren Burger observed: "Our system is too costly, too painful, too destructive, too inefficient for a truly civilized people." As a result, accountants find themselves affected in many ways by the litigation explosion.

What is affecting accountants started with the prudent liability and the notion of strict liability, whereby "strict liability means that whenever a particular product emerges from an assembly line in a defective condition, the manufacturer will be liable for any injury that the defect causes."[30] The notion of strict product liability was later expanded to the area of professional liability affecting, in the process, architects, doctors, lawyers, accountants, and so on. In the case of the accountants, it meant that they should be held responsible for a business that does not function properly. This action has generated a flood of lawsuits against accountants. Each time a company fails, its independent auditors become one of the few potential defendants that are solvent and, therefore, likely targets for a suit. Given this situation, the first step is to identify the five potential sources of legal liability of accountants.

The first source of legal liability is the common liability to clients. This involves contractual liability, negligence liability, and problems of independence.

With respect to contractual liability, the auditor is bound by a contract with the client and an engagement letter specifying the scope of the audit, that his or her audit examinations is to be performed with due care and in accordance with professional standards, and that an opinion is to be issued regarding the quality of the client's financial statement. Without this, the accountant would be subjected to legal liability.

With respect to negligence liability, it would arise not only from a breach of contract, but also from a failure to observe professional standards and from lapses such as the following: (a) inadequate preparation by failing to prepare or revise the audit program for a client to take into account internal or external changes; (b) lapses in examination by omission or misapplication of a procedure required by the generally accepted standards; (c) inadequate supervision, review, and training of the audit staff; (d) shortcomings of evaluation and judgment; and (e) failure in reporting the right opinion. The accountant can avoid negligent liability if he or she can prove that (a) the client's own negligence contributed to the problem in the company; (b) the client failed to supervise its personnel, which contributed to the accountant's failure to fulfill his or her contract and to report the truth; (c) the client disregarded the auditor's recommendations; and (d) the client knew that reliance on the auditor's opinion is unjustified and that such reliance is a form of contributory negligence.

With respect to problems of independence, they arise when the auditor issues an opinion on the financial statements while acting as an advocate for the client or an unjustifiably deferential to the client management's judgment. This usually happens when the accountant is also performing nonaudit accounting services for the client.

The second source of liability for accountants is the common liability to third parties. For a long time accountants were liable at common law for negligence in the performance of their professional engagements only to their clients. This is known as the *privity of contract doctrine*. The test of the privity of contract doctrine involving auditors came in Ultramares Corp. v. Touche.[31] In that case the defendant certified the accounts of a firm, knowing that banks and other lenders were guilty of negligence and fraudulent misrepresentation in not detecting fictitious amounts included in accounts receivable and accounts payable. In his opinion Justice Cardozo drew a sharp distinction between fraudulent conduct and merely negligent conduct, holding that the auditor would not be liable to third parties for the latter:

If liability for negligence exists, a thoughtless slip or blunder, the failure to detect a theft or forgery beneath the cover of deceptive entries, may expose accountants to a liability in an indeterminate amount for an indeterminate time to an indeterminate class. The hazards of a business conducted on these terms are so extreme as to rekindle doubt whether a flaw may not exist in an implication of a duty that espouses to these consequences. The court also stated, however, that if the degree of negligence is so gross as to amount to "constructive fraud," accountants' liability extends to third parties.

Then the defense of lack of privity eroded as the work of the auditors became more and more the subject of lawsuits by non-client plaintiffs.

An accountant may be liable for ordinary negligence to third parties for whom the accountant knows the client has specifically engaged him or her to produce the accounting product. This type of third party is known as the *primary beneficiary*. An accountant may also be liable for ordinary negligence to third parties, those known or reasonably foreseen by the accountant, as well as those the accountant knows will rely on his or her work product in making a particular business decision. This type of third party is known as the *foreseen party*. This liability may extend to all third parties, including merely forseeable third parties. In other words, users of financial statements beyond those actually foreseen could hold a CPA liable.

In addition, accountants may be found liable to third parties for actual or constructive fraud that is inferred from evidence of gross negligence. The plaintiff is required, in this case, to prove that the auditor knew the falsity (or its equivalent) of a representation. This knowledge is known as the *scienter* and the requirement of its proof as the *scienter requirement*. In any case, fraud consists of the following elements: (a) false representation, (b) knowledge of a wrong and acting with the intent to deceive, (c) intent to induce action in reliance, (d) justifiable reliance, and (e) resulting damage.

The third source of liability for accountants arises under the federal securities laws. Everybody relies on accountants to play a role in producing accurate information. This main responsibility lies in making an independent verification of a company's financial statements. The Securities and Exchange Commission (SEC) perceives the purpose of an audit as a public accountant's examination intended to be an independent check on management's accounting of its stewardships. Thus the accountant has a direct and unavoidable responsibility, particularly where his or her engagement relates to a company that makes filings with the commission or where there is a substantial public interest. That audit responsibility is exactly the reason for the potential legal liability of a CPA under the federal securities laws, specifically under Section 11 of the Securities Act of 1933; Section 10(b) of the Securities Exchange Act of 1934 and related Rule 10b-5; Section 12(2) of the 1933 act; Sections 9 and 18 of the 1934 act; Section 17(a) of the 1933 act; and Section 14 of the 1934 act.

Section 11 of the 1933 act defines the rights of third parties and auditors as follows:

In case any part of the registration statement . . . contained an untrue statement of a material fact or omitted to state a material fact required to be stated therein or necessary to make the statements therein not misleading, any person acquiring such security . . . may . . . sue . . . every accountant . . . who has with his consent been named as having . . . certified any part of the registration statement . . . with respect to the statement in such registration . . . which purports to have been . . . certified by him.

Section 11 lists among potential defendants every accountant who helps to prepare any part of the registration statement or any financial statement used in it. It imposes a civil inability on accountants for misrepresentations or omissions of material facts in a registration statement. The leading Section 11 case, Escott v. Barchris Construction Corp.,[32] was a class action against a bowling alley construction corporation that had issued debentures and subsequently declared bankruptcy, and against its accountants. The court ruled that the accountants were liable for not meeting the minimum standard of "due diligence" in their review of subsequent events occurring to the effective date of the registration statement.

Section 10(b) of the 1934 act states:

It shall be unlawful for any person directly or indirectly, by the use of any means or instrumentally of interstate commerce, or of the mails or of any facility of any national securities exchange, a) to employ any device, scheme, or artifice to defraud, b) to make any untrue statement of a material fact or omit to state a material fact necessary in order to make the statements made, in the light of the circumstances under which they are made, not misleading, or c) to engage in any act, practice, or course of business which operates or would operate as a fraud or deceit upon any person in connection with the purchase or sale of any security.[33]

The elements of Section 10(b) violation are, therefore, (a) a manipulative or deceptive practice, (b) in connection with a purchase or sale, (c) which results in a loss to plaintiff. Unlike the case in Section 11 of the 1933 act, here the plaintiff carries the burden of proof under Section 10(b). For a while the courts disagreed on the standard of performance to enforce against an accountant under Rule 10b-5. Then in 1976 the Supreme Court resolved the controversy in Ernst & Ernest v. Hochfelder[34] by ruling that some knowledge and intent to deceive are required before accountants can be held liable for violation of Rule 10b-5. In other words, the private suit must require the allegation of a scienter. Most lower courts have held that "recklessness" by a defendant is sufficient to satisfy the scienter requirement of Section 10(b), although mere negligence is not.

Section 12(2) of the 1933 act provides that any person who offers or sells a security by means of a prospectus or by oral statements that contain untrue statements or misleading opinions shall be liable to the purchaser for the damages sustained. Some courts have taken a broad view by implicating accountants as liable for aiding and abetting Section 12(2) violations.

Section 18(a) of the 1934 act imposes civil liability on accountants for filing a false or misleading statement. To escape liability the defendant must prove that "he acted in good faith and had no knowledge that such statement was false or misleading."

Section 17(a) of the 1933 act states that it should be unlawful for any person in the offer or sale of securities (a) to defraud, (b) to obtain money or property by means of an untrue statement or misleading omission, or (c) to engage in any transaction, practice, or course of business that deceives a purchaser. This section does not state, however, whether a party violating the law is liable. The issue remains to be solved by the Supreme Court.

Section 14 of the 1934 act sets forth a comprehensive scheme governing solicitation of proxies. Rule 14 a-9 outlaws proxy solicitation by use of false statements or misleading omissions.

The fourth source of liability for accountants arises under the Foreign Corrupt Practices Act (FCPA) of 1977. This act makes it illegal to offer a bribe to an official of a foreign country. It also requires SEC registrants under the 1934 act to maintain reasonably complete and accurate records and an adequate system of internal control to prevent bribery. Until now the SEC has refused to take any action against perceived violations of the accounting provisions of the FCPA unless those violations are linked to breaches of other securities.

The fifth source of liability is the criminal liability under both federal and state laws. The criminal provisions are in the Uniform Mail Fraud Statute and the Federal False Statements Statute. All of these statues make it a criminal offense to defraud another person through knowingly being involved with false financial statements. Four of the most widely publicized criminal prosecutions were the Continental Vending, Four Seasons, National

Student Marketing, and Equity Funding cases, in which errors of judgment on the part of the auditors resulted in criminal liabilities. The SEC position on bringing criminal charges against auditors was once stated as follows:

While virtually all Commission cases are civil in character, on rare occasions it is concluded that a case is sufficiently serious that it should be referred to the Department of Justice for consideration of criminal prosecution. Referrals in regard to accountants have only been made when the Commission and the staff believed that the evidence indicated that a professional account certified financial statements that he knew to be false when he reported on them. The Commission does not make criminal references in cases that it believes are simply matters of professional judgment even if the judgments appear to be bad ones.[35]

DEPROFESSIONALIZATION IN ACCOUNTING

Predictions made by sociologists and futurologists spoke of a "post-industrial society" wherein according to Bell,[36] the professional and technical classes will be preeminent, or, according to Friedson,[37] it will be a professionalized society. This professional mood was to be characterized by (a) a body of expert knowledge, (b) autonomy, (c) group solidarity within a professional community, (d) self-regulation, (e) licensing, (f) authority over clients, and (g) a code of ethics.[38] A note of warning was then sounded by Harold Wilensky's paper, "The Professionalization of Everyone,"[39] and by Goode's paper, "The Theoretical Limits of Professionalization."[40] Both Wilensky and Goode argue that few of the occupations that aspire to gain professional status will become fully professionalized. In effect, the predictions of Wilensky and Goode are being fulfilled as the conditions that foster the growth and dominance of the professions are being eroded by social change. A phenomenon of deprofessionalization has begun. It has been defined as "a loss to professional occupations of their unique qualities, particularly their monopoly over knowledge, public belief in their service ethics, and expectations of work autonomy and authority over the client."[41]

Accounting has not been immune to the phenomenon of deprofessionalization. Various social, political, and economic changes have altered the same environment that facilitated the emergence and dominance of the accounting profession, and have precipitated deprofessionalization in accounting, that is, a decline in the autonomy and monopolistic privileges of accountants.

The following arguments may be used to explicate the deprofessionalization thesis in accounting.

First, for a certain amount of time, the accounting profession has based its claim in autonomy and monopoly on the fact that accounting work is nonroutine. However, with the increasing routinization and computerization of all accounting work, the accounting profession has been stripped of its magic elements and is being forced to undergo change. As put by Montagne: "What was once unwritten rule mystique is now rationalized; in the process of formalizing its rules, the profession transforms that knowledge from an intellectual to a mechanical technique."[42] Basically, the Tayloristic urge in accounting to accelerate the specialization and routinization of professional practice has led to a phenomenon of deprofessionalization.

Second, for a certain amount of time the relation between the accountant and his or her client has been ruled by the former's claim to autonomy (freedom from lay control) and authority (the client's duty to obey), by virtue of his or her expertise knowledge and commitment to the client's benefit. The education and knowledge level of the client have progressed and changed as a result of the mass dissemination of the accounting knowledge of transfer and knowledge level of the client have progressed and changed as a result of the mass dissemination of the accounting knowledge of transfer bookkeeping, tax and computer courses, and continuous education. In addition, clients have gotten into the habit of seeking the audit that plays according to their rules; this is known as "auditor switch" or "opinion shopping." *Public Accounting Report*, an industry newsletter, reported that in 1982 the number of publicly held firms that fired their auditors jumped 48% to 442 from 298 the year before. It also reported that 92 of these dismissals came as a direct result of auditors qualifying company reports, and 122 were prompted by "accounting disagreements" or "personality conflicts," which is equivalent to disputes over qualifications. The newsletter failed to report where the qualified firms that switched auditors subsequently received cleaner opinions or fewer qualified opinions. In any case, opinion shopping is a clear indication of a form of "client's revolt" in accounting, an awakening of the client to his or her right to contest implied accounting expertise.[43]

Third, specialization is increasing in accounting.[44] There is an information explosion in accounting, and no individual CPA can be fully competent in all areas of the accounting function. Specialization is unavoidable in most disciplines and particularly in accounting. Not only is there an information explosion, but also an increase in the variety of services demanded from CPA firms. A de facto specialization is already occurring in most CPA firms. It takes the form of a natural segmentation of the typical, large CPA firm into audit, tax, and management-advisory service departments. The socialization has created internal division and threatens the integrity of the firm as the specialists serve different classes of clients, solve different problems, depend on different knowledge bases, and acquire different cultures. What has followed is an internal stratification based on income, taxes, and type of clients served. A normative, cognitive, and attitudinal answer is nearly impossible to obtain in today's Big Eight accounting firms. Specialization in accounting rises to accelerate the decline in homogeneity within the accounting profession and create different subcultures, instead of the shared socialization emergencies and participation in a common "accounting" culture. This situation is not unique in accounting.

The rapid expansion of knowledge has, however, placed strains on each profession and its incumbents in their attempts to keep abreast of developments. The explosion has been of such proportions that no one person could hope to grasp all the new findings and techniques. The Renaissance man with a command of all fields is indeed a creature of the past. For a time the response of the professions has been to retain its knowledge monopoly by specialization. If no one individual could retain everything known in an entire professional field, then groups of individuals could collectively control the body of knowledge by dividing up the expertise pie so that each would master slices in depth, and maintain monopoly through specialization.[45]

Fourth, consumerism is creeping into the accounting profession mostly at the demand of big accounting firm and because of four developments: (1) CPA firms face a competitive practice environment in which the auditing segment of practice is either stabilizing or declining. To offset the declining revenues from the audit function, firms have expanded their areas of activities beyond those considered to be the traditional activities of the profession. In August 1988 the ruling council of the AICPA agreed to permit members to accept contingency fees from clients and commissions from suppliers recommended to clients by accountants. By doing so AICPA members have risked their identity as professionals and accelerated deprofessionalization. (2) Large CPA firms have begun absorbing smaller firms, and expanding by opening operations in most U.S. cities and establishing affiliations worldwide. These firms have resorted to aggressive techniques to draw business in a competitive environment. As a result, a wider gap has been created between them and the remainder of the professions; competitive rivalry rather than camaraderie has become the rule. (3) With the increase in size and the large scope of services offered, the larger firms operate more as large, divisionalized corporate enterprises than as professional partnerships. New characteristics include central management, line divisional officers, a board of directors, and a chief executive. The small firms have remained as true partnerships managed by their partners. As a result of these new organizational and management structures, the large CPA firms have found themselves pursuing a continuous goal of increasing revenues and market share and turning the profession into a true commercial business. The main characteristics of a true profession, which is to put unselfish service to clients and the public ahead of income considerations, does not necessarily apply to large CPA firms. (4) Because of their expanded profile the larger firms have found themselves offering services and agreeing to financial arrangements that may not be permissible under the rules of conduct. The situation has led to an increase in lawsuits with monumental claims for damages. What also followed is an erosion of the confidence that the public places in the independence and objectives of the profession as a whole.

Fifth, the accounting profession is losing its monopoly and the provider of accounting services as closely allied professions, "information specialists," have begun to encroach and expand into areas previously reserved to accountants. What Kronus[46] has labeled the problem of "boundary maintenance" is already a lost cause, as accountants have never tried to protect themselves from the "unauthorized practice of accounting." The case of the NSPA is a good example of another allied profession that in addition is seeking direct confrontation to break the traditional monopolies of the accounting profession.[47]

Sixth, like all professionals, accountants started as self-employed before expanding into the professional bureaucracies of the CPA firms. The professional and bureaucratic principles of organization are either inconsistent of contradictory.[48,49] For accountants the situation may translate into loss of independence, initiative, and judgment, as well as limited professional autonomy. In the CPA firms accountants are bound by specific accepted bureaucratic procedures, and they are seldom in a position to exercise their full judgment about the work situation. In addition, there is in the CPA firm a new breakdown of the accounting work, with tasks being reorganized to fit new categories of new workers, with new titles, new training, and responsibilities. The new workers' expertise may be computer technology, software, information systems, and even social sciences. The term subprofessionals, paraprofessionals, nonprofessionals, or new professionals apply to them but not the term accountants. They find themselves in a struggle with accountants over occupational tasks and territory.

The paraprofessional has in fact been viewed as an essential element of the professional's expertise. Witness the following comment:

Every professional occupation includes a large component of nonprofessional knowledge and technology in its professional practice-intuition, common sense, folkways, and cultural and moral values. There is no reason to believe that professionals are more effective or better equipped in their use of this nonprofessional knowledge and skill because of their more professional (i.e., esoteric) knowledge. In fact, they tend to organize their brand of nonprofessional knowledge and skill for their own purposes rather than the client's. They aggrandize nonprofessional knowledge, pretending to have a much greater range of professional esoteric knowledge and skill, in fact exists.[50]

REGULATION IN THE ACCOUNTING PROFESSION
Less Standard Setting

Certified public accountant (CPA) is the major professional designation of those who practice public accounting. The American Institute of Certified Public Accountants (AICPA) is the professional coordinating organization of practicing CPAs in the United States. One of its many functions is to prepare and grade a rigorous uniform examination that a person must satisfy before becoming a CPA. The examination consists of four parts: accounting practice, accounting theory, auditing, and business law.

Besides providing the uniform examination, the AICPA acts as the main spokesperson on all areas of interest to its members. Its two important senior technical committees- the Accounting Standards Executive Committee (AcSEC) and the Auditing Standards Committee (AuSEC)- are empowered to speak for the AICPA in the areas of financial and cost accounting, and auditing, respectively. These committees issue statements of positions (SOPs) on accounting issues. These SOPs clarify and elaborate on controversial accounting issues and should be followed as guidelines if they do not contradict existing Financial Accounting Standards Board (FASB) pronouncements. Through its monthly publication, *The Journal of Accountancy*, the AICPA communicates with its members on controversial accounting problems and solutions.

The AICPA has always been interested in standard setting. In fact, since its inception in 1887, the AICPA has taken the lead in developing accounting principles. In 1938 it formed the Committee on Accounting Procedures (CAP) to narrow the areas of difference in corporate reporting by eliminating undesirable practice. Rather than develop a set of generally accepted accounting principles, the

CAP adopted an ad hoc and pragmatic approach to controversial problems. During a period of 20 years, through 1958, the CAP issued 51 accounting research bulletins (ARBs) suggesting accounting treatments for various items and transactions. At the time, these ARBs were supported by the SEC and the stock exchanges and, consequently, represented the only source of the "generally accepted accounting principles" in the United States. After World War II the coexistence of many alternative accounting treatments, the new tax laws, financing techniques, and complex capital structure, such as business combination, leasing, convertible debts, and investment tax credit, created the need for a new approach to the development of accounting principles. In 1959 the AICPA created a new body, the Accounting Principles Board (APB), to advance the written expression of what constitutes the generally accepted accounting principles. In addition, the AICPA appointed a director of accounting research and a permanent staff. Between 1959 and 1973 the APB issued opinions intended to be used as guidelines for accounting practices. With the creation of the FASB to replace the APB in 1973 as the standard-setting body, the AICPA issued Rule 203 of the Code of Professional Ethics to define its new relationship with the FASB. Rule 203 constitutes an endorsement of the FASB as the standard-setting body. In spite of Rule 203, the AICPA does not seem comfortable in its new position. One evidence of such an attitude is that the AICPA had begun, right after the FASB was formed, to issue through its executive committee SOPs. In effect, although the AcSEC does not establish generally accepted accounting principles and acts only as the Institute's official spokesperson on all matters concerning financial accounting and reporting, one of its key responsibilities ahs been to respond to the proposals issued by the FASB and the SEC. To provide more guidance to AICPA members, the AcSEC started issuing SOPs. Despite the perception that they are similar to standards, amendments, and interpretations issued by the FASB, SOPs are not enforceable under Rule 203 of the AICPA's Code of Professional Ethics. They merely provide guidance. In fact, each SOP includes a caveat similar to the following:

Statement[s] of position of the AICPA accounting standards division are issued for the general information of those interested in the subject. They present the conclusion of at least a majority of [the members of] the accounting standards['] executive committee, which is the senior technical body of the Institute, authorized to speak for the Institute in the areas of financial accounting and reporting and cost accounting.

The objective of statements of position is to influence the development of accounting and reporting standards in directions the division believes are in the public interest. It is intended that they should be considered, as deemed appropriately [sic], by bodies having authority to issue pronouncements on the subject. However, statements of positions do not establish standards enforceable under the Institute's Code of Professional Ethics. Although these caveats made clear that the SOP's are to be interpreted primarily as guidance, many public accountants attribute to them the status of generally accepted accounting principles (GAAP).

The AcSEC does not limit its guidance role to the issuance of SOPs. Except for special situations, AcSEC's recommendations on emerging problems may take the form of issue papers. They are intended to help the FASB in identifying accounting and financial accounting problems and suggest solutions to the FASB by adding a new topic to its agenda, by interpreting an existing standard, or by issuing a staff technical bulletin. These issue papers are uniformly and rigorously prepared. Typically, they include (a) a background section summarizing the problem; (2) an analysis of current service often based on research through the AICPA's National Automated Accounting Research System; (c) a review of any relevant or analogous authoritative review; (d) a clear statement of the issues that need to be resolved, along with related subissues; and (e) the advisory conclusions of AcSEC and the committee or task force that developed the paper.

Both the SOPs and the issue papers seem to contribute to mutual standard-setting efforts of the FASB and the AICPA, with the FASB still keeping the dominant policy role. In fact, one of the recommendations of the Financial Accounting Foundation structure committee review was that in setting standards, the FASB should rely more heavily on the work of others. As a result, the FASB has resorted to more "leveraging," as evidenced by a substantial increase in its use of task forces and the development of closer working relations with AcSEC, the committee on corporate reporting of the Financial Executives Institute, and other outside groups. Leveraging has increased the board's activity without diminishing its primary role in the standard-setting process and without the possibility that an outside group like the AICPA would end up dictating its agenda.

More Self-regulation

For a long time the accounting profession has been the subject of severe criticism as a result of numerous failures, improper payments, and other misdeeds by corporations. From everywhere in society came calls for more regulation. The question, however, was whether it should be private regulation, public regulation, or peer regulation. *Private regulation* takes place when firms prescribe and enforce operating policies and practices designed to ensure compliance with professional standards. *Public regulation* includes the laws, regulations, and court system meant to deal with fraud, gross negligence, or failure to comply with legally mandated standards governing independent audits of financial statements. *Peer regulation* takes place when firms agree to have their operations and procedures reviewed by other firms. The general consensus in the accounting profession is that private regulation is the most effective form of regulation. As part of this effort of the profession for a self-regulation program, the AICPA established in 1977 the Division for CPA Firms as a ways of monitoring and improving the audit services provided by its members. The division is made up of two sections: the SEC Practice Section (SECPS) and the Private Companies Practice Section (PCPS). Both sections are very active in a peer review program of each firm to be conducted by other practicing CPAs. An AICPA leaflet, *What is Peer Review?* described peer review and nine elements of quality control. It pointed out that the division's

aim is to maintain and improve the quality of the accounting and auditing services performed by member firms. . . .

A peer review provides reasonable assurance that the accounting and auditing work done by the firm is quality work- work that can be relied upon. . . . It means that a profession which plays an important role in the country's business and financial life is serious about self-regulation and actively pursues the goals of quality work by its members. The members . . . are willing to put their dedication to quality work to the challenge of a peer review every three years. Those who use financial statements and rely on a CPA's report reap the benefit of that dedication.

The objective is not only to evaluate each firm's audit policies and procedures, but also to improve the quality of the audit and accounting practices of members. The procedures to be used enable peer reviewers to determine whether a firm's policies and procedures are adequate to achieve the objective inherent in the nine basic elements of quality control for a CPA firm. They are as follows:

1. Independence- to be free from financial, business, family, and other relations involving a client when required by the profession's code of ethics.
2. Assignment of personnel- to have people on the job with the technical training and competence required in the circumstances
3. Consultation- to have personnel seek assistance, when necessary, from competent authorities so that accounting or auditing issues may be properly resolved
4. Supervision- to determine that work is planned and carried out efficiently and in conformity with professional standards
5. Hiring- to have competent, properly motivated people of integrity
6. Continuing professional education- to provide staff with training needed to fulfill their responsibilities and to keep them abreast of current developments
7. Advancement- to select for advancement people who are capable of handling the responsibilities involved
8. Client acceptance and continuance- to anticipate problems and minimize the likelihood of association with a client whose management lacks integrity
9. Inspection- to conduct a periodic internal review to be sure all other elements of the quality control system are working

Under the SECPS, self-regulation is accomplished in a mandatory peer review, sanctions of firms for failure to meet the requirements of the section, mandatory rotation of all audit engagement partners, public reporting of certain firm information, and monitoring of all section activities by a public oversight board (POB). In effect, the AICPA is intended to act as a neutral link or honest broker between the SEC and the profession. The POB gave teeth to the self-regulatory program given its powers to monitor and evaluate the SECPS's performance. The POB is authorized to investigate any matter pertaining to the SECPS, report publicly on such matters, and make recommendations to the section's executive committee. It also serves as a "sounding board" for the public, Congress, and federal agencies in their interactions with the accounting profession. The board consists of knowledgeable and respected people outside the public accounting profession who provide an objective review of the structure and operation of the self-regulatory effort. It also makes an annual report of its findings and comments.

Given this self-regulation program, efforts are continuously being made to encourage as many firms as possible to join one or both sections. In fact, early objections by the executive committee of the PCPS against publication of the Division for CPA Firms directory on the grounds that nonlisted firms would suffer serious competitive disadvantages were quickly dismissed. A directory for CPA firms is published annually.

Various criticisms have been raised against the self-regulation program of the profession. The primary target of criticism of the profession's self-disciplinary process seems to be the response to alleged audit failures. The accounting profession is criticized for being lax in investigating alleged audit failures and for not disciplining substandard performances. The answer to such criticism by D. R. Carmichael, then vice-president, technical services, of the AICPA, is stated as follows:

The disciplinary process often cannot cope with alleged audit failures because of the near impossibility of judging the degree of culpability of the auditor when financial statements are deficient.

There is a spectrum of conduct from honest mistakes to fraud, but along this spectrum it is extremely difficult to distinguish between an honest mistake and negligence. Even more extreme forms of conduct, such as recklessness and fraud, may be difficult to distinguish from negligence. This difficulty is caused by the necessary generality of professional standards, the complexities of professional practice, and the nature of human failure.

The structure of the division in two sections gave the erroneous perception that the profession consisted of two groups of members that provided different quality levels of service. To counter this criticism a joint coordinating committee was formed to facilitate coordination between the two sections in identifying and dealing with common problems. However, a long-term solution would be to restructure the Division for CPA Firms into a more unified organization without sections. Such a unified structure would be able to provide and expanded range of services and ultimately make it feasible to attract all CPAs in public practice into the system.

John C. Burton, a former chief accountant at the SEC, challenged the AICPA's legal authority to achieve effective surveillance and discipline and proposed that legislation be enacted that would create a self-regulatory organization under direct SEC oversight, possibly patterned along the lines of the National Association of Securities Dealers. The governing body of this organization would be a board of directors, half of whose members would be from firms practicing before the SEC and half, public members drawn from the business, financial, professional, and academic communities.

Others have maintained that the AICPA program of self-regulation, if given a good chance, is a likely success and that the current frustrations with the limits of government involvement in regulation should make anyone hesitant to put another layer of regulation on any profession.

Sunset Review

State accountancy boards are essential to the efficient working of accountancy laws. In fact, state accountancy boards are responsible for the efficient conduct of accounting in each state. They are responsible for (a) the adoption of rules and promulgation of rules of conduct; (b) the administration of examinations; (c) the issuance of CPA certificates and permits to practice, and licensing; and (d) the monitoring of all licensed practitioners to ensure ethical conduct. These items would be vital if one opted for self-regulation of the discipline and profession of accounting. It is then essential that their continued existence remain justified. The crucial time for this justification is when, periodically, they come for what is called sunset review. The result of such review determines the way the discipline and the profession will be organized in each state.

The sunset review process resulted from the enactment of the first sunset law in Colorado in 1976. Since then most states have enacted some form of sunset law. A sunset law calls for termination of governmental agencies, programs, and boards engaged in professional licensing on a specific date if their continued existence cannot be justified. When applied to state accountancy boards, a board is called on to justify its existence to a reviewing panel. Interested parties are also allowed to present their views. The panel proceeds with its review and recommendation to the legislature of either reestablishment, modification, or termination of the board. Although most recommendations, so far, have been either reestablishment or minor modification, such as the addition of a public member to a board, they may be more radical, such as a proposal, rejected by the New Hampshire legislature, to terminate the state accountancy board. In fact, the New Hampshire statute survived the sunset review and was reenacted with new features, including mandatory continuing professional education; a requirement that CPA candidates be of "good personal character" rather than of "good moral character"; a change in the composition of the state board to include three CPAs, one public accountant, and one public member; required biannual, rather than annual, renewals; and the establishment of fees by the board rather than by statute.

Given the possibility of the worst case- termination- the profession is risking high stakes and should be thoroughly prepared to survive the scrutiny of the sunset process. Otherwise, the regulation of accounting will cease in those states where an accountancy board is eliminated under sunset. To ensure that the sunset review is favorable , the state accountancy board needs to ensure that the public interest is protected. Various questions need to be examined.

- The review board needs to be reassured that the attest function is vital to the efficient conduct of business and is performed by qualified people who have met strict requirements for licensing.
- The review board needs to be reassured that the entry requirements are not set too high and act as barriers to entry. Although the CPA examinations are difficult and the passing rates are low, the reason lies mainly in the less-than-stringent process that candidates must undergo before taking the examination. In effect in most states, the maximum requirement is an undergraduate degree in accounting. The review panel may inquire whether or not graduate education in accounting may be a better requirement for aspiring CPAs. This is in line with a trend for more graduate programs in accounting and more professional schools of accounting. This position is supported by the 1978 report of the Commission on Auditor's Responsibilities: "The importance of instilling in students an appropriate professional attitude and the need to expose them to the pressures and problems of public accounting practice during the formal educational process support the need for graduate professional schools of accounting similar to law school" (p. 89).
- The review board may need to be reassured again that the CPA examination and advisory-granting service, used by all jurisdictions, is not only fair and appropriate, but also well managed. One solution in this case has been devised by the AICPA and the National Association of State Boards of Accountancy (NASBA) in the form of a special CPA examination review board appointed by the NASBA to conduct an ongoing review of the appropriateness of the CPA examination on behalf of all state boards of accountancy. A second solution, mainly with regard to the fairness of grading in the CPA program, is the critique program of the NASBA, whereby candidates who did not pass all parts of the CPA examination are allowed by the state boards to review their papers. This solution is unique among professions.
- The review board may need to be reassured that the state accountancy boards are effectively handling the enforcement of technical and ethical standards through positive and continuous monitoring of performance and reactive responses to complaints.

Although the sunset review process has definite merits as far as the protection of the public interest is concerned, its popularity is not shared by all. In fact, some states have repealed it, like North Carolina in 1977, criticized it, like Arkansas and Maryland, or revamped it, like Kansas. In the Kansas case a new 1981 law required only the state-supported agencies to be subject to the sunset law. The other boards are just reviewed without the threat of termination by the house and senate governmental organization committees. The major complaints against the sunset review process are that it is sometimes inefficient, duplicative, and not cost-effective. In 1979 a report in the *Washington Monthly* claimed that sunset audits and hearings cost Colorado $212,300, and the result was the abolition of three agencies with a combined annual budget of $6,810. The repeal of the sunset review process in North Carolina was based on the complaints that the Governmental Evaluation Commission had spent more than $200,000 a year since 197 but had terminated only five agencies.

These criticisms may reflect the deregulatory outlook and mood at a given time. Nevertheless, the review process, with or without termination, is essential to the necessary protection of the public interest. To ensure its survival, the accounting profession should not only take the sunset review process seriously, but also prepared for it.

Peer Review: Does It Work?

The question is how to regulate the activities of CPA firms and ensure that the quality of the services offered is adequate with the ultimate purpose of protecting the public from exploitation and inadequate service by accountants. Regulation may be exercised by the government (governmental regulation), the private sector (private regulation), or the profession itself (peer regulation).

Some claim that peer and private regulation are not enough to ensure the quality of services provided by the accounting profession and that governmental regulation should be used. This threat came in 1978 with the introduction of H.R.13175, the so-called Moss Bill (named after John E. Moss, former chairman of the

House Commerce Committee's Subcommittee on Oversight and Investigations), which mainly called for the enactment of the National Organization of Securities and Exchange Commission Accountancy. The bill, officially titled the Public Accounting Regulatory Act, called for action:

To establish a National Organization of Securities and Exchange Commission Accountancy, to require that independent public accounting firms be registered with such an Organization in order to furnish audit reports with respect to financial statements filed with the Securities and Exchange Commission, to authorize disciplinary action against such accounting firms and principals in such firms.

It claimed that the accounting profession has not established and appears unable to establish a self-regulatory environment. It also authorized the proposed Accountancy Commission to regulate the quality of services provided by accounting professionals and to impose various sanctions where necessary. Among its provisions were the following:

- Only one member of the new agency's five-member board could be from a major accounting firm.
- The Accountancy Commission would review the work of individual accounting firms every three years, checking for "acts or omissions" by such accounting firms or principals in such firms that are contrary to the interest of the investor public.
- CPA firms' legal liability would be greatly increased, making them accountable for negligence even without evidence of fraud or intentional conduct.

Fortunately for the accounting profession the Moss Bill never passed the House. The threat did not, however, go unnoticed. The AICPA decided to act to prove that self-regulation or peer regulation is a viable alternative. It first allowed CPAs, in addition to other individuals, to join the Institute. More specifically, it created two sections: the Private Companies Practice Section (PCPS) for small accounting firms serving mostly private companies, and the SEC Practice Section (SECPS), for those firms serving companies registered with the SEC. The AICPA also required that in the future, all firms in both sections undergo independent peer reviews to be conducted every three years. In addition to establishing the system of peer reviews, the AICPA decided that the SECPS would be monitored by the Public Oversight Board (POB), composed of, but not limited to, former public officials, lawyers, bankers, securities industry executives, educators, economists, and business executives.

Central to the AICPA innovation is the peer review requirement, thus keeping the oversight of professional the oversight of professional practice within the profession. The peer review is essentially a form of quality control by peers. In general, a firm is provided the names of available reviewers from a bank of reviewers from which it may select a review team. A firm may also choose a "firm-on-firm" review by selecting another CPA firm to review its quality control. In the latter case, a quality control review panel, selected by the SECPS peer review committee, is appointed to oversee the review.

The review is similar to an audit. In general, it consists of the following testing procedures:

1. A review of the firm's quality control documents, manuals, checklists, and so on. In effect, the 1979 AICPA Statement on Quality Control Standards No. 1, "System of Quality Control for a CPA Firm," states that "to provide itself with reasonable assurance of meeting its responsibility to provide professional services that conform with professional standards, a firm shall have a system of quality control" (para. 2)

2. A testing of the compliance with the documented policies and procedures by interviewing key and selected staff people; reviewing personnel files, administration files, and other evidential matter; or reviewing engagement work papers and reports

3. An exit conference with the directors of the firm to discuss their findings and to report (a) any significant deficiencies in the quality control procedures of the firm, (b) any noncompliance with the documented policies and procedures, and (c) any noncompliance with membership requirements of either SECPS or PCPS

4. A written report and a letter of comments to be sent to the firm's managing partner and to the public file at the Institute. The comments on quality control system design and compliance that seem to attract the peer reviewers' attention focus on categories such as the following: (a) acceptance and continuance of clients, (b) independence, (c) hiring,

(d) advancement, (e) professional development, (f) assignment of personnel, (g) consultation, (h) supervision in engagement planning, (i) supervision in engagement performance, (j) supervision in engagement review, and (k) inspection. In all of these categories the reviewers rely on the profession's standards as a basis for evaluation. As an example, Price Waterhouse's letter to Touche Ross concerning its peer review findings follows.

To the Partners of
Touche Rosse & Co.   October 10, 1979

We have reviewed the system of quality control for the accounting and auditing practice of Touche Ross & Co. in effect for the year ended March 31, 1979, and have issued our reported dated October 10, 1979. This letter should be read in conjunction with that report.

Our review was for the purpose of reporting upon your system of quality control and your compliance with it and with the membership requirements of the SEC Practice Section of the AICPA Division for CPA Firms (the Section). Our review was performed in accordance with the standards promulgated by the peer review committee of the Section; however, our review would not necessarily disclose all weaknesses in the system of lack of compliance with it or with the membership requirements of the Section because our review was based on selective tests.

There are inherent limitations that should be recognized in considering the potential effectiveness of any system of quality control. In the performance of most control procedures, departures can result from misunderstandings of instructions, mistakes of judgment, carelessness, and other personal factors. Projection of any evaluation of a system of quality control to future periods is subject to the risk that the procedures may become inadequate because of changes in conditions or that the degree of compliance with the procedures may deteriorate.

During the course of our review, we noted the following areas which we believe could be improved to further strengthen your system of quality control:

Improved documentation of key issues considered and audit work performed

It is the firm's policy to require for every audit engagement a complete record of audit procedures performed and the facts and rationale for key judgments and conclusions. We believe documentation in the engagement record could be improved in the following areas:

- The facts, discussion of the issues considered, consultations, if any, with designated local office consultants and reviewers, and related reasoning for the conclusions reached on significant accounting, auditing and reporting matters
- Procedures performed when using work of outside specialists and internal auditors
- Effects of EDP control reviews on audit scope
- Procedures followed in limited reviews of interim financial information
- Communications between offices participating in a multi-office engagement

We recommend that the importance of appropriate documentation procedures be reemphasized to the professional staff.

Codify consultation policies

The firm's technical inquiry policy requires consultation with the Executive Office Accounting and Auditing Technical Staff in specific instances, as well as in cases where additional consultation outside the local office consultation process is considered necessary. We believe compliance with the firm's consultation policies could be improved by codifying in one firm publication the instances where such additional consulting is appropriate or required.

Improve compliance with the firm policies on use of the work and reports of other auditors

The firm's written policies on the use of the work and reports of other auditors are reasonable and consistent with authoritative guidance. Firm policy requires timely approval of the National Director of Accounting and Auditing before accepting certain engagements involving other auditors and approval of the Executive Office Accounting and Auditing Technical Staff for exceptions from performing specified audit procedures concerned with the work of other auditors. Based on our review we recommend that the firm review its compliance with firm policy particularly in the areas of (1) acceptance of principal auditor responsibility, (2) reference in the firm's report to the work of other auditors, (3) the performance of appropriate procedures for supervising the work of other auditors, and (4) documentation of other auditor independence.

Improve compliance with firm policy on client representation letters

The firm's policy requires that representation letters obtained from clients conform with a model letter supplied as a part of the firm's reference material and that deletions, except in certain cases, from specified standard paragraphs be cleared with the Executive Office Accounting and Auditing Technical Staff. Firm guidance and professional literature also require consideration of additional representation paragraphs beyond those included in the model letter when unusual accounting or reporting requirements exist. Our review disclosed instances where letters of representation did not conform with firm policy. We recommend that the firm emphasize the importance of obtaining management's representations on all significant matters reflected in the financial statements and clarify the circumstances where deviations from the model letter are to be approved by the Executive Office Accounting and Auditing Technical Staff.

Emphasize importance of timely preparation of staff performance reports

Firm policy requires timely preparation of a formal written staff evaluation report for each staff member assigned to an engagement of appropriate length and complexity. We recommend that the firm emphasize to the appropriate responsible personnel the importance to the firm's overall equality procedures of timely evaluation of staff performance on quality engagements.

The foregoing matters were considered in determining our opinion set forth in our report dated October 10, 1979, and this letter does not change that report.

Price Waterhouse & Co.

When the review is not favorable, sanctions from the appropriate section may be imposed. The possible sanctions considered in the *1983 SECPS Manual* include the following:

1. Requirement of corrective measures by the firm, including consideration by the firm of appropriate actions with respect to individual-firm personnel
2. Additional requirements for continuing professional education
3. Accelerated or special peer reviews
4. Admonishments, censures, or reprimands
5. Monetary fines

6. Suspension from membership
7. Expulsion from membership

    Whether the outcome is favorable or unfavorable, peer review provides various benefits besides the major benefit of keeping governmental regulation off the backs of CPA firms. Among the tangible benefits are the improvement of the quality control before or after the review itself, the educational process created before and during the review, and the improvement in the morale resulting from the discovery and correction of any material failure to perform in compliance with the firm's own quality control document. In addition, the cost of a peer review is manageable. The SECPS' rates range from \$35 to \$90 an hour, depending on the size of the firm reviewed. The PCPS has set one rate for review captains, \$45 an hour, and one rate for reviewers, \$35 an hour. For a one-office firm with three partners and five professional staff, the total fee for the review would be roughly \$2,400 to \$3,300, which amounts to an additional cost to do business of only \$800 to \$1,100 and a guaranteed improvement in quality control.

    Why, then, is the peer review program being criticized? Some of the arguments follow.

    1. Peer review might seem to be something that all public accountants would welcome to avoid the feared alternative of governmental regulation. However, although the large CPA firms have shown a high degree of acceptance and voluntarism, most smaller CPA firms have reacted with either apathy or hostility. Their response is based on the belief that, first, the peer review is going to lead to unnecessary additional expenses and new procedures that are probably irrelevant to the nature of their practices, and that, second, the peer review is of more value to larger CPA firms. But the small practitioners need the peer review system even more than the larger firms, and in most cases the benefits outweigh the cost.

    2. Some small, as well as large, CPA firms are reluctant to let an outside observer, whether or not it is a competitor, evaluate the adequacy of their quality control policies. One may wonder whether the threat is not the outside observer, but the possibility of a qualified report. But these firms should realize that with adequate preparation,

a peer review is much easier to survive than a loss of clients or, in the worst case, a loss of privilege to practice as a result of an inadequate job. Besides, peer review is bound to inspire investors' confidence in the accountants' high professional standards and competency.

3. To date no official sanctions have been imposed by the AICPA's SECPS Executive Committee. The most drastic step taken by the peer review committee is to refuse to accept the review report until an appropriate response or modification has been made. What emerges from this behavior is that the SECPS and the PCPS appear to be avoiding tough actions. The whole peer review exercise could easily be misinterpreted as mutual back scratching.

4. Membership in the SECPS and CPCS was not made mandatory by the AICPA. The argument most often used has been that such requirements should be imposed by the federal government and are not the province of a self-regulatory profession. Although the arguments may have some conceptual merits, the credibility of the peer review system, the integrity of the profession, and the soundness of the quality control may rest on a mandatory membership. It is, however, appropriate to note that the AICPA is taking steps to ensure compliance with quality control. Although the Statement on Quality Control Standards No. 1, "System of Quality Control for a CPA Firm," does not specifically refer to documentation of compliance, a proposed interpretation, "Documentation of Compliance with a System of Quality Control," advises CPA firms that documentation would ordinarily be required to demonstrate a firm's compliance with its policies and procedures for quality control. That is a very positive step toward making potential peer reviews more effective.

5. There is finally the issue of confidentiality, given that the peer review committee's responses to unfavorable reports have been so far nonpublic. As a consequence, the credibility of the program is tarnished. The reason for confidentiality is generally supported by the complexity of the situation involving private rights, the public interest, the litigious nature of the American society, and the misconceptions about the role, rights, and responsibilities of

auditors. Although this reason may be legitimate, there is an urgent need for the profession to find a means of publicizing its sanctions for the sake of credibility of the peer review program in general and self-regulation in particular.

CONCLUSIONS

The coverage of the issues affecting the accounting profession in this chapter indicate the potential of a coming crisis that may threaten the foundation and existence of the accounting profession. The accounting profession appears as failing to impose itself as a true profession. The situation shows an accounting profession in a state of either incomplete professionalization or gradual deprofessionalization. The state of the coming crisis appears more possible as (a) credentialism fails to ensure social credits; (b) accountancy knowledge is in a process of fragmentation, precipitating a conflict that has its roots in the divergence of professional values and intents among people working in CPA firms; (c) a difficult and advisory situation confronts the accountants in courts as either witnesses in the conduct of legal inquiry or defendants in the law of torts; (d) a phenomenon of deprofessionalization is emerging; and (e) a "less than credible" regulatory system is in place.

A realization of the gravity of these problems followed by a process of education and reform is in order for the accounting profession to survive the coming crisis created by these conflicts.

NOTES

1. Herbert Simon, *Administrative Behavior* (New York: Macmillian, 1945).

2. J. G. March and H. Simon, *Organization* (New York: Wiley, 1958), 30.

3. R. L. Satow, "Value-Rational Authority and Professional Organizations: Weber's Issuing Type," *Administrative Science Quarterly* 10 (1975): 526-31.

4. Ray E. Gey, *Professionals in Organizations* (New York: Kaeger, 1985), v. 9.

5. R. M. Khoury, "Demythologizing the Professions," *International Review of History and Political Science* 17 (1980): 5-70.

6. Ibid.

7. D. Klegon, "The Sociology of Professions: An Emerging Perspective," *Sociology of Work and Occupations* (August, 1978): 259-83.

8. E. Friedson, "The Futures of Professionalization," in *Health and the Division of Labor*, ed. M. Stacey et al. (London: Crown Helm, 1977), 13.

9. P. B. Forsyth and T. J. Danisiewing, "Toward a Theory of Professionalization," *Work and Occupations* (February 1985): 59-76.

10. L. Braude, *Work and Workers: Sociological Analysis* (New York: Praeger, 1975), 105.

11. R. K. Merton and A. Kitt, "Contributions to the Theory of Reference Group Behaviors," in *Studies in the Scope and Methods of the American Soldier*, ed. R. K. Merton and P. F. Lazarfeld (New York: Macmillan, 1950), 87-91.

12. E. C. Hugler, *Men and Their Work* (Glencoe, Ill.: The Free Press, 1953), 8.

13. Robert Redwick, "Our Profession in the Year 2000: A Blueprint of the Future," *Journal of Accountancy* (August 1988): 55-56.

14. R. L. Akers and R. Quinney, "Differential Organizations of Professions: A Comparative Analysis," *American Sociological Review* (February 1968): 104-21.

15. J. L. Berlant, *Profession and Monopoly* (Berkeley: University of California Press, 1976).

16. Robert A. Rothman, "Deprofessionalization: The Case of Law in America," *Work and Occupations* (May 1984): 203.

17. A. M. Spence, *Market Signaling: Information Transfer in Hiring and Related Screening Processes* (Cambridge, Mass.: Harvard University Press, 1974).

18. J. F. Barron, "Business and Professional Licensing-California, a Representative Exchange," *Stanford Law Review* 18 (1966): 640-65.

19. Eliot Friedson, *Professional Powers: A Study of the Institutionalization of Formal Knowledge* (Chicago: University of Chicago Press, 1986), 64.

20. Wallace E. Olson, *The Accounting Profession: Years of Trial: 1969-1980* (New York: American Institute of Certified Public Accountants, 1982), 174.

21. Ibid., 188.

22. Friedson, *Professional Powers*, 70.

23. Eliot Friedson, *Professional Dominancy* (New York: Atherton Press, 1976), 115-18.

24. Ahmed Belkaoui, *Public Policy and the Practice and Problems of Accounting* (Westport, Conn.: Greenwood Press, 1985), 82-85.

25. Langdon Winner, "Complexity and the Limits of Human Understanding," in *Organized Social Complexity*, ed. T. R. Laporte (Princeton, N.J.: Princeton University Press, 1975), 112-25.

26. Lee Berton, "Cutting the Pie: Accounting Firms Force a Deepening Division the Consultants' Pay," *Wall Street Journal*, 26 July 1988, 1.

27. Lee Berton,"Peat Marwick Consultant Transferred, Another Sign of Rift with the Accountants," *Wall Street Journal*, 12 August 1988, 17.

28. Harvey Smith, "Contingencies of Professional Differentiation," *American Journal of Sociology* 63 (1958): 410-14.

29. Rue Bucher and Joan Stelhing, "Characteristics of Professional Organizations," *Journal of Health and Social Behavior* 1- (1969): 9.

30. Jethro Weberman, *The Litigious Society* (New York: Basic Books, 1981), 42.

31. Ultramares Corp. v. Touche, 255 N.Y. 170, 174, N.E. 441 (1931).

32. Escott v. Barchis Construction Corp. 283 F. Supp. 643 (S.D. N.Y. 1968).

33. Securities Act of 1934, 17 C.F.R. Section 240, 10b-5 (1971).

34. Ernst & Ernst v. Hochgelder, 425 U.S. 185, 965 Ct. 1375, 47 L.Ed.2d 668 (end ed.).

35. J. C. Burton, "SEC Enforcement and Professional Accountants: Philosophy, Objectives and Approaches," *Vanderbilt Law Review* 78 (January 1975): 88.

36. D. Bell, "The Measurement of Knowledge and Technology," in *Indicators of Social Change*, eds. Eleanor B. Sheldon and Wilbert E. Moore (New York: Russell Sage Foundation, 1968), 152.

37. E. Friedson, "Editorial Foreward," *American Behavioral Scientist* (March/April 1971): 467.

38. Rothman, "Deprofessionalization," 183.

39. H. L. Wilensky, "The Professionalization of Everyone," *American Journal of Sociology* (September 1964): 137-58.

40. W. Goode, "The Theoretical Limits of Professionalization," in *The Semi-Professions and Their Organization*, ed. A. Etzioni (New York: Free Press, 1969), 980-96.

41. Marie R. Haug, "Deprofessionalization: An Alternate Hypothesis for the Future," *Sociological Review Monograph* 20 (1973): 197.

42. P. D. Montagne, "Professionalization and Bureaucratization in Large Professional Organizations," *American Journal of Sociology* (September 1968), 143.

43. Nivia Toren, "Deprofessionalization and Its Sources: A Preliminary Analysis," *Sociology of Work and Occupations* (November 1975): 323-37.

44. W. E. Olson, "Specialization: Search for a Solution," *Journal of Accounting* (September 1982): 70-79.

45. Haug, "Deprofessionalization," 200.

46. C. C. Kronus, "The Resolution of Occupational Power: An Historical Study of Task Boundaries Between Physicians and Pharmacists," *Sociology of Work and Occupations* (February 1976): 3-37.

47. Olson, *The Accounting Profession: Years of Trial*, ch. 9.

48. W. R. Scott, "Professionals in Bureaucracies- Areas of Conflict," in *Professionalization*, eds. H. Vollruer and D. Mills (Englewood Cliffs, N.J.: Prentice-Hall, 1966), 266-82.

49. R. H. Hall, "Professionalization and Bureaucratization," *American Sociological Review* (February 1968): 92-104.

50. R. Reiff, "The Danger of the Techni-Pro: Democratizing the Human Service Professions," *Social Policy* (May/June 1971): 62-64.

REFERENCES

"Auditors' Liability Limited in Draft of Law Codification" (news report). *Journal of Accountancy*, (December 1973): 20, 22.

Austin, K. R., and D. C. Langston, "Peer Review: Its Impact on Quality Control." *Journal of Accountancy* (July 1981): 78-82.

Austin, R. H. "CPA's Social, Civic, and Political Responsibilities" (statements in quotes). *Journal of Accountancy* (December 1971): 64-66.

Bab, D. S. "Current Thoughts About the Legal Liability of the CPA." *New York Certified Public Accountant* 41 (June 1971): 64-66.

Braverman, Harry. *Labor and Monopoly Capital*. New York: Monthly Review Press, 1974.

Brenster, W. G. "Peer Review: Enhancing Quality Control." *Journal of Accountancy* (October 1983): 78-88.

____. "The AICPA Division for Firms: Problems and a Challenge." *Journal of Accountancy* (August 1984): 98-110.

Briloff, A. J. *Effectiveness of Accounting Communication*, with a foreword by Justice William O. Douglas. New York: Frederick A. Praeger, 1967, 338.

____. "Old Myths and New Realities in Accountancy." *Accounting Review* (July 1986): 404-95.

Buchholz, D. L., and J. F. Moraglio. "IRS Access to Auditors' Work Papers: The Supreme Court Decision." *Journal of Accountancy* (September 1984): 91-100.

Buroway, Michael. *Manufacturing Consent*. Chicago: University of Chicago Press, 1975.

Cardechi, Gughielmo. *On the Economic Identification of Social Classes*. London: Routledge & Kegan Paul, 1977).

Carey, G. B. "Problems of the Profession in the United States." *Accountancy* (England), (February 1968): 77-80.

___. "Corporate Disclosure: How Much Is Enough?" *Bankers Monthly*, 15 June 1977, 12-13.

Carmichael, D. R. "Auditor's Statutory Liability to Third Parties: A Landmark Decision." *Texas CPA* (October 1968): 5-12.

___. "BarcChris Case: A Landmark Decision on the Auditor's Statutory Liability to Third Parties." *New York Certified Public Accountant* (November 1968): 780-87.

___. "What Does the Independent Auditor's Opinion Really Mean?" *Journal of Accountancy* (November 1974): 83-87.

___. "Corporate Financial Reporting: The Benefits and Problems of Disclosure." Proceedings of a symposium, edited by D. R. Carmichael and B. Makels. New York: 1976.

___. "Risk and Uncertainty in Financial Reporting and the Auditor's Role." In *Auditing Symposium III*. Lawrence, Kans.: Touche Ross/University of Kansas Symposium on Auditing Problems, 1976, 49-73.

___. "The Auditor's Role and Responsibilities," *Journal of Accountancy* (August 1977): 55-60.

Catlett, G. R. "Relationship of Auditing Standards to Detection of Fraud." *Arthur Andersen Chronicle* (October 1975): 50-62. Reprinted from *CPA Journal* (April 1975).

Causey, D. Y. "Foreseeability as a Determinant of Audit Responsibility." *Accounting Review* (April 1973): 258-67.

Chirm, R. "Deception of Auditors and False Records." *Journal of Accountancy* (July 1979): 1-72.

Davies, J. "Changing Legal Environment of Public Accounting: Lower Court Applications of the Hochfelder Decision" (case notes). *American Business Journal* (Winter 1978): 394-401.

Delfliese, P. L. "The Search for a New Conceptual Framework of Accounting.' *Journal of Accountancy* (July 1977): 59-67.

Denzin, N. K. "Incomplete Professionalization: The Case of Pharmacy." *Social Forces* 46 (1968): 375-82.

Derber, Charles. *Professionals as Workers: Dental Labor in Advanced Capitalism.* Boston: G. K. Holland Co., 1982.

Devine, C. T. "Professional Responsibilities: An Empirical Suggestion," with discussion by L. L. Vance and H. J. Davidson. In *Empirical Research in Accounting: Selected Studies.* Conference on Empirical Research in Accounting. Chicago: University of Chicago Press, May 1966, 160-82.

DeVos, B. H., Jr. "The Top-down Approach (to the Foreign Corrupt Practices Act)." *Financial Executive*, July 1979, 50-57.

"Do the SEC Disclosure Rules Have an Impact on Your Small Business?" *SEC Accounting Report* (May 1978): 5-7.

Doyle, B. R. "Three Company Approaches (to the Foreign Corrupt Practices Act): General Electric Company." *Financial Executive* (July 1979): 32-41.

Earle, V. M. "Accountants on Trial in Theatre of the Absurd." *Fortune* (May 1972): 227-28, 232.

Elliott, R. K., and P. D. Jacobson. "Is Regulation the Answer?" *World* (Spring 1979): 12-16.

Ellyson, R. C., and W. H. Van Rensselaer. "Sunset- Is the Profession Ready for It?" *Journal of Accountancy* (June 1980): 52-61.

Estes, R. W. "Accountant's Social Responsibility." *Journal of Accountancy* (January 1970): 40-43.

Fedders, J. M., and L. G. Perry. "Policing Financial Disclosure Fraud: The SEC's Top Priority." *Journal of Accountancy* (July 1984): 58-64.

Financial Accounting Foundation, Structure Committee. *The Structure of Establishing Financial Accounting Standards.* Stamford, Conn., April 1977.

Flom, J. H., and P. A. Atkins. "Expanding Scope of SEC Disclosure Laws." *Harvard Business Review* (July/August 1974): 109-19.

Francia, A. J., and N. J. Elliott. "Significant Differences in Accountants' Professional Liability Insurance Coverage."

New York Certified Public Accountant (October 1970): 810-15.

Friedson, Eliot. "Professionals and the Occupation Principle." In *The Professions and Their Prospects*, edited by E. Friedson. Beverly Hills, Calif.: Sage Publications, 1971, 12-18.

___. "The Division of Labor as Social Interaction." In *Work and Technology*, edited by Marie Haug and Jacques Dofny. Beverly Hills, Calif.: Sage Publications, 1977, 13-76.

___. *Professional Powers*. Chicago: University of Chicago Press, 1986.

Gavin, T. A., R. L. Hicks, and J. D. Decosimo. "CPAs' Liability to Third Parties." *Journal of Accountancy* (June 1984): 80-84.

Gibson, C. "Analysis of Continental Vending Machine (United States versus Simon)." *Ohio CPA* (Winter 1971): 8-16.

Goode, W. "The Theoretical Limits of Professionalism." In *The Semi-Professions and Their Organization*, edited by A. Etzioni. New York: Free Press, 1969.

Gregory, W. R. "Unaudited, but OK?". *Journal of Accountancy* (February 1978): 61-65.

Hagerman, R. L. "Metcalf Report: Selling Some Assumptions." *Management Accountant* (NAA) (January 1978): 13-16.

Hall, R. H. "Professionalization and Bureaucratization." *American Sociological Review* (February 1968): 92-104.

Hampson, J. J. "Accountant's Liability: The Significance of Hochfelder." *Journal of Accountancy* (December 1976): 69-74.

Hansom, R. E., and W. J. Brown. "CPA's Workpapers: The IRS Zeroes In." *Journal of Accountancy* (April 1977): 60-65.

Haug, Marie. "Deprofessionalization: An Alternative Hypothesis for the Future." In *Professionalization and Social Change*, edited by P. Halmos. Keele: University of Keele, 1970, 100-109.

___. "The Deprofessionalization of Everyone." *Sociological Focus* 8 (1975): 197-213.

___. "Computer Technology and the Obsolescence of the Concept of Profession." In *Work and Technology*, edited by Marie

Haug and Jacques Dofny. Beverly Hills, Calif.: Sage Publications, 1977, 815-28.

Haug, M., and M. B. Sussman. "Professional Autonomy and the Revolt of the Client." *Social Problems* 17 (1969): 153-61.

Hearn, L. "On the Philosophy of Startor Resartus." *Interpretations of Literature*, vol. 1, edited by J. Erskine. New York: Dodd, Mead, 1915, 208-32.

Helstein, R. S. "Guidelines for Professional Liability Insurance Coverage." *CPA Journal* (October 1973), 849-55.

Henry, W. O. E., et al. "Responsibilities and Liabilities of Auditors and Accountants." *Business Lawyer* (March 1975): 169-205.

Herwitz, D. R. "Right to Know." In *Objectives of Financial Statements*, vol. 2. Selected Papers. New York: American Institute of Certified Public Accountants, Accounting Objectives Study Group 1974, 55-56.

Hickok, R. S. "Looking to the Future: A Key to Success." *Journal of Accountancy* (March 1984): 77-82.

Hill, T. W., Jr. "Public Accountant's Legal Liability to Clients and Others." *New York Certified Public Accountant* (January 1958): 21-31.

___. *Theory of Accounting Measurement*. Sarasota, Fla.: American Accounting Association, 1975.

Kaplan, R. S. "Should Accounting Standards Be Set in the Public or Private Sector?" Working paper, Carnegie-Mellon University, April 1979. In *Regulation and the Accounting Profession* (proceedings). Los Angeles: University of California, 1980.

Kay, R. S. "How to Detect Illegal Activity." *Touche Ross Tempo*, 1976, 7-10.

Kripke, H. "Where Are We on Securities Disclosure After the Advisory Committee Report?" *Securities Regulation Law Journal* (Summer 1978): 99-132; *Journal of Accounting, Auditing and Finance* (Fall 1978): 4-32.

___. *The SEC and Corporate Disclosure: Regulation in Search of a Purpose*. New York: Law and Business, 1979.

Krogstad, J. L., M. E. Stark, K. L. Fox, and H. O. Lytle, Jr. "The Faculty Residency: A Concept Worth Considering." *Journal of Accountancy* (November 1981): 74-86.

Lantry, T. L. "Judges as Accountants" (comments). *American Business Law Journal* (Spring 1975): 108-18.

Larson, C. B. "Directors for CPA Firms: A Provocative Proposal." *Journal of Accountancy* (May 1983): 86-94.

Larson, Magali Sargatti. *The Rise of Professionalism: A Sociological Analysis.* Berkeley: University of California Press, 1977.

___. "Proletarianization and Educated Labor." *Theory and Society* 9 (1980): 131-77.

Larson, R. E., and T. P. Kelley. "Differential Measurement in Accounting Standards: The Concept Makes Sense." *Journal of Accountancy* (November 1984): 78-90.

Lee, B. Z., R. E. Larson, and P. B. Chenok. "Issues Confronting the Accounting Profession." *Journal of Accountancy* (November 1983): 78-85.

Levine, A. L., and E. S. Marks. "Accountants' Liability Insurance; Perils and Pitfalls." *Journal of Accountancy* (October 1976): 59-64.

Litter, Graig R. *The Development of the Labour Process in Capitalist Societies.* London: Heineman Educational Books 1982.

___. "Specialization: Search for a Solution." *Journal of Accountancy* (September 1982): 70-79.

Oppenheimer, Martin. "The Proletarianization of the Professional." *Sociological Review Monographs* 20 (1973): 112-32.

Pacter, P. A. "The Conceptual Framework: Make No Mystique About It." *Journal of Accountancy* (July 1983): 76-88.

Palmer, R. E. "Audit Committees: Are They Effective? An Auditor's View." *Journal of Accountancy* (September 1977): 76-79.

Pearson, D. B. "Will Accreditation Improve the Quality of Education?" *Journal of Accountancy* (April 1979): 53-58.

Prentice-Hall. *Accountants on the Firing Line: What Accountants, Corporate Managers, and Lawyers Must Know About Accountants' New and Expanded Duties*. Englewood Cliffs, N.J.: Prentice-Hall, 1975.

Previts, G. J., and E. N. Coffman. "Practice and Education: Bridging the Gap." *Journal of Accountancy* (December 1980): 39-45.

"Proposed Regulation of the Profession." *Week in Review* (Deloitte Haskins and Sells) (June 1, 1978): 1-3.

Rolfe, R. S., and R. J. Davis. "Scienter and Rule 10b-5." Notes, *Columbia Law Review* (June 1969): 1057-83. Reprinted in *Securities Law Review* (1970): 173-204.

Rothman, Robert A. "Deprofessionalization: The Case of Law in America." *Work and Occupations* 11 (1984): 183-206.

Salaman, Graeme. *Work Organization and Class Structure*, Armonk, N. Y.: M. E. Sharp, 1981.

___. *Working*. London: Tavistock Publishers, 1986.

Saxe, E. "Accountants' Responsibility for Unaudited Financial Statements." *New York Certified Public Accountant* (June 1971): 419-23; *Massachusetts CPA Review* (July/August 1971): 21-24; *Michigan CPA* (November/ December 1971): 5-7.

Schnepper, J. A. "Accountants' Liability Under Rule 10b-5 and Section 10(b) of the Securities Exchange Act of 1934: The Hole in Hochfelder." *Accounting Review* (July 1977): 653-57.

"Scienter and SEC Injunction Suits." *Harvard Law Review* (March 1977): 1018-28.

Siegel, G. "Specialization and Segmentation in the Accounting Profession." *Journal of Accountancy* (November 1977): 74-80.

Simonetti, G. "Corporate Accountability System Under Fire." *Price Waterhouse Review* (1977): 2-9.

Skousen, K. F. "Accounting Education: The New Professionalism." *Journal of Accountancy* (July 1977): 38-42.

Slavin, N. S. "The Elimination of Scienter in Determining the Auditor's Statutory Liability." *Accounting Review* (April 1977): 360-68.

___. "Origin of the Present Structure of the Public Accounting Profession: A Historical Analysis," pts. 1 and 2. *National Public Accountant* (August 1977): 15-18; (September 1977): 38-42.

Sloan, D. R. "The Education of the Professional Accountant." *Journal of Accountancy* (March 1983): 56-60.

Smith, B. E. "Reaching the Public: The CPA's New Image." *Journal of Accountancy* (January 1980): 47-52.

Solomons, D. "The Politicization of Accounting." *Journal of Accountancy* (November 1978): 65-73.

Sterling, R. R. *Institutional Issues in Public Accounting.* Lawrence, Kans.: Scholars Book Co., 1974, 9.

Toren, Nina. "Deprofessionalization and Its Source: A Preliminary Analysis." *Sociology of Work and Occupations* 2 (1975): 323-38.

U.S. Senate, Committee on Government Operations. Subcommittee on Reports, Accounting and Management. *Accounting Establishment: A Staff Study.* 1976.

___. *Accounting and Auditing Practices and Procedures* (hearing). 1977.

Vance, L. L. "Changing Responsibilities of the Public Accountant." Stanford, Calif.: Stanford University, 1970, 16. Stanford Lectures in Accounting, presented by the Graduate School of Business, Stanford University, under sponsorship of the Price Waterhouse Foundation, 5 June 1970.

Warren, C. S. "Audit Risk." *Journal of Accountancy* (August 1979): 66-74.

Wilensky, Harold. "The Professionalization of Everyone." *American Journal of Sociology* 20 (1964): 137-58.

FRAUD IN THE ACCOUNTING
ENVIRONMENT
3

Fraud in the accounting environment is on the increase, causing enormous losses to firms, individuals, and society and creating a morale problem in the workplace. It takes place as corporate fraud, fraudulent financial reporting, white-collar crime, or audit failures. This chapter explicates the nature of fraud in the accounting environment, provides some theoretical explanations of the phenomenon from the field of criminology, and explores some outcome situations arising from corporate fraud.

NATURE OF FRAUD IN THE ACCOUNTING ENVIRONMENT

Fraud has many definitions. It is a crime. The Michigan criminal law states:

Fraud is a generic term, and embraces all the multifarious means which human ingenuity can devise, which are resorted to by one individual to get advantage over another by false representations. No definite and invariable rule can be laid down as a general proposition in defining fraud, as it includes surprise, trick, cunning and unfair ways by which another is cheated. The only boundaries defining it are those that limit human knavery.[1]

It is the intentional deception of another person by lying and cheating for the purpose of deriving an unjust, personal, social, political, or economic advantage over that person.[2] It is definitively immoral.

Within a business organization fraud can be perpetrated for or against the firm. It is then *corporate fraud*. It can be perpetrated by management or a person in a position of trust. It is then a *management fraud* or *white-collar crime*. It may involve the use of an accounting system to portray a false image of the firm. It is then a form of *fraudulent financial reporting*. It may also involve a failure of the auditor to detect errors or misstatements. It is then an *audit failure*. In all these cases- corporate fraud, management fraud, white-collar crime, fraudulent financial reporting, audit failure- the accountant as preparer, auditor, or user stands to suffer heavy losses.

Corporate Fraud

Corporate frauds or economic crimes are perpetrated generally by officers, executives, and/or profit center managers of public companies to satisfy their short-term economic needs. In fact, it may be the short-term-oriented management style that creates the need for corporate fraud, given the pressure to increase current profitability in the facc of few opportunities and the need to take unwise risks with the firm's resources. As confirmed by Jack Bologna:

Rarely is compensation based on the longer term growth and development of the firm. As a consequence of this myopic view of performance criteria, the executives and officers of many public companies have a built-in incentive or motivation to play fast and loose with their firm's assets and financial data.[3]

In fact, more than the pressure for short-term profitability, it is the economic greed and avarice that blot social values and lead to corporate fraud. Evidence from the Federal Bureau of Investigation shows that arrests from two categories of corporate fraud have climbed: fraud jumped 75% between 1976 and 1986, and embezzlement rose 26%. See Exhibit 3.1.[4] In fact, corporate fraud goes beyond mere fraud and embezzlement. An exhaustive typology is shown in Exhibit 3.2.

The situation points to a myriad of activities that may result in corporate fraud. The increase in corporate fraud in the United States and elsewhere is the result of the evasion in business ethics. See Exhibit 3.3 for an examination of the contemporary views of ethical behavior.

Fraudulent Financial Reporting

Fraudulent financial reporting is so rampant that a special commission was created to investigate it: the National Commission on Fraudulent Financial Reporting. The commission defined fraudulent financial reporting as "intentional or reckless conduct, whether act or omission, that results in materially misleading financial statements."[5] Such reporting undermines the integrity of financial information and can affect a range of victims: shareholders, creditors, employees, auditors, and even competitors.

Exhibit 3.1
Arrests for Corporate Fraud

Year	Embezzlement[1]	Fraud[2]
1976	10,000	199,300
1977	7,500	247,900
1978	8,100	262,500
1979	8,600	261,900
1980	8,500	291,500
1981	8,700	295,100
1982	9,000	334,400
1983	8,800	309,800
1984	8,100	270,700
1985	11,400	342,600
1986	12,600	349,300

[1]Embezzlement is defined as the misappropriation of money or property entrusted to you, or an attempt at misappropriation

[2]Fraud is defined as obtaining money or property under false pretenses, and includes shoplifting, writing bad checks, learning without paying, confidence games, unauthorized withdrawals from automatic teller machines, and computer crimes.

Exhibit 3.2
Typology of Corporate Fraud

I. Internally generated corporate frauds
  A. For the company
    1. Regulatory violations
      a) OSHA, EEO, ERISA, EPA, FTC, FDA, ICC, OFCC, wage-hour, antitrust, SEC, IRS, FCPA, building and fire codes, state sales, USE, extraction and property taxes, rate regulations, padding government contracts, etc.
    2. Consumer and customer frauds
      a) False labeling, branding, advertising, and packaging
      b) Short weights and counts, defective products, and substitution of inferior goods
      c) Price fixing
    3. Stockholder and creditor frauds
      a) False financial statements and representations
      b) False or forged collateral
      c) Stock manipulation, insider trading, and related party transactions
    4. Frauds against competitors
      a) Theft or compromise of competitors' trade secrets or proprietary information
      b) Predatory pricing and other forms of unfair competition
      c) Copyright and patent infringement
    5. Corruption of customers' and competitors' personnel and/or regulatory authorities or union leaders
  B. Against the company
    1. By executives
      a) False claims for bonuses, benefits, or expenses
      b) Commercial bribery by vendors
      c) Sales of proprietary information or trade secrets to competitors
      d) Theft or embezzlement of corporate assets
      e) Fabrication of operational or financial performance data
    2. By nonmanagement employees
      a) Pilferage
      b) Sabotage of company property
      c) Theft or embezzlement of corporate assets
      d) False claims for bonuses, benefits, or expenses
      e) Intentional waste
      f) Falsifying time and attendance and productivity reports
  C. Frauds from within the accounting system
    1. False input scams (creating fake debits)
      a) False or inflated claims from vendors, suppliers, benefits claimants, and employees, or false refund or allowance claims by customers
      b) Lapping on receivable payments or customer bank deposits
      c) Check kiting
      d) Inventory manipulation and reclassification
        (1) Arbitrary write-ups and write-downs
        (2) Reclassification to lower value-obsolete, damaged, or "sample" status
      e) Intentional misclassification of expenditures

Exhibit 3.2 Continued

  (1) Operational expense versus capital expenditures
  (2) Personal expense versus business expense
 f) Fabrication of sales and cost of sales data
 g) Misapplication and misappropriation of funds and other corporate assets (theft and embezzlement)
 h) Computerized input and fraudulent access scams
  (1) Data diddling and manipulation
  (2) Impersonation and impostor terminal
  (3) Scavenging
  (4) Piggybacking
  (5) Wiretapping
  (6) Interception and destruction of input and source documents
  (7) Fabrication of batch or hash totals
  (8) Simulation and modeling fraud (fraudulent parallel systems)
 i) Forgery, counterfeiting, or altering of source documents, authorizations, computer program documentation, or loan collateral
 j) Overstating revenues and assets
 k) Understating expenses and liabilities
 l) Creating off-line reserves
 m) Related party transactions
 n) Spurious assets and hidden liabilities
 o) "Smoothing" profits
 p) Destruction, obliteration, and alteration of supporting documents
 q) Exceeding limits of authority
2. False thruput scams
 a) Salami slicing, trap doors, Trojan horse, logic bombs
 b) Designed random error during processing cycle
3. Output scams
 a) Scavenging through output
 b) Output destruction, obliteration
 c) Theft of output reports and logs
 d) Theft of programs, data files, and systems programming and operations documentation

D. Frauds from without the accounting system
 1. Confidence schemes by outsiders
 2. Fraudulent misrepresentations by current and prospective vendors, suppliers, customers, and employees

II. Externally generated corporate frauds
 A. Vendors, suppliers, common carriers, warehousemen
  1. False weights, counts, and quality representations
  2. Double billing
  3. Full billing for partial shipments
  4. Diversion and conversion
  5. Intentional overpricing and extension errors
  6. Corruption of purchasing employees
  7. Conspiring with employees to overlook shortages
 B. Customers
  1. Falsification of identity and credit worthiness
  2. False claims for refunds, discounts, returns, and allowances for damage
  3. Shoplifting

Exhibit 3.2 Continued

    4. Switching price tags
    5. Corrupting sales personnel
    6. Conspiring with employees to ship unbilled merchandise

C. Competitors
    1. Predatory sales, advertising, and pricing practices
    2. Theft, conversion, or/of appropriation and technology, trade secrets, proprietary information, patents, and copyrights
    3. Employee pirating
    4. Commercial slander

D. Public enemies
    1. Robbery, larceny, and burglary of corporate assets
    2. Usury
    3. Terrorist or violent acts against the company's assets and human resources — kidnapping, sabotage, extortion, and blackmail by criminal elements and hostile foreign governments
    4. Hostile takeover by financial pirates

Source: Reproduced from Jack Bologna, *Corporate Fraud: The Basics of Prevention and Detection* (Stoneham, MA: Butterworth Publishers, 1984), pp. 60–63. With permission from the publisher.

Exhibit 3.3
Views of Ethical Behavior

I. Factors that erode business ethics	
a. Decay in cultural and social institutions	76%*
b. Increased concentration on short-term earnings	74%
c. Doing business in ethically different cultures	47%
d. Volatile economic conditions	41%
II. A region has ethical standards largely because of	
a. Cultural heritage	75%
b. Religious tradition	10%
c. Education	7%
d. Economic condition of region	4%
III. The main reason for a professional's high ethical standards is	
a. Professional guidelines and accreditation	48%
b. Peer opinion and approval	26%
c. Education	11%
d. Socioeconomic background of practitioners	10%

*Percentages represent proportion of respondents naming that entry from 1,082 respondents in a 1988 survey (directors and top executives of corporations with at least $500 million in annual sales, deans of business schools, and members of Congress).

Source: "Living Up to Standards," *U.S. News and World Report,* March 14, 1988, 76.

It is used by firms that are facing economic crises as well as by those motivated by a misguided opportunism. An exhaustive list of the common types of fraudulent financial reporting with examples of each is shown in Exhibit 3.4. There is a deliberate strategy to deceive by distorting the information and the information records. This results from a number of documented dysfunctional behaviors: smoothing, biasing, focusing, gaming, filtering, and illegal acts. Such behaviors generally occur when managers have a low belief both in the analyzability of information and in the measurability and verifiability of data.[6] Of all these documented dysfunctional behaviors the one most likely to result in fraudulent financial reporting is the occurrence of illegal acts by violation of a private or public law through the type of frauds outlined in Exhibit 3.2. It does not always start with an illegal act. Managers are known to choose accounting methods in terms of their economic consequences. Various studies have argued that managerial preferences for accounting methods and procedures may vary, depending on the expected economic consequences of those methods and procedures. It has been well established that the manager's choice of accounting methods may depend on the effect on reported income,[7] the degree of owner versus manager control of the company,[8] and methods of determining managerial bonuses.[9] This effort to use accounting methods to show a good picture of the company becomes more pressing on managers who are facing some form of financial distress, and are in need of showing the economic events in the most optimistic way. This may lead to suppressing or delaying the dissemination of negative information.[10,11] The next natural step for these managers is to use fraudulent financial reporting. To hide difficulties and to deceive investors, declining and failing companies have resorted to the following fraudulent reporting practices:

(a) prematurely recognizing income, (b) improperly treated operating leases as sales, (c) inflated inventory by improper application of the Last In-First Out (LIFO) inventory method, (d) included fictitious amounts in inventories, (e) failed to recognize losses through write-offs and allowances, (f) improperly capitalized or deferred costs and expenses, (g) included unusual gains in operating income, (h) overvalued marketable securities, (i) created "sham" year-end transactions to boost reported earnings, and (j) charged their accounting practices to increase earnings without disclosing the changes.[12]

One factor in the increase of fraudulent financial reporting that has escaped scrutiny is the failure of accounting educational institutions to teach ways of detecting fraud and the importance of its detection to the entire financial reporting system. The emphasis in the university and the CPA examinations is with financial auditing rather than with forensic, fraud, or investigating reporting. J. C. Threadway, Jr., chairman of the National Commission on Fraudulent Financial Reporting, sees it this way:

If you go back to the accounting literature of the 1920s or earlier, you'll find the detection of fraud mentioned as the objective of an audit much more prominently. Our work to date in looking at the way accounting and auditing are taught today in colleges and business schools indicates that fraud detection is largely ignored. In fact, there are texts currently in use that do not even talk about the detection of fraud.[13]

Because the Securities and Exchange Commission is dedicated to the protection of the interests of investors and the integrity of capital markets, it is concerned that the adequate disclosures are provided for the public to allow a better judgment of the situation. One financial disclosure fraud enforcement program called for disclosures in four areas:

1. Liquidity problems, such as (a) decreased inflow of collections from sales to customers, (b) the lack of availability of credit from suppliers, bankers, and others, and (c) the inability to meet maturing obligations when they fall due.
2. Operating trends and factors affecting profits and losses, such as (a) curtailment of operations, (b) decline of orders, (c) increased competition, or (d) cost overruns on major contracts.
3. Material increases in problem loans must be reported by financial institutions.
4. Corporations cannot avoid their disclosure obligations when they approach business decline or failure.[14]

Corporations need to adopt measures to reduce exposure on causes of fraudulent and questionable financial reporting practices. The potential effects of some suggestions for reducing exposure are shown in Exhibit 3.5

Exhibit 3.4
Common Types of Fraudulent Financial Reporting

Type of Fraud	Examples
Manipulating, falsifying, or altering records or documents	Changing dates on supplier invoices so that expenses are not recorded until the next accounting period.
	Changing dates on shipping documents in order to book sales (and recognize profits) before the time of actual shipment.
	Changing invoice amounts to understate the amount of expense booked in the accounting records.
	Creating false inventory count sheets.
Suppressing or omitting the effects of completed transactions from records of documents	Failing to record supplier invoices at year end.
Recording transactions without substances	Creating fictitious customer orders.
Misapplying accounting policies	Capitalizing start-up and tooling costs and other items that should be expensed according to generally accepted accounting principles.
	Recognizing revenue and profits on sales for which a significant risk of return still existed.
	Purposely booking inadequate reserves to show a predetermined amount of earnings.
	Recording prepayments as expenses of current period.
Failing to disclose significant information	Concealing an impairment in the value of certain assets.
	Concealing pending litigation.
	Not reporting a change in accounting policy.

Source: Kenneth A. Merchant, *Fraudulent and Questionable Financial Reporting: A Corporate Perspective* (Morristown, N.J.: Financial Executives Research Foundation, 1987), 5. Reprinted with permission of the publisher.

Exhibit 3.5
Effects of Suggestions for Reducing Exposure on Causes of Fraudulent and Questionable Financial Reporting Practices

Causes of Fraudulent and Questionable Financial Reporting Practices

Suggestions for Reducing Exposure	Provision of incentives for deceptive financial reporting	Failure to persuade employees that chances of detection are high and penalties are severe	Failure to provide adequate moral guidance and leadership
Formulate desired stands of behavior			X
Maintain effective system of internal control		X	
Maintain effective financial organization with acknowledged responsibility for maintaining good financial-reporting practices		X	X
Main effective internal audit function		X	X
Have the board of directors play an active role in reviewing financial-reporting policies and practices		X	X
Monitor capabilities and circumstances of individuals in positions affecting financial reporting			X
Promise and use strong penalties for violations of policies		X	
Make sure performance targets are realistic	X		
Beware of high emphasis on short-term financial performance	X		

Source: Kenneth A. Merchant, *Fraudulent and Questionable Financial Reporting: A Corporate Perspective* (Morristown, N.J.: Financial Executives Research Foundation, 1987), p. 38. Reprinted with permission of the publisher.

White-collar Crime

White-collar crime was a concern for Durkheim who was convinced that the "anomie state" of "occupational ethics" was the cause "of the incessant recurrent conflicts, and the multifarious disorders of which the economic world exhibits so sad a spectacle."[15] At the same time, Ross noticed the rise in vulnerability created by the increasingly complex forms of interdependence in society and the exploitations of these vulnerabilities by a new class he called "criminaloid."[16] He argued that a new criminal was at large, one "who picks pockets with a railway rebate, murders with an adulterant instead of a bludgeon, burglarizes with a 'rake-off' instead of a jimmy, cheats with a company prospectus instead of a deck of cards, or scuttles his town instead of his ship."[17] The phrase white-collar crime was originated in Edwin Sutherland's presidential address to the American Sociological Society in December 1939.[18] He defined it as "a crime committed by a person of respectability and high social status in the course of his occupation."[19] A debate followed, with Clinard's defining white-collar crime as restricted only to "illegal activities among business and professional men,"[20] and Harting defining it as "a violation of law regulating business, which is committed for a firm by the firm or its agents in the conduct of its business."[21] Basically, one view of white-collar crime focused on occupation and the other focused on the organization. But in fact it is the world of both occupation and organization that are the world of white-collar crime and that constitute what the knife and gun are to street crime.[22] White-collar crimes have not been condemned as vehemently as other common crimes. One reason is that their crime is not to cause physical injury, but to further organizational goals. In fact, individuals were found to consider organizational crimes to be far more serious than those with physical impact.[23] Another reason for the indifference to white-collar crime may be the possibility that members of the general public are themselves committing white-collar crimes on a smaller scale.[24] In addition, the white-collar criminal generally finds support for his behavior in group norms, which places him in a different position from the common criminal. As Aubert explains:

But what distinguishes the white-collar criminal in this aspect is that his group often has an elaborate and widely accepted ideological rationalization for the offenses, and is a group of great social significance outside the sphere of criminal activity- usually a group with considerable economic and political power.[25]

The white-collar criminal is motivated by social norms, accepted and enforced by groups that indirectly give support to the illegal activity. In a lot of cases the organization itself is committing the white-collar crime, sometimes because it may be the only response to economic demands.

White-collar crime may be characterized by five principal components: (1) intent to commit the crime, (2) disguise of purpose, (3) reliance on the naivete of the victim(s), (4) voluntary victim action to assist the offender, and (5) concealment of the violation.[26] Unlike traditional crime, its objective is to steal kingly sums rather than small sums of money, and its modus operandi is to use technology and mass communications rather than brute force and crude tools. In addition, white-collar crime relies on the ignorance and greed of its victim.[27] It inflicts economic harm, physical harm, and damages to the social fabric.

Audit Failure

Auditors are expected to detect and correct or reveal any material omissions or misstatements of financial information. When auditors fail to meet these expectations, an audit failure is the inevitable result. It is then the level of audit quality that can avoid the incurrence of audit failures. Audit quality has been defined as the probability that financial statements contain no material omission or misstatements.[28] It has also been defined in terms of audit risk, with high-quality services reflecting lower audit risk.[29] Audit risk was defined as the risk that "the auditor may unknowingly fail to appropriately modify his opinion on financial statements that are materially misstated."[30]

Audit failures do, however, occur and, as a consequence, bring audit firms face to face with costly litigation and loss of reputation, not to mention court imposed judgments and out-of-court settlements. It is the client's or user's losses that lead to the litigation and situation and the potential of payments to the plaintiff. Litigation can be used as an indirect measure of audit quality using an inverse relation- auditors with relatively low (high) litigation offer higher- (lower-) quality audits. This relation was verified in a study that indicated, as expected, that non-Big Eight firms as a group had higher litigation occurrence rates than the Big Eight, and that supported the Big Eight as quality-differentiated auditors.[31]

But not all litigations follow directly from audit failures. In a study that described the role of business failures and management fraud in both legal actions brought against auditors and the settlement of such actions, Palmrose found that (a) nearly half of the cases that alleged audit failures involved business failures or clients with severe financial difficulties, and (b) most lawsuits that involved bankrupt clients also involved management fraud.[32] These findings point to the fact that business failures and management fraud play a great role in the occurrence of audit failures, which calls for the auditor to take a responsible attitude in the detection of fraud, as it may affect the audit quality, the audit risk, and the potential for costly litigations. As stated by Connor:

Establishing the requirement to identify the conditions underlying fraudulent reporting as an independent objective of the audit process would help to clarify auditor responsibility and increase auditor awareness of this responsibility. Performance of the recommended procedures of management control review and evaluation and fraud risk evaluation would improve the probability of detecting conditions leading to misstated financial statements. The required focus on financial condition would help identify more effectively those entities that would qualify as business failure candidates in the near term.[33]

Although management fraud and business failure may play a great role in audit failures, there are other reasons for such failures. For example, St. Pierre and Anderson's extended analysis of documented audit failure identified three other reasons: (1) error centering on the auditor's interpretation of generally accepted accounting principles; (2) error centering on the auditor's interpretation of generally accepted auditing standards or the implementation of generally accepted auditing standards; and (3) error centering on fraud of the auditor.[34]

FRAMEWORK FOR FRAUD IN THE ACCOUNTING ENVIRONMENT

We have established that fraud is rampant in the accounting environment, taking the shape of corporate fraud, fraudulent financial reporting, white-collar crime, and audit failures. The main issue is to determine the causes and, above all, provide and explanation for the situation. Descriptive characteristics of the person or the situation that may lead to fraud in the accounting environment abound. For example, there is a need to watch for "red flags," which do not necessarily prove management fraud, but when enough of them exist there is the potential for corporate fraud. Red-flag characteristics to be wary of in the course of an audit include the following:

-A person who is a wheeler dealer
-A person without a well-defined code of ethics
-A person who is neurotic, manic-depressive, or emotionally unstable
-A person who is arrogant or egocentric
-A person with a psychopathic personality[35]

An exhaustive list of red flags is shown in Exhibit 3.6. Merchant cities as causes of fraudulent financial reporting organizational factors and personal circumstances.

By providing incentives for deception, by failing to persuade managers and employees that chances of detection are higher and penalties severe, and by failing to provide adequate moral guidance and leadership, corporations increase the use of illegal and unethical practices.[36]

Although these descriptive characteristics may be useful for detecting the potential for fraud in the corporate environment, they do not provide an adequate normative explanation of why fraud happens. The field of criminology offers various models and theories that are very much applicable to fraud in the accounting environment and may offer alternative explanations for the phenomenon.

Exhibit 3.6
Characteristics That Lead to Fraud in Accounting

I. Personal
  A. Financial Pressures
    1. High personal debts
    2. Severe illnesses in family
    3. Inadequate income and/or living beyond means
    4. Extensive stock market speculation that creates indebtedness
    5. Loan shark involvement
    6. Excessive gambling
    7. Heavy expenses incurred from the involvement with other women/men
    8. Undue family, peer, company, or community expectations
    9. Excessive use of alcohol or drugs which cause indebtedness
  B. Revenge Motives
    1. Perceived inequities (e.g., underpaid, poor job assignment)
    2. Resentment of superiors
    3. Frustration, usually with the job
II. Company
  A. Financial Pressures
    1. Unfavorable economic conditions within that industry
    2. Heavy investments or losses
    3. Lack of sufficient working capital
    4. Success of the company is dependent on one or two products, customers, or transactions
    5. Excess capacity
    6. Severe obsolescence
    7. Extremely high debt
    8. Extremely rapid expansion through new business or product lines
    9. Tight credit, high interest rates, and reduced ability to acquire credit
    10. Pressure to finance expansion through current earnings rather than through debt or equity
    11. Profit squeeze (costs and expenses rising higher and faster than sales and revenues)
    12. Difficulty in collecting receivables
    13. Unusually heavy competition (including low-priced imports)
    14. Existing loan agreements with little flexibility and tough restrictions
    15. Progressive deterioration in quality earnings
    16. Significant tax adjustments by the IRS
    17. Long-term financial losses
    18. Unusually high profits with a cash shortage
    19. Urgent need for favorable earnings to support high price of stock, meet earnings forecast, etc.
    20. Need to gloss over a temporary bad situation and maintain management position and prestige
    21. Significant litigation, especially between stockholders and management
    22. Unmarketable collateral
    23. Significant reduction in sales backlog indicating future sales decline
    24. Long business cycle

Exhibit 3.6 Continued

25. Existence of revocable and possibly imperiled licenses necessary for the continuation of business
26. Suspension or delisting from a stock exchange
27. Fear of a merger

Opportunity Red Flags

I. Personal
  A. Personally Developed Opportunities
    1. Very familiar with operations (including cover-up capabilities)
    2. In a position of trust
    3. Close association with cohorts, suppliers, and other key people
  B. Firm Environments Which Foster and/or Create Opportunities
    1. A firm which does not inform employees about rules and disciplines of fraud perpetrators
    2. A firm in which there is rapid turnover of key employees — quit or fired.
    3. A firm in which there are no annual vacations of executives
    4. A firm in which there are no rotations or transfers of key employees
    5. A firm which does not use adequate personnel screening policies when hiring new employees to fill positions of trust
    6. A firm in which there is an absence of explicit and uniform personnel policies
    7. A firm which does not maintain accurate personnel records of dishonest acts or disciplinary actions for such things as alcoholism and/or drug use
    8. A firm which has no documented code of ethics
    9. A firm which does not require executive disclosures and examinations
    10. A firm which has weak leadership
    11. A firm which has a dishonest management and/or environment
    12. A firm which has a dominant top management (one or two individuals)
    13. A firm which is always operating on a crisis basis
    14. A firm which pays no attention to details
    15. A firm in which there is too much trust in key employees
    16. A firm in which there are relatively few interpersonal relationships
    17. A firm which does not have viable dissatisfaction and grievance outlets
    18. A firm which lacks personnel evaluations
    19. A firm which does not have operational productivity measurements and evaluations
II. Company
  A. Nature of Firm
    1. A firm which has related party transactions
    2. A firm which has a very complex business structure
    3. A firm which does not have an effective internal auditing staff
    4. An extremely large and decentralized firm
    5. A highly computerized firm
    6. A firm which has inexperienced people in key positions
  B. Relationship with Outside Parties
    1. A firm which uses several different auditing firms
    2. A firm which has a reluctance to give auditors needed data

Exhibit 3.6 Continued

     3. A firm which changes auditors often
     4. A firm which hires an auditor who lacks expertise
     5. A firm which persistently brings unexpected information to the auditors' attention
     6. A firm which changes legal counsel often
     7. A firm which has a reluctance to give accounting information to their legal counsel
     8. A firm which has several different legal counsels
     9. A firm which uses several different banks, none of which can see the entire picture
    10. A firm which has continuous problems with various regulatory agencies

C. Accounting Practices
     1. A firm which has large year-end unusual transactions
     2. A firm in which there are many adjusting entries required at the time of the audit
     3. A firm which supplies information to auditors at the last minute
     4. A firm which has a poor internal control system or does not enforce internal control procedures
     5. A firm which has unduly liberal accounting practices
     6. A firm which has poor accounting records
     7. A firm which has inadequate staffing in the accounting department

---

Personality Red Flags

I. Personal Traits
  A. A person lacking in the development of personal moral honesty
  B. A person without a well-defined code of personal ethics
  C. A person who is a "wheeler-dealer," i.e., someone who enjoys feelings of power, influence, social status, and excitement associated with rapid financial transactions involving large sums of money
  D. A person who is neurotic, manic-depressive, or emotionally unstable
  E. A person who is arrogant or egocentric
  F. A person with a psychopathic personality
  G. A person with threatened self-esteem
  H. A person who is intrigued by the personal challenge of subverting a system of controls

II. Personal Demographics
  A. A person with a criminal history
  B. A person who has questionable associates
  C. A person with poor references

Reprinted with permission from *Management Fraud: Detection and Deterrence* by R. K. Elliott and J. J. Willingham, (Petrocelli Books, 1980).

The Conflict Approach

The consensus approach and the conflict approach are two major views that hypothesize about law and society.[37] Influence by anthropological and sociological studies of primitive law, the consensus approach sees laws developing out of public opinion as a reflection of popular will. The conflict approach sees laws as originating in a political context in which influential interest groups pass laws that are beneficial to them. A third view argues for an integrated approach that focuses on the different functions of the consensus and conflict approaches, with the conflict approach ideal to explain the creation of criminal law and the consensus perspective, the operation of the law.

In the case of the accountant and fraud it can be argued, using the conflict approach, that accounting interest groups presented a favorable picture of their problematic situation by insisting that they can control for fraud and worked to get their view of the situation more widely recognized. The process led to less stringent regulation enacted for fraudulent reporting cases and white-collar crime. Basically, it fits with the notion that the criminal law that emerges after the creation of the state is designed to protect the interests of those who control the machinery of the state, including the accounting profession.

The consensus approach refers instead to the widespread consensus about the community's reaction to accounting fraud and to the legislation enacted. The consensus approach to accounting fraud may have resulted from either the ignorance or the indifference of the general public to the situation. Another explanation is the idea of differential consensus related to the support of criminal laws.[38] While serious crimes receive strong support for vigorous actions, crimes relating to the conduct of business and professional activities generate an apathetic response.

If one adopts a conflict model of crime, then the origin of the fraudulent practices in accounting may be linked to a society's political and economic development. As society's political and economic development reach higher stages, institutions are created to accommodate new needs and to check aggressive impulses. In the process these restraining institutions create a system of inequality and spur the aggressive and acquisitive impulses that the consensus model of crime mistakes for part of human nature. It is the powerful elites rather than the general will that arises to label the fraudulent practices in accounting as criminal because these crimes affect these elites as they are related to property and its possession and control. At the same time, members of that same elite constitute a major component of those participating in the fraudulent practices in accounting. Their motivation to engage in the practices remain the question. The conflict model of crime would attribute the practices to a system of inequality that values certain kinds of aggressive behavior. Basically, those engaging in fraudulent practices in accounting are reacting to the life conditions of their own social class: acquisitive behavior of the power on one hand and the high-risk property crimes of the powerless on the other. One would conclude that the focus of the attack on the fraudulent practices should be toward the societal institutions that led to the isolation of the individuals. It implies a reorganization of these institutions to eliminate the illegal possession of rights, privileges, and position.[39]

The Ecological Theory

An examination of some of the notorious accounting frauds, white-collar crimes, and audit failures may suggest that some criminal types are attracted to business in general and to accounting in particular. Therefore, the criminal cases are not indicative of a general phenomenon in the field, but the result of the criminal actions of the minority of criminal types that have been attracted to the discipline of accounting. This approach is known as the "Lombrosian" view of criminology. But with the Lombrosian theory of a physical "criminal type" losing its appeal, the ecological theory appears as a more viable and better alternative to an explanation of the fraud phenomenon in accounting. It adopts as a basis of explanation of corporate fraud phenomenon in accounting. It adopts as a basis of explanation of corporate fraud the concept of social disorganization, which is generally defined as the decrease in influence of existing rules of behavior on individual members of the group. Criminal behavior in the accounting field is to be taken as an indicator of a basic social disorganization. First, weak social organization of the discipline of accounting leads to criminal behavior. Second, with the social control of the discipline waning because of the general public indifference, some accountants are freed from moral sensitivities and are predisposed to corporate fraud, white-collar crime, and audit failure. It is then the general public's failure to function effectively as an agency of social control that is the immediate cause of corporate fraud, white-collar crime, fraudulent financial reporting, and audit failure. Basically, some accountants are freed from moral sensitivities when social control breaks down or fails to function properly.

The Cultural Transmission Theory

Unlike the ecological theory, which assumes that criminal behavior is a product of common values incapable of realization because of social disorganization, the cultural transmission theory attempts to identify the mechanisms that relate social structure to criminal behavior. One mechanism is the conception of differential association, which maintains that a person commits a crime because he or she perceived\s more favorable than unfavorable definitions of law violation. A person learns to become a criminal. As explained by Sutherland:

As part of the process of learning practical business, a young man with idealism and thoughtfulness for others is inducted into white-collar crime. In many cases he is ordered by a manager to do things which he regards as unethical or illegal, while in other cases he learns from those who have the same rank as his own how they make a success. He learns specific techniques for violating the law, together with definitions of situations in which those techniques for violating the law, together with definitions of situations in which those techniques may be used. Also he develops a general ideology.[40]

This mechanism assumes, then, that delinquents have different values than condone crime. Criminals have been socialized into the values that condone crime. They were transmitted into a culture of crime. Their behavior is an expression of specific values.[41]

Basically, what is implied is that fraudulent behavior in accounting is learned; it is learned indirectly, or by indirect association with those who practice the illegal behavior. An accountant engages in fraud because of the intimacy of his or her contact with fraudulent behavior. This is called the process of "differential association." Sutherland explains:

It is a genetic explanation of both white-collar criminals generally start their careers in good neighborhoods and good homes, graduate from colleges with some idealism, and with little selection on their part, get into particular business situations in which criminally is practically a folk way. The lower-class criminals generally start their careers in deteriorated neighborhoods and families, find delinquents at hand from whom they acquire the attitudes toward, and the techniques of, crime through association with delinquents and through partial segregation from law-abiding people. The essentials of the process are the same for the two class of criminals.[42]

Anomie Theories

Anomie, as introduced by Durkheim, is a state of normlessness or lack of regulation, a disordered relation between the individual and the social order, which can explain various forms of deviant behavior.[43] Merton's formulation of anomie focuses not on the discontinuity in the life experiences of an individual, but on the lack of fit between values and norms that confuse the individual.[44] As an example in achieving the American dream a person may find himself or herself in a dilemma between cultural goals and the means specified to achieve them. The ways adopted include conformity, innovation, ritualism, retreatism, and rebellion.[45]

Conformity to the norms and use of legitimate means to attain success do not lead to deviance. Innovation refers to the use of illicit means to attain success and may explain white-collar crime in general and fraudulent accounting and auditing practices in particular. Merton alludes as follows:

On the top economic levels, the pressures toward innovation not infrequently erase the distinction between business-like stirrings this side of the mores and sharp practices beyond the mores.[46]

Ritualism refers to an abandoning of the success goal. "Though one draws in one's horizons, one continues to abide almost compulsively by institutional norms."[47] Retreatism is basically a tacit withdrawal from the race, a way of escaping from it all.

Finally, rebellion is a revolutionary rejection of the goals of success and the means of reaching it.

Those adaptations are a result of the emphasis in our society on economic success and on the difficulty of achieving it.

It is only when a system of cultural values extols, virtually above all else, certain *common* success-goals for the population at large while the social structure rigorously restricts or completely closes access to approved modes of reaching these goals *for a considerable part of the same population*, that deviant behavior ensues on a large scale.[48]

Interestingly enough, Merton goes as far as suggesting that deviance develops among scientists because of the emphasis on originality. Given limited opportunity and short supply, scientists would resort to devices such as reporting only data that support one's hypothesis, secrecy, stealing ideas, and fabricating data.[49]

Unlike Durkheim, Merton believes that anomie is a permanent feature of all modern industrial societies. Their emphasis on achievement and the pressures that result lead to deviance. The anomie thesis is further explored in the work of Cohen[50] and Cloward and Ohlin.[51] Cohen attributes the origins of criminal behavior to the impact of ambition across those social positions for which the possibilities of achievement are limited. What results is a nonutilitarian delinquent subculture.[52] Individuals placed in low social positions accept societal values of ambition but are unable to realize them because of lack of legitimate opportunities to do so. Cloward and Ohlin suggest that the resulting delinquent behavior is, however, conditioned by the presence or absence of appropriate illegitimate means.[53]

Corporate fraud, fraudulent reporting practices, white-collar crime, and audit failures are a result of anomie in modern societies. Basically, delinquent accountants emerge among those whose status, power, and security of income are relatively low but whose level of aspiration is high, so that they strive to emerge from the bottom even using illegal ways. Fraudulent behavior among accountants is then the solution to status anxiety. It results from the discrepancy between the generally accepted values of ambition and achievement and the inability to realize them, and the availability of appropriate illegitimate means.

A Framework for Fraud in Accounting

The various theories from the field of criminology offer alternative explanations for corporate fraud, white-collar crime, fraudulent financial reporting, and audit failures. They can be integrated in a framework to be used for identifying the situations most conducive to those phenomena (see Exhibit 3.7). Basically, the framework will postulate that corporate fraud, white-collar crime, fraudulent financial reporting, and audit failures will occur most often in the following situations:

- *In which accounting and business groups have presented a favorable picture of their problematic situation by insisting that they can control for fraud and worked to get their view of the situation more widely recognized.* What may exist is a situation in which the accountants and/or businessmen have stated that they are taking private actions to avoid public regulation of the phenomena, where in fact their actions were mere cosmetic changes or camouflage of serious problems in the profession. There have been many examples of situations in which the accounting profession has argued for private regulation of various problems that affect the profession, the discipline, and standard setting, and has thwarted the actions of legislators who were trying to put a stop to the abuses. One has only to recall the failure of various congressional committees investigating the profession to enact any fundamental regulations to change the nature, character, structure, and behaviors of the profession to illustrate the point. From a conflict approach, this is clearly a situation in which the interests of those who control the machinery of the state, including the power of the accounting profession, are protected from stringent regulation.

Exhibit 3.7
A Framework for Fraud in Accounting

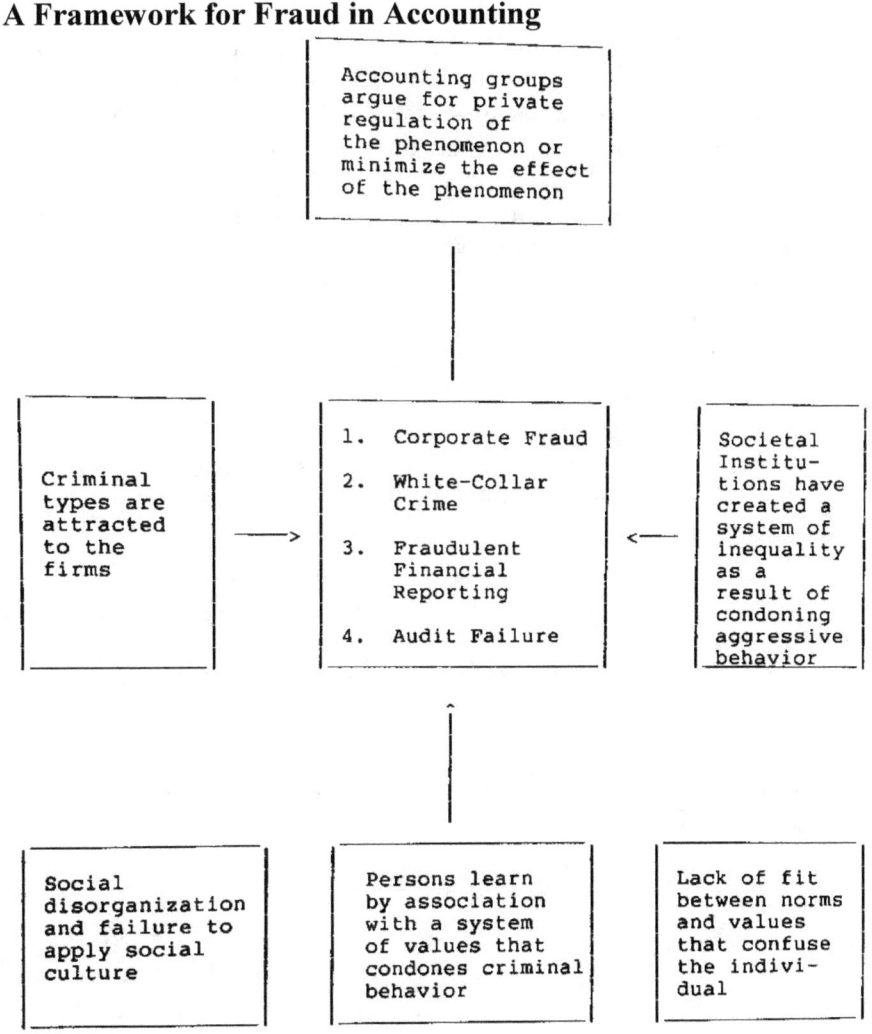

- *In which societal institutions have accumulated power, privileges, and position, creating a perception of inequality in those who are not members of these institutions.* Basically, the situation may lead to an isolation of individuals in a situation in which the acquisitive behavior of the powerful is evident in their daily lives. The lower-level accountant may react to this situation of powerlessness, inferiority, and exclusion by resorting to the various types of illegal activities covered in this chapter. It would be a mere reaction to a system of inequality that values aggressive behavior as explained by the conflict model.
- *In which firms in general have attracted some criminal types.* The Lombrosian view of the phenomena applies to various accounting frauds.
- *In which social disorganization in general and failure to apply social control exist.* Basically, weak social organization of the discipline and failure of the general public to be concerned creates a climate conducive to fraud.
- *In which people are placed in a system of values that condones corporate fraud, white-collar crime, fraudulent financial reporting, and audit failures.*
- *In which there is a lack of fit between values and norms that compose the person.*

OUTCOME SITUATIONS THAT ARISE FROM CORPORATE FRAUD
Away from RICO to ADR

There is definitely a dramatic increase in the number of claims against certified public accountants (CPAs) and in the amounts sought by claimants as a result of the expanding scope of accountants' liability and RICO (Racketeer-Influenced and Corrupt Organizations Act) liability. RICO, originally used by people victimized by a "pattern of racketeering activity" to sue for treble damages and attorney fees, has been used more and more in commercial litigation growing out of fraudulent securities offerings, corporate failures, and investment disappointments. A situation in which co-defendant auditors (sometimes in alleged conspiracy with their client and its management) had violated the federal mail and securities fraud statutes by improperly auditing and issuing audit opinions on their client's financial statements on two or more specified occasions, and by employing in the operations of their firms (in or affecting interstate commerce) the fees received for those audits, by reason of which plaintiffs were injured in their business or property, is claimed to allege a violation of statutory provisions of the RICO Act.[54] Efforts were made in 1987 to reform the civil provisions of RICO. In fact a Senate bill introduced by Senator Howard Metzenbaum continues to permit plaintiffs to seek multiple damages in cases otherwise punishable under the securities laws if the plaintiffs are small investors. The definition of small investor will include more than 50% of the more than 45 million investors in securities in the United States. This spells bad news for the accounting profession. Witness the following statement made by B. Z. Lee, the AICPA's choice for testifying to the need to reform RICO:

Of greatest concern to the accounting profession. . . is the fact that RICO continues to be used to evade the standards of the securities laws and to raise the stakes in ordinary litigation arising from securities transactions.[55]

For now, fraudulent cases that involve auditors will continue to be prosecuted with RICO liability in mind. In these fraudulent cases accountants have found themselves named as co-defendants. The rationale behind the courts' proneness to hold auditors liable for losses associated with business failures results from the belief that auditors" (1) can best prevent the losses associated with business failures and (2) are able to spread their liability through insurance."[56] What auditors face is a dangerous gamble that is trail by jury, especially with the risk of RICO-treble damage judgments. Not only may the average juror not understand the complexities of the cases, but the CPA may face situation of claims without merit because his or her factual and legal positions may be misunderstood or rejected by the same jurors. The trail by jury may also be an expensive alternative even if the CPA's position prevailed. Witness the following assessment of the situation:

Even if the accountant ultimately prevails at trial, the costs of protracted litigation, including attorney's fees and deposition costs, can be prohibitively high. Thus, even a win before a jury often translates into great pecuniary loss. Litigation costs and exposure aside, an additional substantial burden is placed on an accountant defendant who is called away from practice- losing both time and fees- and required to produce and review records, study claimant's documents and testimony, appear as a witness on deposition, defend depositions of other and be in attendance at trial.[57]

The trial by jury can also be detrimental to accountants because of the several often repeated arguments that are increasingly persuasive in courts. These arguments include the perceptions that (a) auditors are equipped to prevent the losses associated with business failures, (b) accountants are deep pockets that can use their insurance to spread the losses, and (c) equity calls for placing losses resulting from business failures on auditors. [58] What appears to be more beneficial options for resolving claims against CPAs are the ADR (alternative dispute resolution) methods: *arbitration, court-assessed arbitration, mediation, and mistrial.*

The AICPA's special committee on accountants' legal liability prepared in 1987 a paper on ADR as a flexible approach to resolving litigation with a client by transforming the typical confrontational positive into one of cooperation to reach a mutually advantageous solution.[59] One suggestion made is for the accountant and his or her client to agree on some element of an engagement letter or on a separate agreement that any disputes between them will be determined by ADR procedures. The following two model paragraphs are offered for an engagement letter, one specifically for arbitration and the other for general procedure:

Model Arbitration Paragraph

Any controversy or claim arising out of or relating to our engagement to [describe service, e.g., audit the company's financial statements] shall be resolved by arbitration in accordance with the Commercial Arbitration Rules of the American Arbitration Association and judgment on the award rendered by the Arbitrator(s) may be rendered in any Court having proper jurisdiction.

Model General ADR Paragraph

In the event of any dispute between us relating to our engagement to [describe engagement, e.g., audit the company's financial statements; prepare the company's tax returns], we mutually agree to try in good faith to resolve the dispute through negotiation or alternative dispute resolution techniques before pursuing full-scale litigation.[60]

Arbitration is now appearing as the more viable option. The pros for arbitration include (a) its informal nature, (b) the choice of knowledgeable professionals as arbitrators, (c) its low cost, (d) its avoidance of the wrong judgments by an unsophisticated jury, (e) the neutralizing of the hostility factor to professionals and sympathy factor to alleged victims prevalent in a jury trial, and (f) the elimination of the risk of a runaway jury's returning a verdict that far exceeds actual losses. These features are summed up as follows:

In arbitration, extensive and time consuming discovery, which has become standard practice in litigation, is generally not permitted. During the prepatory stages of arbitration, lengthy depositions usually aren't allowed and limited documentation is exchanged on an informal basis. At arbitration hearings, the rules of evidence are more relaxed. Because of the expertise of the members of the panel, the need for experts to make detailed explanations to unsophisticated jurors is substantially reduced. Fewer witnesses need to be called to testify, fewer technical requirements need be met and fewer technical evidentiary objections and arguments need to be made.[61]

Naturally there are limitations to arbitration. The major limitations are the absence of judicial review and the loss of the court's requirement that evidence be legally admissible and weighed in accordance with legal principles. Other limitations are expressed as follows:

While the American Institute of CPAs' accountants' legal liability special committee has submitted proposed alternative dispute resolution and arbitration clauses, the inclusion of these clauses in the initial engagement letter may subject a member to a coverage defense in any subsequent litigation. . . . Arbitration includes numerous negative points such as limited discovery, limited appeal and a difficulty in confining the arbitrators' decision to case and statutory law. This is particularly true when a defense may involve a question of privity. These negative points severely affect the insurer's ability to defend an insured in a malpractice claim. It seems to me that a CPA may subject himself to an insurance coverage dispute by including an arbitration clause in the initial engagement letter, since the clause in the initial engagement letter, since the clause binds the CPA and his insurer to submit to future arbitration.[42]

The Liability Exposure Expands

With the number of lawsuits filed in 1987 reaching one private lawsuit for every 15 Americans, accountants were not immune to the epidemic of lawsuits. The consequences include escalating judgments and legal costs and astronomic increases in the premiums for professional liability. Even the AICPA professional liability insurance plan increased the premium to 200% by the end of 1985 along with a coupling of deductibles and reduction in the maximum coverage available from $20 million in 1984 to $5 million in 1985. The situation is explained as follows:

As a result of the premium increase, some medium-sized firms previously paying about $3,400 for $5 million in coverage saw their bills jump to $10,250. In addition, the deductible per claim double from $3,500 to $7,000.[63]

To make things worse, megasuits are now being filed against the eight largest accounting firms. Examples include (a) the $260 million damage suit filed in 1985 by the British government for alleged negligence against the auditors of the Delorean Motor Co. in northern Ireland and (b) the $100 million judgment brought against an Australian accounting partnership in Cambridge Credit Corporation Ltd. v. Hutcheson.[64]

The nature of accounting liability has changed since the first English lawsuit against an auditor in 1887.[65] Two major suits had a profound effect- Judge (later Justice) Benjamin N. Cardozo's opinion in Ultramares Corp. v. Touche in 1931[66] and the McKesson & Robbins business fraud and settlement with accountants in 1938.[67] The Ultramares v. Touche decision was that accountants are liable for negligence to their clients and to those they know will be using their work product. More precisely, Judge Cardozo held that accountants could not be held liable to third parties because it might expose accountants to a liability in an indeterminate amount for an indeterminate time to an indeterminate class. The hazards of business conducted on these terms are so extreme as to enkindle doubt whether a flaw may not exist in the implication of a duty that exposes to these consequences.[68]

The doctrine known as the "privity defense" has recently been eroded with a dramatic expansion in the scope of an auditor's availability for negligence. As Minow states: "The new theory seems to be that the accountant should be held responsible for a business that doesn't function properly."[69] The new *doctrine of indeterminate liability* extends the accountants' liability to any investor or creditor who can convince the court or a jury that the accountant, in hindsight, could have prevented a business failure or fraud by disclosing it. Another new doctrine known as the *fraud-on-the-market theory* allows investors to recover from defendants for alleged misrepresentations of which the investors were completely unaware as long as reliance on the statements by the market affected the price of the security bought or sold by the plaintiff. An example of the new doctrines came in 1983 when the New Jersey Supreme Court, in H. Rosen Blum, Inc. v. Adler, held that the accountants can be held of negligence to nay reasonable "third parties" relying on that information, especially that the accountants are able to use and misuse:

Independent auditors have apparently been able to obtain liability insurance covering these risks or otherwise to satisfy their financial obligation. We have no reason to believe they may not purchase malpractice insurance policies that cover their negligence leading to misstatements relied up on by persons who received the audit from the company pursuant to a proper business purpose. Much of the additional costs incurred either because of more thorough auditing review or increased insurance premiums would be borne by the business entity and its stockholders or its customers.[70]

There is definitely a misperception of the accounting professor and its work product. Victor Earle, general counsel of Peat, Marwick, Main & Co., stated this misperception with prescience a decade ago:

The misconceptions in the public mind are at least fivefold: first, as to *scope*- that auditors make a 100% examination of the company's records, which can be depended upon to recover all errors or misconduct; second, as to *evaluation*- that auditors pass the wisdom and legality of a company's multitudinous business decisions; third, as to *precision*- that the numbers set forth in a company's audited financial statements are immutable absolutes; fourth, as to *reductability*- that the audited results of a company's operations for a year can be synthesized into a single number; and fifth, as to *approval*- that by expressing an option on a company's financial statement, the auditors "certify" its health and attractiveness for investment purposes.[71]

The liability exposure of U.S. accounting firms doing audits of overseas subsidiaries of American companies also increased tremendously in March 1988 when a federal judge ruled that United States- based accounting firms can be sued in U.S. courts for allegedly shoddy audits in other nations. The decision came after the court denied a motion by Arthur Anderson & Co. to throw out a $260 million suit against it by the British government for allegedly negligent audits after the collapse of Delorean Motor Co.'s Irish unit. That the U.S. courts will have jurisdiction in such cases spells more trouble for American accounting firms, as U.S. courts are known to be far tougher on accountants than are English and European courts.[72]

In March 1988 the liability exposure took a different dimension when the Supreme Court made it easier for shareholders to file class-action lawsuits against companies that issue misleading information. In its ruling the Supreme Court endorsed the efficient market hypothesis, which maintained that all publicly available information is reflected in the market price. Therefore, shareholders who allege misleading information and security fraud don't have to prove that they have relied on the misleading information. Basically, nobody can hide anymore behind a white collar.[73]

Those developments put the accounting profession in a dangerous situation, as all business failures could be blamed on the accountant and as the normal risks of investment may be shifted from the investor to the accountant. Frivolous litigation may rise, leading the accounting profession to avoid serving riskier industries and to avoid innovations in its own practice. A case in point is the review of earnings forecasts. Minow explains:

Accountants would be discouraged from innovations within their own practice, such as review of earnings forecasts, which, though potentially highly useful to the investing public, are necessarily speculative and, in the current climate, pose obvious litigation risks to accountants.[74]

Fraud Engagement: The Issues

Fraud as the intentional deception, misappropriation of resources, or distortion of data to the advantage of the perpetrator may involve either a manager or an employee. Management fraud it the most difficult to detect and can cause irreparable damage. The conduct of an audit in accordance with generally accepted accounting principles does not anticipate deceit and may fail to detect fraud. The key to fraud prevention could be effective and functioning internal controls. However, some fraud schemes may be effectively designed to work within the framework of an effective internal control system. The level of assurance of these controls becomes the key, even though fraud is most associated with a problem of integrity and, therefore, not easily quantifiable. What may be needed besides the audit is a fraud engagement. This is different from an audit based on a generally accepted auditing standard in the following way:

In short, the fraud engagement requires a specialized program that is singularly designed for discovery. It is ideally concerned with what lies behind transactions, with regard to materiality, and is not concerned with the application of generally accepted accounting principles unless misapplication has led to fraudulent statements. In its purest form, therefore, it is a hybrid of auditing and management advisory services. And the individual searching for fraud must have a detection mentality that is tempered with a high level of innovation and skepticism.[75]

Fraud engagement should be looking for specifically recurring fraud schemes and watch for specific indicia of fraud. Recurring fraudulent schemes include the following:

- Petty cash embezzlement, generally camouflaged by false or inadequate documentation
- Accounts payable fraud involving the formation of a dummy corporation to invoice the payer and receive the funds
- Cash inventory schemes in which inventory is purchased with cash or its equivalent, rather than by check, and is not placed on the books
- False-payroll schemes involving the creation of a fictitious employee, with management cashing his or her spurious payroll checks

- Lapping schemes in which employees steal from one customer's account and attempt to cover the theft by applying to that account later collections from another customer.
- Kickback schemes.[76]

All these schemes involve some diversion of assets or information followed by the prevention or deferral of the activities' disclosure. They can be detected if certain indicators or indicia are carefully watched, especially those indicators or indicia that are present time and again when fraud occurs. The following irregularities deserve closer scrutiny:

1. High rates of employee turnover, particularly in the accounting or bookkeeping departments
2. Refusal to use serially numbered documents or the undocumented destruction of missing numbers
3. Excessive and unjustified cash transactions
4. Excessive and unjustified use of exchange items, such as cashiers' checks, travelers' checks and money orders
5. Failure to reconcile checking accounts
6. Excessive number of checking accounts with a true business purpose
7. The existence of liens and other financial encumbrances before a bankruptcy, which may indicate that the bankruptcy was planned
8. Photocopies of invoices in files
9. A manager or employee who falls in debt
10. Excessive number of unexplained corporate checks bearing second endorsements
11. Excessive or material changes in bad-debt write-off
12. Inappropriate freight expenses in relation to historical sales or industry norms
13. Inappropriate ratio of inventory components
14. Business dealings with no apparent economic purpose
15. Assets apparently sold but possession maintained
16. Assets sold for much less than they are worth
17. Continuous rollover of loans to management or loans to employees not normally included in the loans accounts
18. Questionable changes in financial ratios, such as net income and inventory
19. Questionable leave practices, such as the failure or refusal of an employee to take leave[77]

It follows that auditors have to expand their role to that of police officers and engage in detecting and reporting fraud and financial weaknesses in the firms they audit. The three-year examination of the auditing profession by the House Subcommittee on Oversight and Investigations that ended in 1988 has a non-negotiable item for the profession, which is to be the voluntary protector of the investor or it will face legislation that will make this role mandatory.[78] For that Congress will use the Treadway findings as a basis for the legislation and increase the SEC power to impose sanctions and push for criminal prosecution. One would not blame Congress, as the typical situation now shows a failure of auditing standards when they allow auditors to wait until a company has failed before notifying the SEC of possible fraud. A case in point is the ZZZZ Best One, in which Ernst and Whinney had good reason to believe long before ZZZZ Best collapsed that many of the statements made by the carpet cleaning company were fraudulent. It was over and of no use to anyone when Ernst and Whinney decided to make its knowledge of fraud public. It is only after the bankruptcy that Ernst and Whinney filed documents with the SEC indicating that it had been tipped off that ZZZZ Best really was little more than a giant Ponzi scheme, costing investors more than $70 million.

Fraud auditing is then one solution to the problem of fraudulent financial reporting and fraud in general. It was referred to as the creation of an environment that encourages the detection and prevention of fraud in commercial transactions.[79] The advent of federal, criminal, and regulatory statutes involving business calls for some form of fraud auditing. When fraud auditing fails to connect the problems and frauds do happen, is there a role for forensic and investigative accounting? Forensic auditing deals with the relation and application of financial factors to legal problems.[80] What, then, is the difference between forensic accounting, fraud auditing, investigative auditing, and financial auditing? The answer to a survey among the staff members of Peak Marqick Lindquist Holmes, a Toronto-based firm of chartered accountants, is illustrative of the difference:

Forensic accounting is a general term used to describe any investigation of a financial nature that can result in some matter that has legal consequence.

Fraud auditing is a specialized discipline within forensic accounting, which involves the investigation of a particular criminal activity, namely fraud.

Investigative auditing involves the review of financial documentation for a specific purpose, which could relate to litigation support and insurance claims as well as criminal matters.[81]

Forensic auditing goes beyond routine auditing. It specializes in uncovering fraud in the ledger of business contracts and bank statements. Forensic auditors will prepare a written profile of every key person involved with the company, including corporate officers, employees, and vendors. Keeping track of everything is the objective. The following comment by Douglas Carmichael illustrates the extend of the investigation under forensic auditing.

When the death of a company (occurs) under mysterious circumstances, forensic accountants are essential. . . . Other accountants may look at the charts. But forensic accountants actually dig into the body.[82]

CONCLUSIONS

The increase of fraud in the accounting environment is definitely an emerging problem for the accounting profession. The credibility of the profession and the field as a guarantor of the integrity of the financial recording system will suffer more unless drastic measures are taken to make the accountant and the auditor face the fraud problem as a major concern. The immorality of the phenomenon should be accentuated in special courses in the ethical problems of the profession. The education community should take the lead in sensitizing the students to the existence, the gravity, the immorality, and the consequences of the problem. The short-term-oriented management style that may account for a large proportion of corporate fraud needs to be de-emphasized because of its myopic view of the environment.

NOTES

1. *Michigan Law Review*, ch. 66, sect. 1529.

2. Jack Bologna, *Corporate Fraud: The Basics of Prevention and Detection* (Boston: Buttersworth Publishers, 1984).

3. Ibid., 10.

4. "Ethics 101," *U.S. News and World Report*, 14 March 1988, 76.

5. National Commission on Fraudulent Financial Reporting, *Report of the National Commission on Fraudulent Financial Reporting* (Washington, D.C.: April 1987): 2.

6. J. G. Birnberg, L. Turopolec, and S. M. Young, "The Organizational Context of Accounting," *Accounting, Organizations and Society* (July 1983): 111-30.

7. S. Lilien and V. Pastena, "Intermethod Comparability: The Case of the Oil and Gas Industry," *The Accounting Review* (July 1981): 690-703.

8. D. S. Dhaliwal, G. L. Salamon and E. D. Smith, "The Effect of Owner Versus Management Control on the Choice of Accounting Methods." *Journal of Accounting and Economics* 1 (1982): 41-53.

9. P. M. Healy, "The Effect of Bonus Schemes on Accounting Decisions," *Journal of Accounting and Economics* 1-3 (1985): 85-107.

10. K. B. Schwartz, "Accounting Changes by Corporations Facing Possible Insolvency," *Journal of Accounting, Auditing and Finance* (Fall 1982): 32-43.

11. K. B. Schwartz and K. Merion, "Auditor Switches by Failure Firms," *The Accounting Review* (April 1985): 248-61.

12. John M. Fedders and L. Glenn Perry, "Policing Financial Disclosure Fraud: the SEC's Top Priority," *Journal of Accountancy* (July 1984): 59.

13. Bill Lietbag, "Profile: James C. Treadway, Jr.," *Journal of Accountancy* (September 1986): 80.

14. Fedders and Perry, "Policing Financial Disclosure Fraud," 59.

15. Emile Durkheim, *The Division of Labor of Society*, trans. George Simpson (New York: Free Press, 1964): 2.

16. E. A. Ross, *Sins and Society* (Boston: Houghton Mifflin, 1907).

17. Ibid., 7.

18. Edwin Sutherland, "White-Collar Criminality," *American Sociological Review* 5 (February 1940): 110-23.

19. Edwin Sutherland, *White Collar Crime* (New York: Dryden Press, 1949): 9.

20. M. B. Clinard and R. F. Reier, *Sociology of Deviant Behavior* (New York: Holt, Rinehard and Winston, 1979): viii.

21. F. E. Hartung, "White Collar Offenses in the Wholesale Meat Industry in Detroit," *American Journal of Sociology* 56 (1950): 25.

22. S. Wheeler and M. L. Rothman, "The Organization as Weapon in White-Collar Crime," *Michigan Law Review* (June 1982): 1403-76.

23. L. S. Shrager and O. F. Short, Jr., "How Serious a Crime? Perceptions of Organizational and Common Crimes," in *White-Collar Crime: Theory and Research*, ed. G. Geis and E. Stotland (London: Sage, 1980): 26.

24. V. Aubert, "White Collar Crime and Social Structure," *American Journal of Sociology* (November 1952): 265.

25. Ibid., 266.

26. H. Edelhertz, E. Stotland, M. Walsh, and J. Weimberg, *The Investigation of White Collar Crime: A Manual for Law Enforcement Agencies*. U.S. Department of Justice, LEAA (Washington, D.C.: Government Printing Office, 1970).

27. August Bequai, *White-Collar Crime: a 20th Century Crisis* (Lexington, Mass.: Lexington Books, 1978): 13.

28. Zoe-Vonna Palmrose, "An Analysis of Auditor Litigation and Audit Service Quality," *The Accounting Review* (January 1988): 56.

29. Linda E. DeAngelo, "Auditor Size and Audit Quality," *Journal of Accounting and Economics* (December 1981): 183-99.

30. American Institute of Certified Public Accountants, *Professional Standards*, Vol. 1 (New York: AICPA, 1985), SAS no. 47.

31. Palmrose, "Analysis of Auditor Litigation," 72.

32. Zoe-Vonna Palmrose, "Litigation and Independent Auditors: The Role of Business Failures and Management Fraud," *Auditing: A Journal of Practice and Theory* (Spring 1987): 90-103.

33. J. E. Connor, "Enhancing Public Confidence in the Accounting Profession," *Journal of Accountancy* (July 1986): 83.

34. K. St. Pierre and J. Anderson, "An Analysis of Audit Failures Based on Documented Legal Cases," *Journal of Accounting Auditing and Finance* (Spring 1988): 229-47.

35. Bologna, *Corporate Fraud*, 39.

36. K. A. Merchant, *Fraudulent and Questionable Financial Reporting* (New York: Financial Executives Research Foundation, 1987): 12.

37. James T. Carey, *Introduction to Criminology* (Englewood Cliffs, N.J.: Prentice-Hall, 1978): 8.

38. Don L. Gibbons, "Crime and Punishment: A Study in Social Attitudes," *Social Forces* (June 1969): 391-97.

39. Carey, *Introduction to Criminology*, 36-41.

40. Sutherland, *White Collar Crime*, 240.

41. Walter B. Miller, "Lower Class Culture as a Generating Milieu of Gang Delinquency," *Journal of Social Issues*, 14:3 (1958): 5-19.

42. Sutherland, "White Collar Criminality," 12.

43. Durkheim, *The Division of Labor in Society*.

44. Robert K. Merton, "Social Structure and Anomie," *American Sociological Review* (October 1938): 672-82.

45. Robert K. Merton, *Social Theory and Social Structure* (New York: Free Press, 1957): 131-160.

46. Ibid., 144.

47. Ibid., 150

48. Ibid., 146.

49. Robert K. Merton, "Priorities in Scientific Discovery: A Chapter in the Sociology of Science," *American Sociological Review* (December 1957): 635-59.

50. Albert K. Cohen, *Delinquent Boys: The Culture of the Gang* (New York: Free Press, 1955).

51. Richard A. Cloward and Lloyd E. Ohlin, *Delinquency and Opportunity* (New York: Free Press, 1960).

52. Albert K. Cohen, "The Study of Social Disorganization and Deviant Behavior," in *Sociology Today: Problems and Prospects*, ed. Robert K. Merton, Leonard Boorm, and Leonard S. Cottrell, Jr. (New York: Harper & Bros., 1959).

53. Cloward and Ohlin, *Delinquency and Opportunity*, 72.

54. R. James Gomley, "RICO and the Professional Accountant," *Journal of Accounting, Auditing and Finance* (Fall 1982): 51-60.

55. "AICPA Testifies at RICO Hearings: Support Boucher Proposal," *Journal of Accountancy* (January 1988): 82.

56. Richard S. Banick and Douglas C. Broeker, "Arbitration: An Option for Resolving Claims Against CPAs," *Journal of Accountancy* (October 1987): 124.

57. Ibid., 126.

58. Stevens H. Collins, "Professional Liability: The Situation Worsens," *Journal of Accountancy* (November 1985): 66.

59. American Institute of Certified Public Accountants, Special Committee on Accountants' Legal Liability, *Alternative Dispute Resolution* (New York: AICPA, 1987).

60. Ibid., 2, 8.

61. Ibid., 126.

62. Joseph D. Steward, "Arbitration," *Journal of Accountancy* (February 1988): 12-13.

63. Collins, "Professional Liability," 57.

64. Ibid., 57.

65. Leeds Estate, Building & Investment Co. v. Shepherd, 36, Ch. D. 787 (1887).

66. Ultramares Corp. v. Torche, 225 N.Y. 170, 174 N.E. 441 (1931).

67. See Denzil Y. Causey Jr., *Duties and Liabilities of Public Accountants* (Home-wood, Ill.: Dow-Jones-Irwin, 1982): 16-17.

68. Ultramares Corp. v. Torche, 225 N.Y. 170, 179-180, 174 N.E. 441, 444 (1931).

69. Newton N. Minow, "Accountants' Liability and the Litigation Explosion," *Journal of Accountancy* (September 1984): 72.

70. Rosenblaum v. Adler, Slip Op. A-39/85 (N.J.: June 9, 1983): 21.

71. Victor Earle, "Accountants on Trial in a Theater of the Absurd," *Fortune* (May 1972): 227.

72. Lee Berton, "Accounting Firms Can Be Sued in U.S. Over Audits Done Abroad, Judge Rules," *Wall Street Journal*, 10 March 1988, 2.

73. Lawrence J. Tell, "Giliam's Legacy: Nobody Can Hide Behind a White Collar," *Business Week* (February 8, 1988): 69.

74. Minow, "Accountants' Liability and the Litigation Explosion," 80.

75. Marvin M. Levy, "Financial Fraud: Schemes and Indicia," *Journal of Accountancy* (August 1985): 79

76. Ibid., 79-86.

77. Ibid., 86-87.

78. Sallie Gaines, "From Balance Sheet to Fraud Beat," *Chicago Tribune*, 28 February 1988, sect. 7, p. 5.

79. Jack G. Bologna and Robert J. Lindquist, *Fraud Auditing and Forensic Accounting* (New York: John Wiley & Sons, 1987), 22.

80. Ibid., 85.

81. Ibid., 91.

82. D. Akst and L. Berton, "Accountants Who Specialize in Detecting Fraud Find Themselves in Great Demand," *Wall Street Journal*, 26 February 1988, sect. 2, p. 17.

REFERENCES

"AICPA Testifies at RICO Hearings: Support Boucher Proposal." *Journal of Accountancy* (January 1988): 82.

Akst, D., and L. Berton. "Accountants Who Specialize in Detecting Fraud Find Themselves in Great Demand." *Wall Street Journal*, 26 February 1988, sect. 2, p. 17.

American Institute of Certified Public Accountants, Special Committee on Accountants' Legal Liability. *Alternative Dispute Resolution*. New York: AICPA, 1987.

American Institute of Certified Public Accountants, *Professional Standards*, vol. 1. New York: AICPA, 1985, SAS no. 47.

Aubert, V. "White Collar Crime and Social Structure." *American Journal of Sociology* (November 1952): 265.

Banick, R. S., and D. C. Broeker. "Arbitration: An Option for Resolving Claims Against CPAs." *Journal of Accountancy* (October 1987): 124.

Bequai, A. *White-Collar Crime: A 20th Century Crisis*. Lexington, Mass.: Lexington Books, 1978, 13.

Berton, L. "Accounting Firms Can Be Sued in U.S. Over Audits Done Abroad, Judge Rules." *Wall Street Journal*, 10 March 1988, 2.

Birnberg, J. G., L. Turopolec and S. M. Young. "The Organizational Context of Accounting." *Accounting, Organizations and Society* (July 1983): 111-30.

Bologna, J. *Corporate Fraud: The Basics of Prevention and Detection*. Boston: Butterworths Publishers, 1984, 39.

, and R. J. Lindquist, *Fraud Auditing and Forensic Accounting*. New York: John Wiley & Sons, 1987, 22, 91.

Carey, J. T. *Introduction to Criminology*. Englewood Cliffs, N.J.: Prentice-Hall, 1978, 8, 36-41.

Causey, D. Y., Jr. *Duties and Liabilities of Public Accountants*. Homewood, Ill. Dow-Jones-Irwin, 1982, 16-17.

Clinard, M. B. and R. F. Reier, *Sociology of Deviant Behavior* (New York: Holt, Rinehard and Winston, 1979).

Cloward, R. A., and L. E. Ohlin. *Delinquency and Opportunity*. New York: Free Press, 1960.

Cohen, A. K. *Delinquent Boys: The Culture of the Gang*. New York: Free Press, 1955, 77-82.

___. "The Study of Social Disorganization and Deviant Behavior." In *Sociology Today: Problems and Prospects*, edited by Robert K. Merton, Leonard Boorm, and Leonard S. Cottrell, Jr. New York: Harper & Bros., 1959.

Collins, S. H. "Professional Liability: The Situation Worsens." *Journal of Accountancy* (November 1985): 57, 66.

Connor, J. E. "Enhancing Public Confidence in the Accounting Profession." *Journal of Accountancy* (July 1986): 83.

DeAngelo, L. E. "Auditor Size and Audit Quality." *Journal of Accounting and Economics* (December 1981): 183-99.

Dhaliwal, D. S., G. L. Salamon, and E. D. Smith. "The Effect of Owner Versus Management Control on the Choice of Accounting Methods." *Journal of Accounting and Economics* 1 (1982): 41-53.

Durkheim, E. *The Division of Labor of Society*, translated by George Simpson. New York: Free Press, 1964, 2.

Earle, V. "Accountants on Trial in a Theater of the Absurd." *Fortune* (May 1972): 227.

Edelhertz, H., E. Stotland, M. Walsh, and J. Weimberg. *The Investigation of White Collar Crime: A Manual for Law Enforcement Agencies*. U.S. Department of Justice, LEAA. Washington, D.C.: Government Printing Office, 1970.

"Ethics 101." *U.S. News and World Report*, 14 March 1988, 76.

Fedders, J. M., and L. G. Perry. "Policing Financial Disclosure Fraud: The SEC's Top Priority." *Journal of Accountancy* (July 1984): 59.

Gaines, S. "From Balance Sheet to Fraud Beat." *Chicago Tribune*, 28 February 1988, sect. 7, p. 5.

Gibbons, D. L. "Crime and Punishment: A Study in Social Attitudes." *Social Forces* (June 1969): 391-97.

Gomley, R. J. "RICO and the Professional Accountant." *Journal of Accounting, Auditing and Finance* (Fall 1982): 51-60.

Hartung, F. E. "White Collar Offenses in the Wholesale Meat Industry in Detroit." *American Journal of Sociology* 56 (1950): 25.

Healy, P. M. "The Effect of Bonus Schemes on Accounting Decisions." *Journal of Accounting and Economics* 1-3 (1985): 85-107.

Leeds Estate, Building & Investment Co. v. Shepherd, 36, Ch. D. 787 (1887).

Levy, M. M. "Financial Fraud: Schemes and Indicia." *Journal of Accountancy* (September 1986): 80.

Lietbag, B. "Profile: James C. Treadway, Jr. *Journal of Accountancy* (August 1985): 79.

Lilien, S., and V. Pastena. "Intermethod Comparability: The Case of the Oil and Gas Industry." *The Accounting Review* (July 1981): 690-703.

Merchant, K. A. *Fraudulent and Questionable Financial Reporting.* New York: Financial Executives Research Foundation, 1987, 12.

Merton, R. K. "Social Structure and Anomie." *American Sociological Review* (October 1938): 672-82.

___. "Priorities in Scientific Discovery: A Chapter in the Sociology of Science." *American Sociological Review* (December 1957): 635-59.

___. *Social Theory and Social Structure.* New York: Free Press, 1957, 131-60.

Michigan Law Review, ch. 66, sect. 1529.

Miller, W. B. "Lower Class Culture as a Generating Milieu of Gang Delinquency." *Journal of Social Issues* 14:3 (1958): 5-19.

Minow, N. N. "Accountants' Liability and the Litigation Explosion." *Journal of Accountancy* (September 1984): 72, 80.

National Commission on Fraudulent Financial Reporting. *Report of the National Commission on Fraudulent Financial Reporting.* Washington, D.C.; April 1987, 2.

Palmrose, Zoe-Vonna. "Litigation and Independent Auditors: The Role of Business Failures and Management Fraud." *Auditing: A Journal of Practice and Theory* (Spring 1987): 90-103.

___. "An Analysis of Auditor Litigation and Audit Service Quality." *The Accounting Review* (January 1988): 56, 72.

Rosenblaum, v. Adler, Slip Op. A-39/85. N.J. June 9, 1983, 21.

Ross, E. A. *Sins and Society.* Boston: Houghton Mifflin, 1907.

Russell, H. F. *Foozles and Fraud.* Altamonte Springs, Fla.: Institute of Internal Auditors, 1977.

Schwartz, K. B. *White Collar Crime*. New York: Dryden Press, 1949, 240.

___. "Accounting Changes by Corporations Facing Possible Insolvency." *Journal of Accounting, Auditing and Finance* (Fall 1982): 32-43.

Schwartz, K. B. and K. Merion. "Auditor Switches by Failure Firms." *The Accounting Review* (April 1985): 248-61.

Shrager, L. S., and O. F. Short, Jr. "How Serious a Crime? Perceptions of Organizational and Common Crimes." In *White-Collar Crime: Theory and Research*, edited by G. Geis and E. Stotland. London: Sage, 1980, 26.

Steward, J. D. "Arbitration." *Journal of Accountancy* (February 1988): 12-13.

St. Pierre, K., and J. Anderson. "An Analysis of Audit Failures Based on Documented Legal Cases." *Journal of Accounting, Auditing and Finance* (Spring 1982): 229-47.

Sutherland, E. "White-Collar Criminality." *American Sociological Review* (February 1940): 210-31.

___. *White Collar Crime*. New York: Dryden Press, 1949, 9.

Tell, L. "Giliam's Legacy: Nobody Can Hide Behind a White Collar." *Business Week*, 8 February 1988, 69.

Uecker, W. C., A. P. Brief, and W. R. Kinney, Jr. "Perception of the Internal and External Auditor as a Deterrent to Corporate Irregularities." *The Accounting Review* (July 1981): 465-78.

Ultramares Corp. v. Torche, 255 N.Y. 170, 179-80, 174 N.E. 441, 444 (1931).

Wheeler, S., and M. L. Rothman. "The Organization as Weapon in White-Collar Crime." *Michigan Law Review* (June 1982): 1403-76.

THE DECLINE OF THE WORK PROCESS IN ACCOUNTING

IN ACCOUNTING

4

The nature of accounting work is tedious, uninspiring most of the time. It involves specialization, subdivision, and fragmentation of tasks. In addition, it is experiencing a general decline as a result of the phenomena of proletarianization, alienation, and de-skilling. These problems, which if left uncorrected can precipitate a crisis, are examined in this chapter to explicate their nature and the gravity of the situation they create.

PROLETARIANIZATION OF THE ACCOUNTANT'S WORK

The division of labor in an accounting firm follows a rigid hierarchy composed of four levels, with the titles, in ascending order, of junior, senior, manager, and partner. The accountants work in either the auditing, tax, or management advisory department. In both the auditing and tax departments the work is technical, structured, and highly subdivided into various components. As Boland describes:

The task of every component is broken down into a large number of subdivided steps; the steps are allocated to specialized functionaries; and task accomplishment is coordinated and controlled by a bureaucratic chain of command that verifies task performance, bundles exceptions and controls quality. Task accomplishment is controlled through checklist technology. A checklist specifies the step to be performed and expresses official expectations of efficiency through time estimates. It also serves as a framework for budget control, because each working hour of each individual is characterized by one of the steps on the checklist. Movement through the hierarchy constitutes professional development for an individual. Each firm has an understood pattern of progression, with two to five years spent at each level before and individual emerges as a partner.[1]

The subdivision and specialization of the accounting are at the core of the proletarianization of the accountant's work.

Proletarianization occurs as clerical workers, like most of the accountants, lose the features that have traditionally placed them among the middle class. As defined by Glenn and Feldberg, proletarianization "occurs as clerical work loses these special characteristics, i.e., as work is organized around manual rather than mental activities, as tasks become externally structured and controlled and as relationships become depersonalized."[2] The proletarianization of accountants has occurred because of (a) the increase in size of certified public accounting (CPA) firms, (b) the overwhelming use of machine technology in the form of computer work, and (c) organizational goals that favor the proletarianization of accounting workers.

First, the clerical work in the accounting office is heavily oriented toward the use of computers in the processing and verification of financial statements and the increasing use of expert systems in the auditing process. Second, the size of accounting firms has increased to accommodate the growth of services provided to a more complex economic environment. Both features call for the organization of accounting firms into specialized units in which accountants are subdivided according to the task and required to be specialized. As a result of the heavy computer use, work has to be structured by the requirements of the computer, subjecting the accountant to the requirements of the machine. The skills required to accomplish the level of accounting task delegated to a single junior accountant has become more mechanical, lower level, and narrower. What has taken place in the accountant's labor process is a systematic subdivision and standardization of the work process followed by more rational and impersonal methods of control, aimed at increasing profitability. The debate in the sociological literature points to the thesis that the subdivision and specialization of the clerical work in general and the accountant's work in particular may be less for reasons of efficiency[3,4] and more for the objective of controlling the labor process.[5] In fact, because of the sheer size of CPA firms, administrative controls were added to the personal controls exercised by supervisors, managers, and/or partners. The use of these supervisors is needed, as the subdivision of the work makes the workers lose control and overview of the total product and makes external coordination a must for a successful completion of the total accounting work. The subdivision itself allows constant inspection of the accounting labor process and easy quantification of the performance measures. Both constant inspection and easy quantification of the performance measures. Both constant inspection and easy quantification of the performance measures are the direct result of the whole process of proletarianization of the accountant. Another direct result is the feeling by the junior accountant that his manual, structured job is too simple, and therefore, his or her services are interchangeable and replaceable.

The junior accountant is, as for all the new professional workers, becoming both an agent of capitalist control and a professionally trained servant of capitalism. His or her situation bears the mark of the proletarian condition. As Braverman states:

For those employees the social form taken by their work, their true place in the relations of production, their fundamental condition of subordination as so much hired labor increasingly makes itself felt, especially in the mass occupations that are part of this stratum. We may cite here particularly the mass employments of draftsmen and technicians, engineers and accountants, nurses and teachers, and the multiplying ranks of supervisors, foremen and petty managers.[6]

The increasing job dissatisfaction with accounting work and staff turnover in CPA firms is a good indication of an increasing awareness of the "proletarian" aspects of accounting work.

The new situation of the accountant provides support to the notion that through the logic of capitalism, the accounting profession, like other professions, is becoming "proletarianized" and that accountants are simply acting as service agents for the providers of capital, governments, and so on. As stated by Martin Appenheimer in his paper "The Proletarianization of the Professional":

The . . . professional is thus caught between the requirements of performing bureaucratic tasks and maintaining the system (and this job) and a professional commitment to do something about social problems, which is presumably what the workplace was set up for. In short, many of the professional and semi-professional jobs in the public sector are related to the oppressive functions of government- keeping welfare clients quiet, policing, regulating- while both the professional's training and the demands of clients emphasize problem solving and delivering service in a human way. Thus, just as the professional begins to grapple with the real function of the job (as opposed to the rhetoric he has been educated on), that job becomes even more onerous due to deteriorating conditions stemming from budget cuts and other symptoms of the fiscal crises of the public sector.[7]

This is in fact part of a general view of professionals as proletarians rather than a technocrats, basically a view where a white-collar, proletarian-type worker is replacing the autonomous professional in the upper strata of professional bureaucracies.[8] The proletarianization results from a *devaluation in the form of work* of the professional. The new labor environment is characterized by (a) an extensive division of labor, leaving the worker to perform only some of the tasks in a total process; (b) a worker's subordination to a higher authority that determines all the parameters of the labor process; (c) a worker's reward restricted to his salary; and (d) a worker's defense in the form of collective bargaining rather than individual face-to-face bargaining.[9] This new labor environment is accepted by the accountants as they espouse a working-class consciousness and face a new social organization in which interests of the actual producers and management dominate the system. The urgency of livelihood as obtained from work requires them to show accommodation and ingenuity. As stated by Matza and Wellman, commenting on the ordeal of consciousness of workers:

Equally taken for granted is a political subordination: the free speech of civic life is alien to the job. Censorship- and thus enforced existence outside of anything resembling "distorted speech communities"- is a basic feature of supervised work, whether white-collar or blue-collar. Being able to say anything one wishes, and having the freedom to do so, is one of the substantial privileges of any society. Control of communication, ranging from the imposition of complete silence during work, to the invention of self-protective etiquettes of interaction with superiors, is part of the ordeal. Whatever it is that consciousness thinks and says when things come to that, it must think and say those things in the light of an understanding that it will not be allowed to speak. Thus it is in the nature of working class consciousness that it frequently has to be whispered or winked; a certain subtlety is involved.[10]

COMPUTERIZATION IN THE ACCOUNTING PROFESSION AND THE DOWNGRADING HYPOTHESIS

Since the 1960s the accounting industry has been characterized by rapid expansion and continual technical change. Accountants have been required to acquire computer skills as a response to increase in size, changes in the types of job that are rapidly created (and just as rapidly transformed), and change in the character of the accounting labor process itself.

The computerization of the accounting labor process has evolved as a result of the emphasis on efficiency and as a result of the need to introduce the new technology in the accounting workplace. Like all other computer works, the one associated with the accounting, auditing, and tax tasks became heavily routinized as a result of the development of "high-level" software languages, so-called canned or packaged programs, and structured programming and its corollaries.[11] Basically, accountants with remedial software skills are able to program and use the machines, relying on canned programs, structured programming, and various forms of modularization. This allows the accounting firms and departments (a) to be free from dependence on individual, highly skilled accounting workers and (b) to produce an efficient task-based fragmentation of accounting work. This may explain the increase in women aspiring to become accountants, as traditionally, women were allowed to move into skilled occupations only during severe labor shortages or when an occupation had been drained of skill through social and technological innovation.[12]

Another consequence of the computerization of the accounting labor process is the downgrading of the computer workers. This is generally accomplished by the establishment of a sharper division of labor and status hierarchy among computer workers in accounting firms or departments. This downgrading is followed by a diminished status of the accountant despite its white-collar connotation, followed by an increase in alienation, dissatisfaction, and even the potential for revolutionary attitudes.[13] It is the need to remain competitive that is the main determinant of downgrading, as it encourages cutting the personnel expenditures, standardizing accounting tasks, and reducing turnover.[14]

COMPUTER TECHNOLOGY AND ALIENATION FROM WORK

Computer technology is becoming more and more important in the accounting, auditing, and tax labor processes. The impact of the introduction of such technology on alienation from work in the accounting field has not yet adequately been researched. One, therefore, cannot make the Marxian assumption that advanced technology has resulted in increased alienation in the accounting field. There is, however, ample evidence of an inverted U-curve relation between technological advance and alienation. Known as the Blauner's hypothesis,[15] it has been verified in both blue-collar and white-collar settings.[16-18]

Blauner maintains that the transition from craft to mass production processes results in an increasingly detailed division of labor (i.e., high functional specialization) that, together with other factors, raises worker alienation to high levels. The trend is assumed to reverse with the development of fully automated, continuous process technology. In an accounting context, the alienation that may be created depends on the type of effect it has on the division of labor and the degradation of skills. If the finely subdivided jobs are perceived to be meaningless, then alienation will settle in the accounting arena. It is the powerlessness and repetition, rather than the complexity, of work that causes the alienation.[19] As it may apply to accountants, the Blauner's hypothesis may be serious. As derived from Seeman,[20] Blauner's hypothesis includes four dimensions: powerlessness, meaninglessness, and social isolation, and self-estrangement.

In the case of the accountants, it is more their separation from the total product of their labor than the introduction of new technology that may be the source of the alienation, job dissatisfaction, and turnover observed in accounting firm. Two conditions are assumed to result from the alienation of workers in general from the product of their labor:

(1) Workers come to be controlled by their own creation (congealed labor, in the form of machinery), and are therefore rendered passive objects of the production process, not active subjects; and (2) the work has

lost its intrinsic purpose for the workers; for them it appears as but a means to the end of subsistence.[21]

Marxist theory suggests various subjective responses to this state of alienation: (a) aversion toward one's work, (b) displacement of one's needs into a sphere of nonwork, and (c) preoccupation with one's basic needs.

DE-SKILLING OF THE ACCOUNTANT'S WORK
The De-skilling Hypothesis

The basis of Bravermans' thesis is that work, at least in capitalism, is geared to the creation of profit rather than the satisfaction of one's need.[22] Given the conflict that may arise between workers and management, control is necessary for the profit objective to be achieved. Management imposes a differentiation between the conception and execution of work such that conception in terms of planning and design of work tasks is the responsibility of management and execution, the responsibility of workers. In essence, it establishes a separation of manual and mental labor leading to a degradation of work, as all elements of knowledge, responsibility, and judgment are taken from the workers and all their tasks are programmed, routinized, and specialized. It amounts to a deskilling of the workers, a control of the workers, and a satisfaction of the profit objective. Management, in Marxist terms, is acting as a class for itself, fully cognizant of its interests and the need to realize them, whereas the working class is acting as a class in itself, living in accordance with the force that act on it. To Braverman, it is the logic of Taylorism that is the logic of capitalism, that control of the labor process remains in the hands of management. Braverman's view of the logic of Taylorism goes as follows:

Workers who are controlled only by general orders and discipline are not adequately controlled, because they retain their grip on the actual processes of labor . . . [and] they will thwart efforts to realize the full potential in their labor power. To change this situation control of the labor process must pass from the hands of management not only in a formal sense but by the control and dictation of each step of the process including its mode of performance.[23]

Basically, Braverman maintains that capitalism produced one classic form of work- Taylorism- which articulated in clear and classic form the requirements of work under capitalism: cheapness, control, and transferability.

To Braverman, the degradation of work takes place because of two concerns of the capitalist organization or the labor process: (a) the need to cheapen labor, reducing the value of labor power by substituting simple for complex labor, and (b) the need to ensure effective control of the labor process by eliminating the esoteric skills that may slow down the reorganization the production in the hands of capital and its agents. The first concern is at the core of the de-skilling hypothesis. It consists of three dimensions: (1) the worker's loss of the right to design and plan work, (2) the fragmentation of work into meaningless segments, and (3) the redistribution of risks among unskilled and semi-skilled labor in an attempt to cheapen labor.

The De-skilling of the Accountant's Work

The de-skilling hypothesis was extended to clerical and accounting work by Crompton and Reid.[24] They argue that clerical de-skilling, which includes the de-skilling of the accountant's work, involves the fragmentation, simplification and standardization of work tasks and a decrease in the accountant's role as an intermediary between management and the mass of routine workers.[25] Basically, accounting managers can reduce the cost of labor by dividing complex accounting tasks into simple routinized steps and by hiring for low wages unskilled accounting graduates to do the resulting detail work. Cost considerations arising from fierce competition between the accounting firms dictate the de-skilling of accounting work and a fine division of accounting labor. Control remains in the hands of the accounting managers by their complete knowledge of the total accounting labor process and by their efforts to reduce accounting workers to mere executors of work. As accounting labor becomes meaningless, accounting workers become more alienated.

One may ask, what factors favor the de-skilling of the accounting work? Arguments may be made in favor of the de-skilling as follows:

1. The skill of the skilled accountant is essentially artificial, socially constructed to maintain differentials in wages and status.
2. The accounting groups have been unable to fight management's interference with their traditional autonomy and independence.
3. The accountants have failed, sometimes by mere inaction and inertia, to reverse or counter the de-skilling trend.
4. The attempts to humanize accounting work are simply cosmetic or doomed to failure.
5. The introduction of computer technology in the accounting work has increased the de-skilling.

An argument may also be used that accounting has not been de-skilled, given its involvement in key decision-making positions within the global function of capital. The argument is without value, as Johnson showed that the involvement itself has created a *horizontal fission* within the profession, whereby the activities of the elite that installs control systems have the effect of routinizing, fragmenting, and de-skilling the work of their nominal professional colleagues.[26-28] The de-skilling works in fact in favor of the accounting elite, as it creates a certain *indetermination* of its own activities, and thus reinforces its monopoly of high-level jobs. What results is that subordinates who finally break into the high-level positions face problems of adjustment because of the "indetermination" of the activities of the partners and managers of accounting firms and other high-level positions in accounting.[29] It is a clear argument for (a) the close links in accounting firms between issues of work design and control and (b) the political (i.e., class-nature of work arrangements and technologies).

That junior accountants fail to see their work situation in class terms in evidence of their false consciousness. The exclusionary tactics by managers of accounting firm through the restrictive practices of the horizontal fission described above, and the failure of the accountants to comprehend the situation and react to it force them into their lower economic class and explain their social, and thus work, structures.

CONCLUSION

This chapter argues about the decline, loss of sovereignty, deprofessionalization, and proletarianization of the accounting profession. It follows from a thesis of accounting professionals as workers in the capitalist system. Because of the decrease in self-employment and the need to work for big CPA firms, accounting workers have come to lose control and autonomy at work, and they become subordinate to an administration and bureaucratic system. In addition, sweeping invasion of professional markets by large-scale capital and expansion of the knowledge and services market put the professional accountant at the service of the large public or private bureaucracies. The proletarianization of the professional accountant is a result of the capitalization of mental labor and human services, which has swallowed up the last remaining realms of "free" labor in the economy and signifies consolidation of corporate and state power. One is reminded in CPA firms of a comparison between prisons and factories. As Foucault asks:

Is it surprising, therefore, that the cellular prison, with its regular chronologies, forced labor, its authorities of surveillance and registration, its experts in normality which continue and multiply the functions of the judge, should become a modern instrument of penalty? Is it surprising that prisons resemble factories, schools, barracks, hospitals, which all resemble prisons?[30]

NOTES

1. Richard N. Boland, Jr., "Myth and Technology in the American Accounting Profession," *Journal of Management Studies* 19:1 (1982): 111.

2. Evelyn Nakano Glenn, and Roslyn L. Feldberg, "Degraded and Deskilled: The Proletarianization of Clerical Work," *Social Problems* (October 1977): 52-64.

3. Andre Gorz, "Technical Intelligence and the Capitalist Division of Labor," *Science for the People*, 19 May 1973, 26-29.

4. Stephen Maglin, "What Do Bosses Do? The Origins and Functions of Hierarchy in Capitalist Production," *Review of Radical Political Economics* (Summer 1974): 60-112.

5. Philip Kraft, "Deskilling Work: The Case of Computer Programmers." Paper presented at Political Economy Colloqiuium, Department of Sociology, Boston University, 1975.

6. H. Braverman, *Labor and Monopoly Capital: The Degradation of Work in the Twentieth Century* (New York: Monthly Review Press, 1974), 407.

7. M. Opphenheimer, "The Proletarianization of the Professional," in *Professionalization and Social Change*, ed. P. Halmos (University of Keele, Monograph No. 20, 1973), 216.

8. Ibid., 213.

9. Ibid.

10. David Matza and David Wellman, "The Ordeal of Consciousness," *Theory and Society* 9 (1980): 2.

11. Philip Kraft, "The Routinizing of Computer Programming," *Sociology of Work and Occupations* 6: 2 (1979): 139-55.

12. Ibid., 152.

13. D. Bell, *The Coming of Post-Industrial Society* (New York: Basic Books, 1973), 148.

14. Teresa A. Sullivan and Daniel B. Cornfield, "Downgrading Computer Workers: Evidence from Occupational and Industrial Redistribution," *Sociology of Work and Occupations*, 6 (May 1979): 184-204.

15. R. Blauner, *Alienation and Freedom* (Chicago: University of Chicago Press, 1964).

16. J. Sheppard, "Technology, Alienation, and Job Satisfaction," *Annual Review of Sociology* 3 (1977): 121-28.

17. B. A. Kissch and J. J. Lengermann, "An Empirical Test of Robert Blauner's Ideas of Alienation in Work As Applied to Different Jobs in a White Collar Setting," *Social Science Research* 56 (1971): 180-94.

18. B. Tudor, "A Specification of Relationships Between Job Complexity and Powerlessness," *American Sociological Review* 37 (1979): 596-604.

19. Ibid., 596-604.

20. M. Seeman, "On the Meaning of Alienation," *American Sociological Review* 24 (1959): 783-79.

21. Steven Peter Vallas and Michael Yarrow, "Advanced Technology and Worker Alienation: Comments on the Blauner/Marxism Debate," *Work and Occupations* 14:1 (1987): 130.

22. Braverman, *Labor and Monopoly Capital.*

23. Ibid., 1100.

24. Rosemary Crompton and Stuart Reid, "The Deskilling of Clerical Work," in *The Degradation of Work? Skill, Deskilling and the Labor Process*, ed. Stephen Wood (London: Hutchinson, 1982), 163-78.

25. Ibid., 175.

26. Terry Johnson, "What Is to Be Known?" *Economy and Society*, 2 (1977): 194-233.

27. Terry Johnson, "The Professions in Class Structure," in *Industrial Society: Class, Cleavage and Control*, ed. R. Scase (London: Allen & Unwin, 1977), 93-110.

28. Terry Johnson, *Work and Power*, in *The Politics of Work and Occupations*, ed. G. Esland and G. Salaman (Milton Keynes, England: Open University Press, 1980), 335-71.

29. E. F. McKenna, *The Management Style of the Chief Accountant* (London: Saxon House, 1978).

30. M. Foucault, *Discipline and Punish* (London: Allen Lane, 1977).

REFERENCES

Anderson, Ronald E., and Jeylan T. Mortimer. "Sociology of Computer Work." *Sociology of Work and Occupations* (May 1979): 131-38.

Armstrong, Peter. "Changing Management Control Strategies: the Role of Competition Between Accountancy and Other Organizational Professions." *Accounting, Organizations and Society* 10:2 (1985): 129-48.

Attewell, Paul. "The Deskilling Controversy." *Work and Occupations* (August 1987): 323-46.

Boland, Richard W., Jr. "Myth and Technology in the American Accounting Profession." *Journal of Management Studies* 19: 1 (1982): 109-27.

Braverman, Harry. *Labor and Monopoly Capital: The Degradation of Work in the Twentieth Century*. New York: Monthly Review Press, 1974.

Chandler, Alfred D., Jr., and Herman Daems. *Managerial Hierarchies*. Cambridge, Mass.: Harvard University Press, 1980.

Chawson, Dan. *Bureaucracy and the Labor Process*. New York: Monthly Review Press, 1980.

Cooley, M. "The Taylorisation of Intellectual Work." In *Science, Technology and the Labor Process: Marxist Studies*, edited by L. Levidow and R. Young, Vol. 1. London: CSE Books, 1981, 45-63.

Crompton, S., and S. Reid. "The Deskilling of Clerical Work." In *The Degradation of Work?* edited by S. Woods. London: Hutchinson, 1982, 62-73.

Edwards, Richard C., Michael Reich, and David M. Gordon, eds. *Labor Market Segmentation*. Lexington, Mass.: D. C. Heath & Co., 1975.

Esland, Geoff, and Solaman Graeme, eds. *The Politics of Work and Occupations*. Milton Keynes, England: Open University Press, 1982.

Giddens, Anthony, and Gavin MacKenzie. *Social Class and the Division of Labor*. Cambridge: Cambridge University Press, 1982.

Glenn, E., and R. L. Feldberg. "Degraded and Deskilled: The Proletariantization of Clerical Work." *Social Problems* (October 1977): 52-64.

___. "Proletarianizing Clerical Work: Technology and Organizational Control in the Office." In *Case Studies on the Labor Process*, edited by A. Zimbalist. (New York: Monthly Review Press, 1979, 51-72.

Gorz, A. "Technology, Technicians and Class Struggle." in *The Division of Labor*, edited by A. Gorz. New York: Harvester Press, 1976, 149-85.

Hales, Mike. *Living Thinkwork: Where Do Labor Processes Come From?* London: CSE Books, 1980.

Hull, F., N. S. Friedman, and T. F. Rogers. "The Effect of Technology on Alienation from Work: Testing Blauner's Inverted U-Curve Hypothesis." *Work and Occupations* 9:1 (1982): 31-57.

Ingram, David. *Hobermas and the Dialectic of Reason*. New Haven, Conn.: Yale University Press, 1987.

Kraft, Philip. *Programmers and Managers: The Routinization of Computer Programming in the United States*. New York: Springer-Verlag, 1977.

___. "The Routinizing of Computer Programming." *Sociology of Work and Occupations*, 6:2 (1979): 139-55.

Larson, Magali Sarfatti. *The Rise of Professionalism: A Sociological Analysis*. Berkeley: University of California Press, 1977.

Lee, D. J. "Skill, Craft and Class: A Theoretical Critique and Critical Case." *Sociology* 15 (1981): 56-78.

Levidown, Les, and Bob Young, eds. *Science, Technology and the Labor Process Marxist Studies*. Vol. 1. London: CSE Books, 1981.

Littler, Craig R. *The Development of the Labor Process in Capitalist Societies*. London: Heinemann Educational Books, 1982.

Littler, C., and G. Salaman. "Braverman and Beyond: Recent Theories of the Labor Process." *Sociology* (May 1982): 251-69.

McKenna, E. F. *The Management Style of the Chief Accountant*. London: Saxon House, 1978.

Periucci, Robert, and Foel E. Gerstt. *Profession Without Community: Engineers in American Society*. New York: Random House, 1969.

Ponlantzas, Nicos. *Classes in Contemporary Capitalism*. London: Lowe & Brydone Printers, Ltd., 1978.

Puxty, Anthony G. *Organization and Management: An Accountant's Perspective*. London: Pitman, 1986.

Scase, Richard, ed. *Industrial Society Class, Cleavage and Control*. London, George Allen & Unwin, Ltd., 1977.

Sullivan, Teresa A., and Daniel B. Cornfield. "Downgrading Computer Workers: Evidence from Occupational and Industrial Redistribution." *Sociology of Work and Occupations*, 6 (May 1979): 184-204.

Vallas, Steven Peter, and Michael Yarrow. "Advanced Technology and Worker Alienation: Comments on the Blauner/Marxism Debate." *Work and Occupations* 14:1 (1987): 126-42.

Wood, S. *The Degradation of Work?* London: Hutchinson, 1982.

Wright, E. O., and J. Singlemann. "Proletarianization in the Changing American Class Structure." *American Journal of Sociology* 88 (Suppl., 1982): S176-S209.

Zicklin, Gilbert. "Numerical Control Machining and the Issue of Deskilling." *Work and Occupations* (August 1987): 452-66.

THE ORGANIZATIONAL CLIMATE IN ACCOUNTING FIRMS
5

The primary asset for a certified public accounting (CPA) firm is its professional staff. The success of the firm depends on motivating them, retraining them, and keeping them satisfied. As a result, research in human resource considerations in public accounting firms is necessary to identify the factors that may create the ideal atmosphere for members of accounting firms to function efficiently and be job satisfied. This type of research has identified serious problems in such areas as (a) job satisfaction in public accounting firms, (b) the organizational climate in public accounting firms, (c) the performance evaluation in public accounting firms, (d) the staff turnover in public accounting firms, (e) the motivation in the accounting environment, and (f) the personal and situational characteristics of accountants and their consequences. The purpose of this chapter is to cover this type of research as it describes potential problems facing the accounting profession.

JOB SATISFACTION IN PUBLIC ACCOUNTING FIRMS

Job satisfaction in all types of work environments and work groups resulted in the general conclusion that an increase relationship existed between job satisfaction and turnover, in the sense that as job satisfaction increases, turnover decreases and as job satisfaction decreases, turnover increases.[1] Another general finding is that job satisfaction and performance are not necessarily positively related.[2,3] Various studies attempted to provide evidence on the degree of job satisfaction in public accounting firms. Using a Porter[4] need satisfaction questionnaire, Strawser and co-workers investigated the job satisfaction of accountants in large and small CPA firms.[5] The results showed that the relative satisfaction of the self-actualization need depended on the type of occupation and the type of firms, with the Big Eight firms showing the higher level of satisfaction. Nevertheless, the accountants working in small firms showed the highest degree of satisfaction with the autonomy needs. Carpenter and Strawser examined the satisfaction levels of academic accountants.[6] Their results showed that those academics in small schools were the most deficient in total satisfaction in four of the six needs categories studied (social, self-esteem, self-actualization, and compensation). Security and autonomy needs were the deficiencies found in large schools for accounting academics.

Similarly, a comparison of the job satisfaction of industrial managers and CPAs showed that the largest perceived need deficiencies are found in the self-actualization category.[7]

Aranya and others examined the accountants' job satisfaction as a process model by examining the influences of organizational and professional commitments and of need deprivation on job satisfaction and on migration intentions.[8] The results of a path analysis showed that the migration tendencies of the accountants were not related to their job satisfaction and organizational commitment of accountants in public practice, but rather to the organizational commitment of accountants in industry or in government. In addition, with the exception of accountants in nonprofessional organizations, professional commitment had an effect on both satisfaction and organizational commitment. "It suggests that the fulfillment of work needs is a determinant of both job satisfaction and commitment to the organization which allows for much fulfillment."[9] This confirms an earlier finding that job satisfaction is affected by professional deprivation.[10]

The impact of environmental uncertainty in job satisfaction was examined in the accounting environment. Ferris provided survey evidence showing that as the level of perceived environmental uncertainty increases, the level of job satisfaction decreases.[11] Other important implications are drawn from the findings:

First, the presence of even moderate levels of uncertainty may be sufficient to explain, in part, the relatively high turnover rate among staff accountants. Second, if perceived uncertainty impacts job satisfaction, then it should also be expected to impact the antecedents of job satisfaction, for example, employee motivation. And, finally, perceived uncertainty may be a causal factor of diminished employee performance.[12]

Benke and Rhode investigated the job satisfaction of higher-level employees in large CPA firms with the objective of (a) determining the possible difference between audit, tax, and management services with respect to job satisfaction, personal characteristics, and job features, and (b) predicting the job satisfaction of audit, tax, and management services, using personal characteristics and job features as independent variables.[13] The findings on the first objective indicate various differences between management service specialists and audit and tax specialists as a combined group. The findings on the second objective pointed to the possibility of predicting the job satisfaction of audit and tax specialists, but not of management service specialists. The results point to the need by large CPA firms (a) not to treat higher-level professional employees as a professional group and to use different personnel policies in the audit, tax, and management service sections, and (b) not to assume that policies aimed at increasing the level of satisfaction and reducing turnover among one kind of specialist may have no impact in the job satisfaction of the other kinds of specialists.[14]

Harrell and Stahl used McClelland's trichotomy of needs theory to provide a conceptual explanation of the job satisfaction and work performance of CPA firm professionals.[15] The theory assumes that individuals are motivated by three needs: need for affiliation, need for power, and need for achievement. A survey of practicing CPAs in one office of a large international firm indicated that the need for power and the need for achievement were positively related to job satisfaction and superior work performance.

ORGANIZATIONAL CLIMATE IN PUBLIC ACCOUNTING FIRMS

The organizational climate in public accounting firms is of importance because of its impact on employee attitudes and behavior. It has been investigated in terms of (a) the accountants' organizational-professional conflict, (b) the impact of role conflict and role ambiguity, (c) the role of informal, nonformal communications and mentoring, (d) the impact of the leadership style of supervisors, and (e) the management strategy of public accounting firms.

The Accountants' Organizational-Professional Conflict

The relationship between organizations and their professional employees ahs been a subject of concern and research because of its effect in the work environment and its impact on employee attitudes and behavior. Organizations do vary in the degree to which they allow professionals the opportunity to act in accordance with their professional judgment. In addition, the incompatibility of the norms and values of the profession and the organization create a conflict in the relationship between the organization and its professional employees.[16] In organizational behavior, results on the notion of "inherent compatibility" was, however, mixed. In accounting, the dysfunctional outcomes of the professional-organizational conflict in public accounting firms were supported in some studies[17,18] and de-emphasized in others.[19,20] In the study in which the conflict was supported it was found to result in job dissatisfaction and migration.[21]

Norris and Nielbuhr, however, provided results showing that accountants who reported high levels of professionalism also reported high levels of organizational commitment.[22]

In reexamining the accountants' organizational-professional conflict, Aranya and Ferris focused on the relationship between the antecedents and outcomes of organizational-professional conflict and examined the relationship between organizational and professional commitments, perceived conflict, job satisfaction, and turnover intentions.[23] A survey of 2,016 U.S. and Canadian accountants showed the potential of organizational-professional conflict to be greater in nonprofessional organizations and to vary inversely with the position in the hierarchy of professional organizations. In addition, the conflict seems to result in lower job satisfaction and higher employee turnover intentions.

Impact of Role Conflict and Role Ambiguity

The organizational climate in public accounting firms may be affected by factors other than the organizational-professional conflict. For example, Senatra argued that perceived role conflict and role ambiguity in public accounting firms by audit seniors may have three potential consequence in terms of (1) job-related tension,

(2) job satisfaction, and (3) propensity to leave the organization.[24] The following ten potential sources of role conflict and role ambiguity are identified from the organizational climate of public accounting firms:

1. Violation in chain of command
2. Formalization of rules and procedures
3. Emphasis on subordinate personnel development
4. Tolerance of error
5. Top management receptiveness
6. Adequacy of work coordination
7. Decision timeliness
8. Information suppression
9. Adequacy of authority
10. Adequacy of professional autonomy.[25]

The results of a survey of seniors in eight offices of one Big Eight public accounting firm verified the model and showed that high levels of both role conflict and role ambiguity would be significantly related to high job-related tension, low job satisfaction, and a high propensity to leave the firm.

Role of Informal and Nonformal Communication

The organizational climate in a public accounting firm is also a function of the role of informal and nonformal communications and mentoring in coordinating and controlling members. Using a naturalistic, qualitative research methodology, Dirsmith and Covaleski confirmed (a) the existence of informal communications in public accounting firms that benefit lower-level individuals despite its limited role in informing organizational members of the politics and power within the organization; and (b) the important role of nonformal communications and mentoring in the performance of audit tasks, socialization of the individual firm, instruction as to politics and power in the firm, and benefit to the protégé, mentor, and firm.[26] Calls were also made for future research to examine the relationship among these three forms of communication. They are adequately defined as follows:

One analogy which we feel may prove useful is that formal communications are used to convey organizational rules and laws, while nonformal communications convey and enculture people to conform to organizational norms, while informal communications instruct as to organizational and group moves.[27]

Impact of Leadership Style of Supervisors

The problems of organizational communications in general, and of supervisor-subordinate communication in particular may have an impact on the organizational climate in public accounting firms. In studies of superior-subordinate communications, researchers have focused attention on how a superior's influence in the organizational hierarchy affects relationships with subordinates.[28] The nature of the accounting work environment, with its regular job interactions between superior and subordinates, suggests that the nature of a superior's influence may provide a framework for analyzing the satisfaction and motivations of public accountants, and the firm's organizational climate. Researchers of superior-subordinate communication have studied the effect of a superior's upward influence in the organizational hierarchy on his or her relationship with subordinates. This effect has commonly become known as the "Pelz effect." In his seminal study, Pelz reported the existence of a positive association between a supervisor's upward hierarchical influence and a subordinate's satisfaction with the performance of the superior, provided the supervisor *also* exhibited a "supportive" leadership style in interactions with the employee.[29] He states: "If the supervisor has *little* power or influence, then neither his helpful behavior nor his restraining behavior will have much concrete effects on the employees."[30]

Wager also explored the effects of supervisors' hierarchical influence and of leadership style on the fulfillment of their supervisory role obligations toward others lower in the organization.[31] His findings were similar to those of Pelz. He observed that a supportive style of leadership was a more powerful variable than hierarchical influence in contributing to the fulfillment of supervisory role obligations, and that the magnitude of the moderating effect of influence varies markedly with the organizational status of the respondent. "The more organizationally marginal the status occupied by subordinates, the greater will be the pervasiveness of the effect of a supervisor's influence on his style of leadership as it bears on fulfillment of his supervisory role."[32]

Other related studies also support the Pelz effect.[33-36] The uniqueness of CPA firms, in terms of composition, organization, tasks, and purposes, creates a different relationship between a supervisor's upward influence and a subordinate's satisfaction with a superior and his or her job. For example, the organizational status and autonomy of subordinates in CPA firms differ from status and autonomy of individuals in the organization studied.

Studying the phenomena in an accounting context, Belkaoui advanced the following research question:

For subordinates in a CPA firm- who perceive their supervisors as supportive or not supportive leaders- does the level of supervisor's hierarchical influence affect subordinates' intention to leave the firm, job satisfaction and level of anxiety stress?[37]

A survey of seniors and managers of two Big Eight public accounting firms located in a large metropolitan area verified the research question for senior accountants with regard to satisfaction with superiors and colleagues when the superior is viewed as having work-related influence.

While not using the Pelz effect, Pratt and Jiambalvo identified, in a field experiment, a number of leader behaviors that relate, either directly or through some intermediary factors, to audit team performance.[38] They state:

For instance, in-charge auditors who were considerate to the personal needs of staff assistants allowed staff innovation and administered frequent positive reinforcement, infrequent negative reinforcements, and complete and timely feedback, supervised those audit teams rated to be most effective by audit managers.[39]

In a follow-up survey the authors found that leader behavior in an audit environment was related to three variables: (1) the match between the accountant in charge's perception of the complexity of the task assigned to the staff assistant and the staff assistant's job experience, (2) the staff assistant's intolerance of ambiguity, and (3) the accountant in charge's personality dominance.[40] The effects of the leader behavior (i.e., consideration and initiation structure) were also found to be contingent on the assistant's perception of task complexity.[41]

The Management Strategy of Public Accounting Firms

Like any other type of organization, the public accounting firm faces a complex and changing environment, if not a turbulent one. It needs, therefore, an adequate strategy to deal with the situation. Little is known about the strategies of public accounting firms. One exception is provided by Baker's use of participant observation to investigate the management strategy of a large public accounting firm.[42] A descriptive model of the management strategy developed included three components: doing, representing, and being. They were defined as follows:

Doing may be defined as those activities which the firm undertakes to maintain and improve its relationship with its clients. . . . Representing may be defined as those activities which the firm undertakes to maintain and improve its relationships to outside parties other than clients. . . . Being may be defined as the image of the firm.[43]

Basically doing, or delivery of a tangible product, and representing, or practice development, act to create an image and a name for the firm, or being, to serve an environment composed of clients, the government, the business community, and the profession. Because of a possible conflict between the delivery of a tangible product, mandated by an economic contract with the client, and the delivery of a social value, mandated by the social contract with the government and society, Baker suggests the need for three tactical, if not strategic, responses: (1) the advent of audit committees, (2) the institutionalization of peer review system, and (3) the provision of an "audit of business" rather than an "audit of books."[44]

The management strategy in public accounting firms faces some differences, however, in the differentiated environments of audit services and management services. The project teams in both environments may face different task environment uncertainty and different formalization of their structure. Watson investigated both research questions in an exploratory study using both a questionnaire and an interview format.[45] The results confirmed both research questions in the sense that (a) the task environmental uncertainty was higher for management services than for auditing, and (b) different structural relations developed in the teams. These findings are then related to Sorensen's observations that (a) there is a conflict between bureaucratism and professionalism in large CPA firms, (b) job satisfaction is affected by professional deprivation, and (c) migration is affected by the task of managing a hybrid professional-bureaucratic orientation.[46] The observed differences in the two functional areas of management services and auditing point to the fact that (a) the conflict between bureaucratism and professionalism may be different between the two functional areas, given the mechanistic organization of the auditing department and the organismic organization of the auditing department and the organismic organization of the management service function, and that (b) the job satisfaction and migration may be different between the two functional areas, with a higher job satisfaction and a lower migration in the management services area.

PERFORMANCE EVALUATION IN PUBLIC ACCOUNTING FIRMS

Performance evaluation results are used as a basis of the reward system and as a way of providing development-oriented feedback to employees.[47] In accounting research, the performance evaluation is often cited to be a major source of dissatisfaction by those leaving public accounting.[48] As a result, various research studies examined the performance evaluation question in public accounting firms.

Jiambalvo used an expectancy theory model, called an "evaluation model of directed job effort," to predict the amount of time CPAs working as auditors direct toward various aspects of their job and their job performance.[49] It was expressed as follows:

$$W_i = f(E_{si} \cdot E_{2i} \cdot E_{3i}(_{j=1}^{m}I_jV_j) + IAV_i)$$

where w_i = effect directed toward activities related to evaluative dimension i; E_{si} = the expectancy that effort leads to effective performance on evaluative dimension i; E_{2i} = the expectancy that being effective on evaluative dimension i leads to being judged as effective on dimension i by a superior; E_{3i} = the expectancy that being judged effective on evaluative dimension i contributes to a high overall evaluation of performance; I_j = the instrumentality of a high overall evaluation of performance for the attainment of job outcome j; V_j = the desirability (valence) of job outcome j; and IAV_i = the intrinsic value or desirability of engaging in activities related to evaluative dimension i.

The IAV was added after Turney's findings that it was a better predictor of job effort and performance than typical expectancy theory constructs.[50] The results o fa survey using senior accountants and their audit managers verified the model by showing that it was possible to predict the amount of time CPAs direct toward various aspects of their job and their performance on job dimensions based on (a) their perceptions of effort-rewards relationships and (b) the intrinsic value of the activities associated with the job performance under both a multiplicative and an additive formulation.

Because large CPA firms are segmented along three distinct and minimally independent functional areas- auditing, tax services, and management services- and the task subenvironment in these firms differ with respect to their uncertainty,[51] it follows that the behavior of the organizational members will be affected by this organizational differentiation. Performance evaluation would be one of the behaviors that may be affected by the segmentation. As a result, Jiambalvo and colleagues advanced the following hypothesis: That organizational differentiation impacts the decision model used by subunit members in the evaluation of personnel, in particular, the weights assigned to different evaluation categories, the consistency in the application of evaluation policies, the self-insight of decision makers and inter-rater agreement.[52]

A survey of partners, managers, and session staff accountants from a large international CPA firm were asked to evaluate hypothetical individuals rated on each of the following eight categories:

1. Willingness and ability to accept responsibility;
2. Ability to effectively utilize staff and plan work assignments;
3. Ability to identify and develop practical workable solutions to problems;
4. Ability to win confidence and respect of clients;
5. Level of creativity exhibited in adapting to unique problems;
6. Knowledge and experience reflected in adherence to known and acceptable procedures and principles;
7. Ability and desire to work effectively with people;
8. Level of judgment exercises.[53]

The results confirmed the hypothesized substantial disagreements among firm members on overall evaluations and on the importance attached to the performance evaluation categories. No differences emerged as far as consistency or self-insight.

Wright found that engagement reviews were the primary source of information on which staff auditor salary and promotion decisions are based.[54] A follow-up experiment showed that for the appraisal of staff auditors, seniors focused almost strictly on examining technical skills, whereas personnel administrators called for several measures of short-run (technical skills) and long-run (e.g., communication skills, motivation) performance.[55]

Kida investigated two essential performance appraisal processes that occur between managers and seniors of international CPA firms: (1) the determination of overall evaluations and (2) the interpersonal characteristics of the feedback meeting.[56] Managers and seniors of international CPA firms were administered an instrument designed to capture their design strategies and review meeting perceptions. The results indicated similar weighting schemes between managers and seniors in the aggregate, but differences among individual raters' strategies. The decision strategies were affected by the leadership style. Subjects with higher consideration scores placed more weight on client relations and communication skills, whereas those higher on initiation structure placed more weight on technical competence. Perceived feedback characteristics such as supportive behavior, initiation to participate, and anticipation in goal setting were found to be related to the seniors' improved job performance. Instead, criticism directed at certain aspects of the seniors' job was strongly correlated with improving performance.

The evaluation system may have an influence on both turnover and quality control as evidenced by the following results:

- Dissatisfaction may result from the appraisal process leading to staff turnover.[57,58]
- Because meeting time budgets is an important factor in performance evaluation, great pressure results from the situation. A consequence of this pressure is the signing off on uncompleted audit procedures[59] and working excessive hours on personal time.[60]

Maher and co-workers[61] and later Jiambalvo[62] found that performance ratings were highly related to accuracy and congruence measures, where accuracy refers to the person's ability to correctly assess the key success factors and congruence refers to the situation in which a person agrees with perceived major factors and directs work accordingly.

Given all these results in the appraisal process in CPA firms and to improve the process, Wright proposed a behaviorally anchored rating scale (BARS).[63] "BARS scales attempt to provide descriptions for the rater to *observe staff actions* rather than forcing one to subjectively judge a person as 'excellent,' 'above average,' or 'below average.'"[64]

STAFF TURNOVER IN PUBLIC ACCOUNTING FIRMS

High rates of staff turnover characterize the public accounting firms.[65-67] About 85% of the accounting graduates who join the big CPA firms will leave within ten years for positions in government, education, or smaller CPA firms.[68] Benke and Rhode[69] estimated the replacement cost of each entry-level staff accountant to exceed $20,000; for one large CPA firm with a turnover of 10,000 employees over a recent ten-year period[70] that price would be $200,000,000 in replacement costs. The reasons behind this high turnover need to be known, as the cost to the CPA firms and the discipline are relatively high and serious. Among the reasons suggested are the following:

1. The turnover is due to both lack of challenge to qualified people and the easing out of unqualified people.[71]

2. The best of a lower-quality set of students are attracted to accounting coupled with a cultural lag experienced by those students in the educational and guidance areas.[72-74] The best students opt for majors other than accounting.[75] What may result is the technical competence that may explain turnover.[76]

3. The needs of young accountants are not met by the right work-related activities in public accounting firms.[77-79] In addition, the work is tedious enough to lead to turnover.[80]

4. Although the views of managing partners and their professional staff are congruent on most strategic goals, the staff is asking for greater variety and better communication of performance criterion.[81]

5. An elevated personality profile as well as a preference for analytic or scientific orientations characterizes a group of accountants that remained in public accounting.[82] Therefore, personality characteristics as well as the vocational interests of entry-level staff accountants may be a strong determinant of turnover in public accounting firms.

6. The personality profiles of managers, partners, juniors, and seniors are known to differ and may result in high turnovers.

    Those personality differences may be a partial predictor of turnover since CPA firms, like other large organizations with few permanent positions at the top and a large staff, often have personnel evaluation criteria that indicate "if you want to be one of us, then you should be like us- in terms of ability, interests, and personality characteristics."[83]

7. The turnover decision in public accounting firms may be a function of negatively valued task outcomes and the likelihood of obtaining those outcomes in one's current position, and the greater chance of realizing certain positive outcomes in alternative positions.[84]

8. A poor communication atmosphere may exist in public accounting firms because not only are the relationships between supervisors and workers not perfect, but also the staff accountants are not fully integrated in the firms and are left on their own about job expectations. The situation is destructive of the job performance of individuals and may explain their turnover decision.[85] The following advice is offered: The data analyzed represent open and legitimate concerns from a selected group of staff accountants during the first 3 ½ years of professional employment. Their concerns are objectively reported and do not represent what someone suspects is the cause of turnover. They are the reasons for turnover actually experienced by staff personnel. It is now up to the CPA firms to act individually to remedy their

unwanted staff losses. This can be done if CPA firms can increase the positive aspects of their work environments and minimize the negative aspects.[86]

9. Satisfaction is inversely related to turnover.[87,88]
10. Turnover is affected by the task of managing a hybrid professional-bureaucratic orientation in public accounting firms.[89]

MOTIVATION IN AN ACCOUNTING ENVIRONMENT

Motivation is important, as it may affect performance and job satisfaction. Expectancy theory models have generally been used to study the subject of work motivation and performance in various research settings.[90] Basically, the theories postulate relationships for the determination of motivation (M) and/or job performance (P). With regard to motivation, the theory holds that the motivation (M) of an individual to perform at a particular effort level (E) is a function of the algebraic sum of the products of (a) the individual's expectancies that specific outcomes or rewards (O) will follow from exerted effort and (b) the perceived valances of the specific rewards (V) or outcomes associated with performing at the effort level.[91] Basically, two models have been used to express the individual's motivation as formulated in expectancy theory. The first model holds that an individual will opt for a particular behavior and a given effort level on the basis of his or her expectancies that effort will lead to certain outcomes and the valences placed on these outcomes. In other words,

$$M=[(E \rightarrow O)(V)].$$

The second model includes two expectancies, given that an individual usually encounters two outcomes: first, the actual task performance and, second, an outcome resulting from the realization of the first outcome.[92] It holds that an individual will offer a particular behavior and effort level on the basis of, first, his or her expectancy that effort will result in task performance and, second, his expectancy that the task accomplishment will lead to a second-level outcome. In other words,

$$M = (E{\rightarrow}P) \, [(P{\rightarrow}O)(V)].$$

With regard to performance, expectancy theory holds that an individual job performance (P) is a joint function of the ability (A) to perform the job, the role perceptions (R) with respect to the job, and the motivation (M) to perform the job. In other words,

$$P = f(A, R, M).$$

The function has been shown to be multiplicative or additive. Then expectancy models were used to argue that when there is a high performance$\rightarrow$outcomes expectancy, there should be a positive correlation between job performance and job satisfaction.[93,94] Known as the Porter and Lawler-Lawler job satisfaction model, it as first tested in an accounting environment by Ferris.[95] The results indicate that the expectancy models were not good predictors of audit staff performance, but good predictors of employee job satisfaction.

A valence-instrumentality-expectancy model refers to a theory of work motivation to explain either job effort or job choice.[96] Basically, it holds that the level of motivation (W) of an individual to perform at a particular effort level is a joint function of (a) V_j, the valence of the outcomes associated with the job; (b) I_{ij}, the instrumentality of these outcomes; and (c) E_i, the expectancies of the performance. In other words,

$$W = E_i \left(\sum_{j=1}^{n} I_{ij} V_j \right).$$

The model also holds that the utilities of rewards (U_i) is a function of I_{ij} and V_j:

$$U_i = \sum_{j=1}^{n} I_{ij} V_j.$$

Although this model has been used in accounting to predict performance[97] and turnover,[98,99] it was also used to compare the motivational levels in Australia and the U.S.[100]

The results indicate that few differences exist between the two groups of accountants from the U.S. and Australia with regard to personal value structure, motivational levels, and perceptions of the work environments.

PERSONAL CHARACTERISTICS OF ACCOUNTANTS AND CONSEQUENCES

Evidence in the behavioral sciences indicate that the personal characteristics of individuals affect how they respond to the work environment. These characteristics include, for example, an individual's personality and personal interests[101] and an individual's feelings toward the work environment.[102] The thesis was also tested in the accounting work environment. Research included (a) research on the general and distinctive characteristics of those who deal with accounting, (b) professional commitment in public accounting, (c) career intentions, and (d) job stress in public accounting.

The Stereotype Accountant

Various studies investigated the general and destructive characteristics of those who deal with accounting, especially to counteract the general traits of inflexibility, introversion, quantitative thinking, and lack of interest in interpersonal relations that are attributed to accountants. The findings were mixed. The stereotypic image was confirmed in various instances as follows:

1. Accountants may exhibit a low level of verbal competency, prefer working with numbers, are precise and exact when it comes to detail, and avoid facing new things without being prepared for them.[103]
2. Conformity, low social interests, and a poorly developed aesthetic sensitivity characterize the accountants.[104]
3. Unlike other students, accounting students were found to prefer a moderate, but stable income, aspire less to work with people and to creative work.[105]
4. When compared with teachers, they scored high in domination and esteem, but low on perception and acceptance of themselves.[106]

5. When compared with creative writing students, a group of accounting students indicated a primarily positive identification with their parents and had a largely accepting attitude toward authority and adhering to external regulations, as well as toward people in general.[107] They confirmed earlier positive results on a hypothesis that suggested that signs of a more rigid fearful identification are seen in accounting students as compared with a seeking for the completion of multiple identification in creative writing students.[108] A study by Aranya and associates found that accounting students tend to show stronger adherence to social values and norms than psychology students.[109] The same study found that accounting students showed vocational interests in business and organization and not in general culture and in arts and entertainment areas.

6. Accounting subjects were found to be primarily characterized by the enterprising and social types and not the investigative type.[110]

   The results were partially confirmed in another study with the additional findings of the conventional type being dominant among sole practitioners and partners in small firms, and the enterprising types dominant among partners in large firms.[111] Those studies were investigated in the framework of Holland's theory, which (a) postulates that the individual, through his or her choice of occupation, attempts to fulfill a way of life, and (b) accountants for six types of people- realistic, investigative, artistic, social, enterprising, and conventional- and assumes that there is a professional environment that corresponds to each.[112-114]

7. In comparison with accountants, a survey of Estes showed that physicians and attorneys come from families with significantly higher socioeconomic status, and the children of physicians are entering careers with significantly higher social economic status scores.[115] Engineers are comparable to accountants. Estes concluded:

   These results suggest that the accounting profession is, along with engineering, drawing its people more from blue collar and rural families, in contrast to other professions. This situation reflects an opportunity, in that law and medicine are apparently not competing effectively in this human resource pool. It also presents a challenge: are we recruiting an appropriate share of young people from families in the upper socioeconomic strata?[116]

   The stereotypic image of accountants was, however, disconfirmed in one case by the evidence that a group of accountants scored higher in friendliness, personal acceptance, and psychological sensitivity than other professional groups included in the survey.[117]

To trace the stereotypical accountant, Aranya and colleagues used the framework of an inclusive theory of professional stereotypes.[118] That framework for the characterization of the stereotypical accountant was based on Holland's theory that an individual, by work.[119] Both vocational interests, and conformity and adherence to socially accepted values were examined for both accounting and psychology students. The results showed that accounting students opted to vocational interests in business and organization and not in general culture and in arts and entertainment areas, whereas psychology students opted for vocational interests in the areas of service, arts and entertainment, and general culture. In addition, accounting students exhibited a stronger adherence to social norms and values, as predicted by Holland's theory.

An examination of the personality profiles of juniors, seniors, managers, and partners in selected national accounting firms showed that partners were oriented toward conforming, conservative, and inflexible behavior, whereas the other categories of accountants tended toward a behavior characterized as competitive aggressive, and directed toward independence through achievement.[120]

Vocational interests and organizational or professional attitudes toward public accounting were found to differ between young CPAs and partners and other CPAs with more extensive work experience.[121] In fact, an existing generation gap of ideals and values existed between partners and staff personnel.[122]

Professional Commitment in Public Accounting

The professional commitment in public accounting, that is, the relative strength of the accountant's identification with and involvement in his or her profession, was the subject of investigation. The concern with both organizational and professional commitment is important because of (a) the fact that better performance is obtained from highly committed employees,[123] (b) turnover may be predicted from the level of organizational commitment to a greater extent than job satisfaction,[124] and (c) the organizational effectiveness is also related to organizational commitment.[125]

Sorensen and Sorensen examined the effects of related variables, that is, holding professional versus bureaucratic orientations and values.[126] They found that conflict between professionalism and bureaucratization leads to job dissatisfaction and job migration. Hastings and Hastings showed that chartered accountants in industry had lower levels of attachment to professional values than those in public practice.[127]

Aranya and co-workers' model assumed three major factors that may influence professional commitment to a profession: organizational commitment, professional organizational conflict, and satisfaction with rewards.[128] The relationship was also assumed to be moderated by the organizational level, following Sorenson and Sorenson's findings, an increase in bureaucratic orientations, and a decrease in professional orientations from lower to higher positions, junior to senior partners.[129] A survey of Canadian chartered accountants showed the primacy of organizational commitment in predicting professional commitment on all organizational levels. In addition, professional commitment was found to be negatively related to professional organizational conflict and positively related to satisfaction with income.

In a follow-up study Aranya and Wheeler found that the accountants' commitment to both profession and organization was essentially related to their scores as conventional and enterprising types.[130]

Career Intentions

Following McClelland's theory[131] suggestion that individuals consciously or unconsciously seek an environment that is congruent with the size of their application, power, and achievement needs, Harrell and Eickoff suggested that influence-oriented auditors may be predisposed to have more positive affective responses than others to the Big Eight public accounting work environment.[132] The results of a survey verified their hypothesis by showing that influence-oriented auditors (a) had experienced higher job satisfaction in the future than others, (b) had greater organizational commitment in the future than others, and (c) had more positive Big Eight career intentions in the future than others. In addition, they exhibited lower levels of voluntary personnel turnover behavior in the future than others.

Other research studies examined the need for achievement as a factor that may explain the career intentions of accounting students. Belkaoui examined the likelihood of an association between accounting students' need for achievement and their career aspirations, with the hypotheses that (a) high need for achievement would be associated with a desire for mobility out of lower-status accounting positions and into higher-status accounting positions and (b) very low need for achievement may be associated with unrealistic career aspirations.[133] An experiment yielded results that supported the first hypothesis for both male and female subjects, and the second hypothesis, for only the female group for their late career aspirations (i.e., 25 years from now).

Dillard used a goal expectancy model of occupation-position choice behavior.[134,135] The model is explained as follows:

Stated succinctly, this model predicts that an individual makes choices based on occupation-position goals. These goals are a function of perceived rewards and punishments associated with the position, the likelihood of obtaining these outcomes, and the chances for acquiring the position.[136]

The model was supported by showing that the measured occupation-position goals were significantly related to the position with the highest expected utility.

Job Stress in Public Accounting

Stress has been defined as "a state which arises from an actual or perceived demand-capability imbalance in the organism's vital adjustment actions and which is partially manifest by a nonspecific response."[137] It is caused by a type of stressor, "a demand made by internal or external environment of an organism that upsets its homeostasis, restoration of which depends on nonautomatic and not readily available energy-expending action."[138] Examples of stressors cited by Antonovosky include accidents and the survivors; the untoward experiences of others in social networks; the horror of history in which we are involved; intrapsychic, unconscious conflicts and anxieties; the fear of aggression, mutilation and destruction; the events of history brought in our living rooms; the changes of the narrower world in which we live; other normative life crises- role entries and exits, inadequate socialization, underboard and overboard; the inherent conflicts in all social relations; and the gap between culturally inculcated goals and socially structured means.[139]

Stress is not a stranger to the accounting world. In fact, it may be considered an important accompaniment of accounting practices, as accounting procedures affect perceptions of control and predictability of those who impose these procedures as well as those who are the target of them.[140,141] Various authors pointed to the effect of job-related stress on professional auditors.[142-146] Other studies elaborated on some of the non-personality factors that may have an impact on stress in accounting firms, such as type and quality of supervision, promotional procedures, job autonomy, career opportunities, and social supports.[147-149] One study hypothesized that personality variables may also be significantly linked to job stress, and investigated four personality dispositions that are potential determinants of job-related stress: Type A, control, commitment, and challenge.[150] Type A personality is characterized by a life style of behavioral responses leaning toward extremes such as competitiveness, hard-driving, intense striving for achievement, sense of time urgency, aggressiveness, hostility, hyperalertness, and inability to respond to bodily signals of stress.[151] Such an individual is generally unable to cope with job stress. Control disposition in an individual implies that the individual tends to believe and act as if he or she is in control of events. It can reduce the effects of a stressful situation.[152] Commitment disposition in an individual implies that the individual likes to get involved with events that are happening to them.[153] It is a good way to cope with stress. Challenge disposition in an individual implies that the individual refers change to stability in working life because these changes offer interesting incentives to growth rather than threats to security.[154] A survey of practicing auditors indicated the existence of a positive relationship between job stress and type A personality, and a negative relationship between job stress on one hand and control, commitment, and challenge personality dispositions on the other hand.[155] The same survey supported the presence of an invested U relationship between stress and performance in the auditing profession. Such a relationship, called the Yerkes-Dodson law,[156] assumes the stress in the work environment leads job performance to improve up to a point after which a situation of stress overload can hinder performance.

SOURCES OF FEEDBACK IN A CPA FIRM

Performance feedback in the work setting has been considered important to employee training, performance, motivation, and satisfaction. Research questions primarily focus on identifying sources of feedback,[157] work as an information environment,[158] and defining the construct of feedback.[159] In assessing the importance of potentially difference sources of job performance information, these studies viewed the worker as an information receiver in an environment capable of providing a variety of information from different sources. They relied on either student subjects or faculty members, and opened an interesting research area on feedback sources in the worker environment.

Three methods have been used to investigate the concept of feedback: knowledge of results, management appraisal, and job quality.[160-162] Although each approach demonstrated the importance of feedback, they have been criticized (a) for using single tasks with unidimensional feedback in the case of the knowledge of results approach; (b) for taking a simplistic and prescriptive stand (e.d., "feedback is important") in the case of the management appraisal literature; and (c) for restricting the importance of feedback to a component of job design, and ignoring the various possibilities of what other feedback aspects might exist. A different research approach was used by Greller and Herold[163] and Hansen and Muchinsky.[164] It relied on a deductive strategy to assess the importance of different potential sources of job performance information and viewed the worker as an information receiver in an environment containing different possible sources of feedback information. In their attempt to clarify the feedback construct, Greller and Herold[165] dimensionalized feedback according to five potential sources: company, supervisor, co-workers, task, and self. Using student subjects, their findings indicate that there is a greater reliance on intrinsic sources (sources psychologically "closer" to the individual) than on more external sources of feedback information, this reliance being reduced for referent information.[166] Hansen and Muchinsky[167] replicated the study, using faculty members as subjects, and found similar results. Both studies' findings may be due to the subject population and environment, since performance is experienced and measured in terms of personal creativity. They may have attached more importance to psychologically closer sources than to external sources. The work environment of a CPA firm is defined in terms of firm policies, closer supervision, and cooperation with co-workers, rather than on personal creativity. Thus one might expect to find different results regarding the informativeness of feedback sources examined. Accordingly, Belkaoui and Picur[168] examined the nature of CPA work environments regarding sources, types, and reliability of the information received. Five sources of information- the formal organization, immediate supervision, co-workers, the task, and personal feelings and ideas- were rated by seniors and managers in the metropolitan offices of two Big Eight CPA firms as to their informativeness in providing referent and appraisal information. The study's results supported the main conclusion of earlier research that referent and appraisal information can be viewed as emanating from different sources that vary in their degree of informativeness. The most notable finding of this study was the consistent importance of the supervisor as the most reliable source of both referent and appraisal information. The findings suggest that CPA firms should develop the interpersonal skills of supervisory personnel.

CONCLUSIONS

Many survey and laboratory experiments have examined the human resource problems in public accounting firms. Various strong results emerge mainly with regard to job dissatisfaction and high turnover in public accounting firms. Various determinants of this situation have emerged, providing the beginning of a clear picture of what may be wrong and/or right in the organizational climate of public accounting firms. A lot remains to be done, as other human resource variables need to be examined. Examples include absenteeism, administrative intensity, autonomy, power stratification, communication, complexity, violence of conflict, coordination, departmentalization, distributive justice, effectiveness, formalization, general training, ideology, innovation, motivation, need strength, pay stratification, bases of power, prestige stratification, productivity, routinization, size, standardization, work group cohesion, and workload in public accounting firms, to name only a few well-researched variables.[169]

NOTES

1. L. W. Porter and R. M. Steers, "Organizational Work and Personal Factors in Employee Turnover and Absenteeism," *Psychological Bulletin* 2 (1973): 151-76.

2. E. E. Lawler, *Pay and Organizational Effectiveness: A Psychological View* (New York: McGraw-Hill, 1971).

3. E. A. Locke, "The Nature and Causes of Job Satisfaction," in *Handbook of Industrial and Organizational Psychology*, ed. M. D. Dunnett (Chicago: Rand McNally, 1976), 1297-1349.

4. L. W. Porter and V. F. Mitchell, "Comparative Study of Need Satisfaction in Military and Business Hierarchies," *Journal of Applied Psychology* (April 1967): 139-44.

5. R. H. Strawser, J. M. Ivancevich, and H. L. Lyon, "A Note on the Job Satisfaction of Accountants in Large and Small CPA Firms," *Journal of Accounting Research* (Autumn 1969): 339-45.

6. G. Carpenter, and R. H. Strawser, "A Study of the Job Satisfaction of Academic Accountants," *The Accounting Review* (July 1971): 509-18.

7. J. M. Ivancevich and R. H. Strawser, "A Comparative Analysis of the Job Satisfaction of Industrial Managers and Certified Public Accountants," *Academy of Management Journal* 3 (1969): 193-203.

8. N. Aranya, R. Lachman, and J. Armevic, "Accountants' Job Satisfaction: A Path Analysis," *Accounting, Organizations and Society* (December 1982): 201-15.

9. Ibid., 210.

10. J. E. Sorensen, "Professional and Bureaucratic Organization in Public Accounting Firms," *The Accounting Review* (July 1967): 553-65.

11. K. R. Ferris, "Perceived Uncertainty and Job Satisfaction in the Accounting Environment," *Accounting, Organizations and Society* 2:1 (1977): 23-28.

12. Ibid., 28.

13. R. L. Benke, Jr., and J. C. Rhode, "The Job Satisfaction of Higher Level Employees in Large Certified Public Accounting Firms," *Accounting, Organizations and Society* (July 1980): 187-201.

14. D. C. McClelland, *Power: The Inner Experience* (New York: Irvington, 1975).

15. A. M. Harrell and M. J. Stahl, "McLelland's Trichotonomy of Needs Theory and the Job Satisfaction and Work Performance of CPA Firm Professionals," *Accounting, Organizations and Society* (June 1984): 241-52.

16. P. M. Blau and W. R. Scott, *Formal Organization* (San Francisco: Chandler, 1962).

17. Sorensen, "Professional and Bureaucratic Organization," 553-65.

18. R. G. Schroeder and L. F. Imdieke, "Local-Cosmopolitan and Bureaucratic Perceptions in Public Accounting Firms," *Accounting, Organizations and Society* (October 1977): 39-45.

19. R. H. Hall, "Professionalization and Bureaucratization," *American Sociological Review* (February 1968): 92-104.

20. P. D. Montagna, "Professionalization and Bureaucratization in Large Professional Organizations," *American Journal of Sociology* (September 1968): 138-45.

21. J. E. Sorensen and T. E. Sorensen, "The Conflict of Professionals in Bureaucratic Organizations," *Administrative Science Quarterly* (March 1974): 58-106.

22. D. R. Norris and R. E. Nielbuhr, "Professionalism, Organizational Commitment and Job Satisfaction in an Accounting Organization," *Accounting, Organizations and Society* (December 1983): 49-60.

23. N. Aranya and K. R. Ferris, "A Reexamination of Accountant's Organizational-Professional Conflict," *The Accounting Review* (January 1984): 1-15.

24. P. T. Senatra, "Role Conflict, Role Ambiguity, and Organizational Climate in a Public Accounting Firm," *The Accounting Review* (October 1980): 594-603.

25. Ibid.

26. M. W. Dirsmith and M. A. Covaleski, "Informal Communications, Nonformal Communications and Mentoring in Public Accounting Firms," *Accounting, Organizations and Society* (May 1985): 149-69.

27. Ibid., 166.

28. F. M. Jablin, "A Reexamination of the 'Pelz Effect,'" *Human Communication Research* 3 (1980): 210-20.

29. D. Pelz, "Influence: A Key to Effective Leadership in the First Line Supervisor," *Personnel* 29 (1952): 209-71.

30. Ibid., 213.

31. L. W. Wager, "Leadership Style, Influence and Supervisory Role Obligations," *Administrative Science Quarterly* 9 (1965): 391-420.

32. Ibid., 418.

33. K. H. Roberts and C. A. O'Reilly, "Failures in Upward Communication: Three Possible Culprits," *Academy of Management Journal* 1 (1974): 205-15.

34. A. P. Jones, L. R. James, and J. R. Bruni, "Perceived Leadership Behavior and Employee Confidence in the Leader as

Moderated by Job Involvement," *Journal of Applied Psychology* 63 (1978): 146-49.

35. C. A. O'Reilly and K. H. Roberts, "Supervisor Influence and Subordinate Mobility Aspirations as Moderators of Consideration and Initiating Structure," *Administrative Science Quarterly* 13 (1968): 65-105.

36. Jablin, "Supervisor's Upward Influence," 210-20.

37. A. Belkaoui, "Leadership Style, Dimensions of Superior's Upward Influence and Job Perception in a Public Accounting Firm: A Reexamination of the 'Pelz Effect'" (unpublished manuscript, University of Illinois at Chicago, June 1989).

38. J. Pratt and J. Jiambalvo, "Relationships Between Leader Behaviors and Audit Team Performance," *Accounting, Organizations and Society* (August 1981): 133-42.

39. Ibid., 139.

40. J. Pratt and J. Jiambalvo, "Determinants of Leader Behavior in an Audit Environment," *Accounting, Organization and Society* (December 1982): 369-79.

41. J. Jiambalvo and J. Pratt, "Task Complexity and Leadership Effectiveness in CPA Firms," *The Accounting Review* (October 1982): 734-50.

42. C. Richard Baker, "Management Strategy in a Large Accounting Firm," *The Accounting Review* (July 1977): 576-86.

43. Ibid., 579-81.

44. Ibid., 582-83.

45. David J. H. Watson, "The Structure of Project Teams Facing Differentiated Environments: An Exploratory Study in Public Accounting Firms," *The Accounting Review* (April 1975): 259-73.

46. J. E. Sorensen, "Professional and Bureaucratic Organization in Public Accounting Firms," *The Accounting Review* (July 1967): 553-65.

47. J. Kane and E. Lawler, "Performance Appraisal Effectiveness: Its Assessments and Determinants," *Research in Organizational Behavior* 2 (1979): 425-78.

48. A. Wright, "Performance Appraisal of Staff Auditors," *CPA Journal* (November 1980): 37-43.

49. J. Jiambalvo, "Performance Evaluation and Directed Job Effort: Model Development and Analysis in a CPA Firm Setting," *Journal of Accounting Research* (Autumn 1979): 436-55.

50. J. R. Turney, "Activity Outcome Expectancies and Intrinsic Activity Values as Predictors of Several Motivation Indexes for Technical-Professionals," *Organizational Behavior and Human Performance* (February 1974): 65-82.

51. Watson, "Structure of Project Teams Facing Differentiated Environments," 259-73.

52. J. Jiambalvo, D. J. H. Watson, and J. V. Baumler, "An Examination of Performance Evaluation Decisions in CPA Firm Subunits," *Accounting, Organizations and Society* (March 1983): 13-29.

53. Ibid., 18-19.

54. Wright, "Performance Appraisal of Staff Auditors," 37-43.

55. A. Wright, "An Investigation of the Engagement Evaluation Process for Staff Auditors," *Journal of Accounting Research* (Spring 1982): 227-39.

56. T. E. Kida, "Performance Evaluation and Review Meeting Characteristics in Public Accounting Firms," *Accounting, Organizations and Society* (February 1984): 137-48.

57. J. Rhode, J. Sorensen, and E. Lawler, "Sources of Professional Staff Turnover in Public Accounting Revealed by Exit Interview," *Accounting, Organizations and Society* (March 1977): 165-75.

58. D. Hellriegal and G. White, "Turnover of Professionals in Public Accounting: A Comparative Analysis," *Personnel Psychology* 2 (1973): 239-49.

59. J. Rhode, *Survey on the Influence of Selected Aspects of the Auditors' Work Environment on Professional Performance of Certified Public Accountants: A Study and Report for the Commission on Auditors' Responsibilities* (New York: AICPA, 1977).

60. S. Lightner, S. Adams, and K. Lightner, "The Influence of Situational, Ethical, and Expectancy Theory Variables on

Accountants' Underreporting Behavior," *Auditing: A Journal of Practice and Theory* (Fall 1982): 1-12.

61. M. Maher, K. Ramanathan, and R. Patterson, "Preference Congruence, Information Accuracy, and Employee Performance," *Journal of Accounting Research* (Autumn 1979): 476-503.

62. J. Jiambalvo, "Measures of Accuracy and Congruence in the Performance Evaluation of CPA Personnel: Replications and Extensions," *Journal of Accounting Research* (Spring 1982): 152-61.

63. A. Wright, "Performance Evaluation of Staff Auditors: A Behaviorally Anchored Rating Scale," *Auditing: A Journal of Practice and Theory* (Spring 1986): 95-108.

64. Ibid., 97.

65. R. S. Capui, "How to Cope with the Staff Man Shortage," *The Practical Accountant* 3 (1969): 22.

66. R. C. Ellyson and B. S. Shaw, "The Psychological Assessment and Staff Recruiting," *Journal of Accountancy* (1970): 35-42.

67. C. Konstans and K. Ferris, "Female Turnover in Professional Accounting Firms: Some Preliminary Findings," *Michigan CPA* (Winter 1981): 11-15.

68. F. P. Kollaritsh, "Job Migration Patterns of Accounting," *Management Accounting* (September 1968): 52-55.

69. Ralph L. Benke, Jr., and J. G. Rhode, "Intent to Turnover Among Higher Level Employees in Large CPA Firms," *Advances in Accounting* 1 (1984): 157-74.

70. J. Healy, "The Drudge Is Dead," *MBA* (November 1976): 48-56.

71. J. Carey, *The CPA Plans for the Future* (New York: AICPA, 1965).

72. J. Ashworth, "People Who Become Accountants," *Journal of Accounting* 2 (1968): 43-49.

73. J. Ashworth, "The Pursuit of High Quality Recruits," *Journal of Accountancy* 1 (1969): 53-57.

74. J. Ashworth, "A Must for Effective Recruiting: Mutual Understanding Between Students and the Accounting Profession," *Journal of Accountancy* 1 (1969): 84-86.

75. F. C. Pierson, *The Education of American Businessmen* (New York: McGraw-Hill, 1959).

76. R. Cruse, "What Can the Behavioral Contribute to the Selection of CPAs," *Journal of Accountancy* 2 (1965): 88.

77. J. Zweig, "Individualisms- A Recruiting Aid for Local Practitioners," *Journal of Accountancy* 1 (1969): 80.

78. C. G. Carpenter and R. H. Strawser, "Job Selection Preference of Accounting Students," *Journal of Accountancy* 2 (1970): 84-86.

79. V. C. Brenner, P. E. Dasher, and W. J. Grasty, "Attitude Change After College Campus Recruiting Interview," *The New York Certified Public Accountant* 2 (1971): 165.

80. P. E. Leathers, *The Staff Retention Problem in Public Accounting: Background and Questions for Discussion* (Subcommittee on Staff Retention of the Committee on Education) (New York: AICPA, 1970).

81. K. V. Ramanathan, R. B. Peterson, and M. W. Maher, "Strategic Goals and Performance Criteria in CPA Firms," *Journal of Accountancy* 141 (1976): 56-64.

82. J. G. Rhode, J. E. Sorensen, and E. E. Lawler III, "An Analysis of Personal Characteristics Related to Professional Staff Turnover in Public Accounting Firm," *Decision Sciences* 7 (1976): 771-800.

83. Ibid., 773.

84. J. F. Dilard and K. R. Ferris, "Sources of Professional Staff Turnover in Public Accounting Firms: Some Further Evidence," *Accounting, Organizations and Society* (February 1980): 179-86.

85. Rhode, Sorensen, Lawler, "Sources of Professional Staff Turnover," 165-75.

86. Ibid., 174.

87. Porter and Steers, "Organizational Work and Personnel Factors," 151-76.

88. M. L. Bullen and E. G. Flamholtz, "A Theoretical and Empirical Investigation of Job Satisfaction and Intended Turnover in Large CPA Firm," *Accounting, Organizations and Society* (August 1985): 287-302.

89. Sorensen, "Professional and Bureaucratic Organizations," 553-65.

90. V. H. Vroom, *Work and Motivation* (New York: John Wiley & Sons, 1964).

91. O. C. Behling, C. Shriesheim, and J. Toliver, "Alternatives to Expectancy Theories of Work Motivation," *Decision Sciences* (January 1975): 449-61.

92. J. R. Galbraith and L. L. Cummings, "An Empirical Investigation of the Motivational Determinants of Task Performance: Interactive Effects Between Instrumentality-Valance and Motivation-Ability," *Organizational Behavior and Human Performance* 2 (1967): 237-57.

93. Lawler, *Pay and Organizational Effectiveness* 12.

94. L. W. Porter and E. E. Lawler, *Managerial Attitudes and Performance* (Homewood, Il: Irwin, 1968).

95. K. R. Ferris, "A Test of the Expectancy Theory of Motivation in an Accounting Environment," *The Accounting Review* (July 1977): 605-15.

96. T. R. Mitchell, "Expectancy Models of Job Satisfaction, Occupational Preference and Effort: A Theoretical, Methodological and Empirical Appraisal," *Psychological Bulletin* 2 (1974); 1053-77.

97. J. Jiambalvo, "Performance Evaluations in CPA Firms: An Empirical Test of an Evaluation Model of Directed Job Effort," *Journal of Accounting Research* 1 (Fall 1979): 436-55.

98. J. F. Dillard, "Valence Instrumentality-Expectancy Model Validation Using Selected Accounting Groups," *Accounting, Organizations and Society* 2 (1979): 31-38.

99. Dillard and Ferris, "Sources of Professional Staff Turnover," 179-86.

100. K. R. Ferris, J. F. Dillard, and L. Nethercott, "A Comparison of V-I-E Mode Predictions: A Cross National Study in Professional

Accounting Firms," *Accounting, Organizations and Society* (December 1980): 361-68.

101. W. Mobley, R. Griffith, H. Hand, and B. Meglino, "Review and Conceptual Analysis of the Employee Turnover Process," *Psychological Bulletin* 2 (1979): 493-522.

102. H. Arnold and D. Felchman, "A Multivariate Analysis of the Determinants of Turnover," *Journal of Applied Psychology* 1 (1982): 350-60.

103. A. Maslow, *Eupsychian Management* (Homewood, Il.: Irwin, 1965).

104. D. D. O'Dowd and P. c. Beardslee, "College Student Images of a Selected Group of Professions and Occupations" (Mideletown, Conn.: Wesleyan University, April 1960).

105. W. Thielen, Jr., "Recruits for Accounting: How the Class of 1961 Entered the Profession" (unpublished report, American Institute of Certified Public Accountants, 1966).

106. J. T. Gray, "Need and Values in Three Occupations," *Personnel Guidance* 42 (1963): 238-44.

107. S. J. Segal and R. Szabo, "Identification in Two Vocations: Accountants and Creative Writers," *Personnel and Guidance Journal* (November 1964): 252-55.

108. S. J. Segal, "A Psychoanalytic Analysis of Personality Factors in Vocational Choice," *Journal of Counseling Psychology* 8 (1961): 202-10.

109. N. Aranya, E. I. Meir, And A. Bar-Ilan, "An Empirical Examination of the Stereotype Accountant Based on Holland's Theory," *Journal of Occupational Psychology* 51 (1978: 139-45.

110. N. Aranya and A. Barak, "A Test of Holland's Theory in a Population of Accountants," *Journal of Vocational Behavior* 19 (1981): 15-24.

111. N. Aranya and J. T. Wheeler, "Accountants' Personality Types and Their Commitment to Organization and Profession," *Contemporary Accounting Research* (Fall 1986): 184-99.

112. J. L. Holland, "Some Explorations of a Theory of Vocational Choice: One and Two-Year Longitudinal Studies," *Psychological Monographs* 76 (1962): 211-21.

113. J. L. Holland, "Explorations of a Theory of Vocational Choice. Part I: Vocational Images and Choice," *Vocational Guidance Quarterly* 2 (1965): 232-39.

114. J. L. Holland, "Explorations of a Theory of Vocational Choice. Part IV: A Longitudinal Study Using a Sample of Typical College Students," *Journal of Applied Psychology* (February 1968): 1-37.

115. Ralph Estes, "An Intergenerational Comparison of Socioeconomics Statistics Among CPAs, Attorneys, Engineers, and Physicians," *Advances in Accounting* 1 (1984): 3-17.

116. Ibid., 16.

117. T. D. DeCoster and J. G. Rhode, "The Accountant's Stereotype: Real or Imagined, Deserved or Unwarranted," *The Accounting Review* 4 (1971): 651-64.

118. Aranya, Meir, and Bar-Ilan, "An Empirical Examination of the Stereotype Accountant," 139-45.

119. J. L. Holland, *The Psychology of Vocational Choice* (Englewood Cliffs, N.J.: Prentice-Hall, 1973).

120. DeCoster and Rhode, "Accountant's Stereotype," 651-64.

121. Sorensen, "Professional and Bureaucratic Organization," 553-65.

122. J. E. Sorensen, J. G. Rhode, and E. E. Lawler, "The Generation Gap in Public Accounting," *Journal of Accountancy* (December 1973): 42-50.

123. L. R. Juach, W. F. Gluck, and R. N. Osbom, "Organizational Loyalty, Professional Commitment, and Academic Research Productivity," *Academy of Management Journal* (June 1978): 84-92.

124. L. W. Porter, R. M. Steers, R .T. Mowday, and P. V. Boulian, "Organizational Commitment, Job Satisfaction and Turnover Among Psychiatric Technicians," *Journal of Applied Psychology* (October 1974): 603-9.

125. R. N. Steers, "Antecedents and Outcomes of Organizational Commitment," *Administrative Science Quarterly* (March 1977): 46-56.

126. Sorensen and Sorensen, "Conflict of the Professionals," 98-106.

127. H. Hastings and C. R. Hastings, "Role Relations and Value Adaptation: A Study of the Professional Accountant in Industry," *Sociology* (September 1970): 353-66.

128. N. Aranya, J. Pollock, and J. Armenic, "An Examination of Professional Commitment in Public Accounting," *Accounting, Organizations and Society* (December 1981): 271-80.

129. Sorensen and Sorensen, "Conflict of Professionals" 98-106.

130. Aranya and Wheeler, "Accountants' Personality Types" 184-99.

131. D. McClelland, "Is Personality Consistent?" in *Further Explorations in Personality*, ed. A. Rubin, J. Aronoff, A. Barcaly, and R. Zucker (New York: John Wiley & Sons, 1981).

132. A. M. Harrell and R. Eickhoff, "Auditors' Influence-Orientation and Their Affective Responses to the 'Big Eight' Work Environment" (unpublished manuscript, University of South Carolina, 1988).

133. A. Belkaoui, "The Accounting Students' Need for Achievement and Career Aspirations: An Experiment," *Issues in Accounting Education* (Fall 1986): 197-206.

134. J. F. Dillard, "A Longitudinal Evaluation of an Occupation Goal-Expectancy Model in Professional Accounting Organizations," *Accounting, Organizations and Society* (February 1981): 17-26.

135. J. F. Dillard, "Applicability of an Occupational Goal-Expectancy Model in Professional Accounting Organizations," *Decision Sciences* 10 (1979): 161-76.

136. Ibid., 164.

137. A. Mikhail, "Stress: A Psychophysical Conception," *Journal of Human Stress* (June 1981): 9-15.

138. A. Antonovsky, *Health, Stress and Coping* (San Francisco: Jossey-Bass, 1979).

139. Ibid., 72.

140. K. E. Weick, "Stress in Accounting Systems," *The Accounting Review* (April 1983): 350-69.

141. R. Libby, "Comments on Weick," *The Accounting Review* (April 1983): 370-74.

142. J. Kusel and N. J. Deyonb, "Internal Auditor Burnout," *The Internal Auditor* (October 1983): 22-25.

143. K. J. Smith and M. S. Katzman, "Stress and Internal Auditors," *Accountants' Journal* 1 (1983): 27-32.

144. T. Helliwell, "The Wages of the Overwork-Burnout," *The Chartered Accountant Magazine* (August 1982): 83-87.

145. G. Firth, "The Impact of Size and Stress in Accounting Firms," *The Chartered Accountant in Australia* (August 1982): 20-33.

146. J. D. Kimes, "Handling Stress in the Accounting Profession," *Management Accounting* (September 1977): 17-23.

147. R. H. Strawser, J. P. Kelly, and R. Wise, "What Causes Stress for Management Accountants?" *Management Accounting* (March 1982): 32-35.

148. R. W. Sapp and R. Seiler, "Accounting for Performance: Stressful- But Satisfying," *Management Accounting* (August 1980): 29-35.

149. C. L. Cooper and R. Payne, *Stress at Work* (London: John Wiley & Sons, 1978).

150. F. Choo, "Job Stress, Job Performance, and Auditor Personality Characteristics," *Auditing: A Journal of Practice and Theory* (Spring 1986): 17-34.

151. F. Choo, "Accountants and Occupational Stress," *The Australian Accountant* (November 1982): 633-38.

152. S. Cohen, "After-Effects of Stress on Human Performance and Social Behavior: A Review of Research and Theory," *Psychological Bulletin* (July 1980): 82-108.

153. S. R. Maddi, M. Hoover, and S. C. Kobasa, "Alienation and Exploratory Behavior," *Journal of Personality and Social Psychology* 3 (1981): 112-19.

154. M. Csikzentmihalyi, *Beyond Boredom and Anxiety* (San Francisco: Jossey-Bass, 1975).

155. Choo, "Job Stress." 17-34.

156. P. L. Broadhurst, "The Interaction of Task Difficulty and Motivation: The Yerkes-Dodson Law Revised," *Acta Psychologica* 16 (1959): 321-38.

157. M. M. Greller and D. M. Herold, "Sources of Feedback: A Preliminary Investigation," *Organization Behavior and Human Performance* 13 (1975): 244-56.

158. L. M. Hansen and P. M. Muchinsky, "Work as an Information Environment," *Organizational Behavior and Human Performance* 21 (1978): 47-60.

159. D. M. Herold and M. M. Greller, "Feedback: The Definition of the Construct," *Academy of Management Journal* 20 (1977): 142-47.

160. J. Annett, *Feedback and Human Behavior* (Baltimore: Penguin, 1969).

161. A. N. Turner and P. R. Lawrence, *Industrial Jobs and the Workers* (Boston: Harvard University Graduate School of Business Administration, 1965).

162. J. R. Hackman and E. E. Lawler III, "Employee Reactions to Job Characteristics," *Journal of Applied Psychology* 55 (1971): 259-86.

163. Greller and Herold, "Sources of Feedback," 244-251.

164. Hansen and Muchinsky, "Work as an Information Environment," 47-60.

165. Greller and Herold, "Sources of Feedback," 244-51.

166. Ibid., 244.

167. Hansen and Muchinsky, "Work as an Information Environment," 47-60.

168. A. Belkaoui and R. D. Picur, "Sources of Feedback in a CPA Firm," *Journal of Business Finance and Accounting* (Summer 1987): 175-86.

169. J. L. Price and C. W. Mueller, *Handbook of Organizational Measurement* (Marshfield, Mass.: Pitman Publishing, 1986).

REFERENCES

Annett, J. *Feedback and Human Behavior*. Baltimore: Penguin, 1969.

Antonovsky, A. *Health, Stress and Coping*. San Francisco: Jossey-Bass, 1979.

Aranya, N., and A. Barak. "A Test of Holland's Theory in a Population of Accountants." *Journal of Vocational Behavior* 19 (1981): 15-24.

Aranya, N., and K. R. Ferris. "A Reexamination of Accountant's Organizational-Professional Conflict." *The Accounting Review* (January 1984): 1-15.

Aranya, N., R. Lachman, and J. Armevic. "Accountants' Job Satisfaction: A Path Analysis." *Accounting, Organizations and Society* (December 1982): 201-15.

Aranya, N., E. I. Meir, and A. Bar-Ilan. "An Empirical Examination of the Stereotype Accountant Based on Holland's Theory." *Journal of Occupational Psychology* 51 (1978): 139-45.

Aranya, N., J. Pollock, and J. Armenic. "An Examination of Professional Commitment in Public Accounting." *Accounting, Organizations and Society* (December 1981): 271-80.

Aranya, N., and J. T. Wheeler. "Accountants' Personality Types and Their Commitment to Organization and Profession." *Contemporary Accounting Research* (Fall 1986): 184-99.

Arnold, H., and D. Felchman. "A Multivariate Analysis of the Determinants of Turnover." *Journal of Applied Psychology* 2 (1982): 350-60.

Ashworth, J. "People Who Become Accountants." *Journal of Accounting* (March 1968): 66-72.

___. "The Pursuit of High Quality Recruits." *Journal of Accountancy* (December 1969): 53-57.

___. "A Must for Effective Recruiting: Mutual Understanding Between Students and the Accounting Profession." *Journal of Accountancy* (January 1969): 84-86.

Baker, C. Richard. "Management Strategy in a Large Accounting Firm." *The Accounting Review* (July 1977): 576-86.

Behling, O. C., C. Schriesheim, and J. Tolliver, "Alternatives to Expectancy Theories of Work Motivation." *Decision Sciences* (January 1975): 449-61.

Belkaoui, A. "The Accounting Students' Need for Achievement and Career Aspirations: An Experiment." *Issues in Accounting Education* (Fall 1986): 197-206.

___. "Leadership Style, Dimensions of Superior's Upward Influence and Job Perception in a Public Accounting Firm: A Reexamination of the 'Pelz Effect.'" Unpublished manuscript, University of Illinois at Chicago, June 1989.

Belkaoui, A., and R. D. Picur. "Sources of Feedback in a CPA Firm." *Journal of Business Finance and Accounting* (Summer 1987): 175-86.

Benke, R. L., Jr., and J. C. Rhode. "The Job Satisfaction of Higher Level Employees in Large Certified Public Accounting Firms." *Accounting, Organizations and Society* (July 1980): 187-201.

___. "Intent to Turnover Among Higher Level Employees in Large CPA Firms." *Advances in Accounting* 1 (1984): 157-74.

Blau, P. M., and W. R. Scott. *Formal Organization*. San Francisco: Chandler, 1962.

Brenner, V. C., P. E. Dasher, and W. J. Grasty. "Attitude Change After College Campus Recruiting Interview." *The New York Certified Public Accountant* 2 (1971): 165.

Broadhurst, P. L. "the Interaction of Task Difficulty and Motivation: The Yerkes-Dodson Law Revised." *Acta Psychologica* 16 (1959): 321-38.

Bullen, M. L., and E. G. Flamholtz. "A Theoretical and Empirical Investigation of Job Satisfaction and Intended Turnover in Large CPA Firm." *Accounting, Organizations and Society* (August 1985): 287-302.

Capui, R. S. "How to Cope with the Staff Man Shortage." *The Practical Accountant* 1 (1969): 22.

Carey, J. *The CPA Plans for the Future*. New York: AICPA, 1965.

Carpenter, C. G., and R. H. Strawser. "Job Selection Preference of Accounting Students." *Journal of Accountancy* (1970): 84-86.

___. "A Study of the Job Satisfaction of Academic Accountants." *The Accounting Review* (July 1971): 509-18.

Choo, F. "Accountants and Occupational Stress." *The Australian Accountant* (November 1982): 633-38.

___. "Job Stress, Job Performance, and Auditor Personality Characteristics." *Auditing: A Journal of Practice and Theory* (Spring 1986): 17-34.

Cohen, S. "After-Effects of Stress on Human Performance and Social Behavior. A Review of Research and Theory." *Psychological Bulletin* (July 1980): 82-108.

Cooper, C. L., and R. Payne. *Stress at Work*. London: John Wiley & Sons, 1978.

Cruse, R. "What Can the Behavioral Contribute to the Selection of CPAs." *Journal of Accountancy* 2 (1965): 88.

Csikzentmihalyi, M. *Beyond Boredom and Anxiety*. San Francisco: Jossey-Bass, 1975.

DeCoster, T. D., and J. G. Rhode. "The Accountant's Stereotype: Real or Imagined, Deserved or Unwarranted." *The Accounting Review* 4 (1971): 651-64.

Dillard, Jesse F. "Applicability of an Occupational Goal-Expectancy Model in Professional Accounting Firms: Some Further Evidence." *Accounting, Organizations and Society* (February 1980): 179-86.

Dirsmith, M. W., and M. A. Covaleski. "Informal Communications, Nonformal Communications and Mentoring in Public Accounting Firms." *Accounting, Organizations and Society* (May 1985): 149-69.

Ellyson, R. C. and B. S. Shaw. "The Psychological Assessment and Staff Recruiting." *Journal of Accountancy* 3 (1970): 35-42.

Estes, Ralph. "An Intergenerational Comparison of Socioeconomic Statistics Among CPAs, Attorneys, Engineers, and Physicians." *Advances in Accounting* 1 (1984): 3-17.

Ferris, K. R. "Perceived Uncertainty and Job Satisfaction in the Accounting Environment." *Accounting, Organizations and Society* 2:1 (1977): 23-28.

___. "A Test of the Expectancy Theory of Motivation in an Accounting Environment." *The Accounting Review* (July 1977): 605-15.

Ferris, K. R., J. F. Dillard, and L. Nethercott. "A Comparison of V-I-E Mode Predictions: A Cross National Study in Professional Accounting Firms." *Accounting, Organizations and Society* (December 1980): 361-68.

Firth, G. "The Impact of Size and Stress in Accounting Firms." *The Chartered Accountant in Australia* (August 1982): 20-33.

Galbraith, J. R., and L. L. Cummings. "An Empirical Investigation of the Motivational Determinant of Task Performance: Interactive Effects Between Instrumentality-Valence and Motivation-Ability." *Organizational Behavior and Human Performance* 2 (1967): 237-57.

Gray, J. T. "Need and Values in Three Occupations." *Personnel Guidance* 42 (1963): 238-44.

Greller, M. M., and D. M. Herold. "Sources of Feedback: A Preliminary Investigation." *Organizational Behavior and Human Performance* 13 (1975): 244-56.

Hackman, J. R., and E. E. Lawler III. "Employee Reactions to Job Characteristics." *Journal of Applied Psychology* 55 (1971): 259-86.

Hall, R. H. "Professionalization and Bureaucratization." *American Sociological Review* (February 1968): 92-104.

Hansen, L. M., and P. M. Muchinsky. "Work as an Information Environment." *Organizational Behavior and Human Performance* 21 (1978): 47-60.

Harrell, A. M., and R. Eickhoff. "Auditors' Influence-Orientation and Their Affective Responses to the 'Big Eight' Work Environment." Unpublished manuscript, University of South Carolina, 1988.

Harrell, A. M., and M. J. Stahl. "McClelland's Trichotonomy of Needs Theory and the Job Satisfaction and Work Performance of CPA Firm Professionals." *Accounting, Organizations and Society* (June 1984): 241-52.

Hastings, H., and C. R. Hastings. "Role Relations and Value Adaptation: A Study of the Professional Accountant in Industry." *Sociology* (September 1970): 353-66.

Healy, J. "The Drudge Is Dead." *MBA* (November 1976): 48-56.

Helliwell, T. "The Wages of the Overwork-Burnout." *The Chartered Accountant Magazine* (August 1982): 83-87.

Hellriegal, D., and G. White. "Turnover of Professionals in Public Accounting: A Comparative Analysis." *Personnel Psychology* 4 (1973): 239-49.

Herold, D. M., and M. M. Greller. "Feedback: The Definition of the Construct." *Academy of Management Journal* 20 (1977): 142-47.

Holland, J. L. "Some Explorations of a Theory of Vocational Choice: One and Two-Year Longitudinal Studies." *Psychological Monographs*, 76 (1962): 22-32.

___. "Explorations of a Theory of Vocational Choice, Part I. Vocational Images and Choice." *Vocational Guidance Quarterly* 2 (1965): 232-39.

___. "Explorations of a Theory of Vocational Choice. Part IV: A Longitudinal Study Using a Sample of Typical College Students." *Journal of Applied Psychology* (February 1968): 1-37.

___. *The Psychology of Vocational Choice*. Englewood Cliffs, N.J.; Prentice-Hall, 1973.

Ivancevich, John M., and Robert H. Strawser. "A Comparative Analysis of the Job Satisfaction of Industrial Managers and Certified Public Accountants." *Academy of Management Journal* 3 (1969): 193-203.

Jablin, F. M. "Supervisor's Upward Influence, Satisfaction, and Openness in Superior-Subordinate Communication: A Reexamination of the 'Pelz Effect,'" *Human Communication Research* 2 (1980): 210-20.

___. "A Reexamination of the 'Pelz Effect,'" *Human Communication Research* 3 (1980): 210-20.

Jauch, L. R., W. F. Gluck, and R. N. Osbom. "Organizational Loyalty, Professional Commitment, and Academic Research Productivity." *Academy of Management Journal* (June 1978): 84-92.

Jiambalvo, J. "Performance Evaluation and Directed Job Effort: Model Development and Analysis in a CPA Firm Setting." *Journal of Accounting Research* (Autumn 1979): 436-55.

___. "Measures of Accuracy and Congruence in the Performance Evaluation of CPA Personnel: Replications and Extensions." *Journal of Accounting Research* (Spring 1982): 152-61.

___. "Performance Evaluations in CPA Firms: An Empirical Test of an Evaluation Model of Directed Job Effort." *Journal of Accounting Research* (Autumn 1979): 436-55.

Jiambalvo, J., and J. Pratt. "Task Complexity and Leadership Effectiveness in CPA Firms." *The Accounting Review* (October 1982): 734-50.

Jiambalvo, J., D. J. H. Watson, and J. V. Baumler. "An Examination of Performance Evaluation Decisions in CPA Firm Subunits." *Accounting Organization and Society* (March 1983): 13-29.

Jones, A. P., L. R. James, and J. R. Bruni. "Perceived Leadership Behavior and Employee Confidence in the Leader as Moderated by Job Involvement." *Journal of Applied Psychology* 63 (1978): 146-49.

Kane, J., and E. Lawler. "Performance Appraisal Effectiveness: Its Assessments and Determinants." *Research in Organizational Behavior* 3 (1979): 425-78.

Kida, T. E. "Performance Evaluation and Review Meeting Characteristics in Public Accounting Firms." *Accounting, Organizations and Society* (February 1984): 137-48.

Kimes, J. D. "Handling Stress in the Accounting Profession." *Management Accounting* (September 1977): 17-23.

Kollaritsh, F. P. "Job Migration Patterns of Accounting." *Management Accounting* (September 1968): 52-55.

Konstans, C., and K. Ferris. "Female Turnover in Professional Accounting Firms: Some Preliminary Findings." *Michigan CPA* (Winter 1981): 11-15.

Kusel, J., and N. J. Deyonb. "Internal Auditor Burnout." *The Internal Auditor* (October 1983): 22-25.

Lawler, E. E. *Pay and Organizational Effectiveness: A Psychological View*. New York: McGraw-Hill, 1971.

Leathers, P. E. *The Staff Retention Problem in Public Accounting: Background and Questions for Discussion*. Subcommittee on Staff Retention of the Committee on Education. New York: AICPA, 1970.

Libby, R. "Comments on Weick." *The Accounting Review* (April 1983): 370-74.

Lightner, S., S. Adams, and K. Lightner. "The Influence of Situational, Ethical, and Expectancy Theory Variables on Accountants' Underreporting Behavior." *Auditing: A Journal of Practice and Theory* (Fall 1982): 1-12.

Locke, E. A. "The Nature and Causes of Job Satisfaction." In *Handbook of Industrial and Organizational Psychology*, edited by M. D. Dunnett. Chicago: Rand McNally, 1976, 1297-1349.

McClelland, D. C. *Power: The Inner Experience*. New York: Irvington, 1975.

____. "Is Personality Consistent?" In *Further Explorations in Personality*, edited by A. Rubin, J. Aronoff, A. Barclay, and R. Zucker. New York: John Wiley & Sons, 1981.

Maher, M., K. Ramanathan, and R. Patterson. "Preference Congruence, Information Accuracy, and Employee Performance." *Journal of Accounting Research* (Autumn 1979): 476-503.

Maddi, S. R., M. Hoover, and S. C. Kobasa. "Alienation and Exploratory Behavior." *Journal of Personality and Social Psychology* 3 (1981): 262-73.

Maslow, A. *Eupsychian Management*. Homewood, Il: Irwin, 1965.

Mikhail, A. "Stress: A Psychophysical Conception." *Journal of Human Stress* (June 1981): 9-15.

Mitchell, T. R. "Expectancy Models of Job Satisfaction, Occupational Preference and Effort: A Theoretical, Methodological and Empirical Appraisal." *Psychological Bulletin* 2 (1974): 1053-77.

Mobley, W., R. Griffith, H. Hand, and B. Meglino. "Review and Conceptual Analysis of the Employee Turnover Process." *Psychological Bulletin* 3 (1979): 493-522.

Montagna, P. D. "Professionalization and Bureaucratization in Large Professional Organizations." *American Journal of Sociology* (September 1968): 138-45.

Norris, D. R., and R. E. Nielbuhr. "Professionalism, Organizational Commitment and Job Satisfaction in an Accounting Organization." *Accounting, Organizations and Society* (December 1983): 49-60.

O'Dowd, D. D., and P. C. Beardslee. "College Student Images of a Selected Group of Professions and Occupations." Middletown, Conn.: Wesleyan University, April 1960.

O'Reilly, C. A., and K. H. Roberts. "Supervisor Influence and Subordinate Mobility Aspirations as Moderators of Consideration and Initiating Structure." *Administrative Science Quarterly* 13 (1968): 65-105.

Pelz, D. "Influence: A Key to Effective Leadership in the First Line Supervisor." *Personnel* 29 (1952): 209-71.

Pierson, F. C. *The Education of American Businessmen*. New York: McGraw-Hill, 1959.

Porter, L. W., and E. E. Lawler. *Managerial Attitudes and Performance*. Homewood, Il: Irwin, 1968.

Porter, L. W., and V. F. Mitchell. "Comparative Study of Need Satisfaction in Military and Business Hierarchies." *Journal of Applied Psychology* (April 1967): 139-44.

Porter, L. W., and R. M. Steers. "Organizational Work and Personal Factors in Employee Turnover and Absenteeism." *Psychological Bulletin* 3 (1973): 151-76.

Porter, L. W., R. M. Steers, R. T. Mowday, and P. V. Boulian. "Organizational Commitment, Job Satisfaction and Turnover Among Psychiatric Technicians." *Journal of Applied Psychology* (October 1974): 603-9.

Pratt, J., and J. Jiambalvo. "Relationships Between Leader Behaviors and Audit Team Performance." *Accounting, Organizations and Society* (August 1981): 133-42.

___. "Determinants of Leader Behavior in an Audit Environment." *Accounting, Organizations and Society* (December 1982): 379-79.

Price, J. L., and C. W. Mueller. *Handbook of Organizational Measurement*. Marshfield, Mass.: Pitman Publishing, 1986.

Ramanathan, K. V., R. B. Peterson, and M. W. Maher. "Strategic Goals and Performance Criteria in CPA Firms." *Journal of Accountancy* 141 (1976): 56-64.

Rhode, J. *Survey on the Influence of Selected Aspects of the Auditors' Work Environment on Professional Performance of Certified Public Accountants: A Study and Report for the Commission on Auditors' Responsibilities*. New York: AICPA, 1977.

Rhode, J., J. E. Sorensen, and E. E. Lawler III. "An Analysis of Personal Characteristics Related to Professional Staff Turnover in Public Accounting Firm." *Decision Sciences* 7 (1976): 771-800.

___. "Sources of Professional Staff Turnover in Public Accounting Revealed by Exit Interview." *Accounting, Organizations and Society* 2 (1977): 165-75.

Roberts, K. H., and C. A. O'Reilly. "Failures in Upward Communication: Three Possible Culprits." *Academy of Management Journal* 17 (1974): 205-15.

Sapp, R. W., and R. Seiler. "Accounting for Performance: Stressful-But Satisfying." *Management Accounting* (August 1980): 29-35.

Schroeder, R. G., and L. F. Imdieke. "Local-Cosmopolitan and Bureaucratic Perceptions in Public Accounting Firms." *Accounting, Organizations and Society* 1 (1977): 39-45.

Segal, S. J. "A Psychoanalytic Analysis of Personality Factors in Vocational Choice." *Journal of Counseling Psychology* 8 (1961): 202-10.

Segal, S. J., and R. Szabo. "Identification in Two Vocations: Accountants and Creative Writers." *Personnel and Guidance Journal* (November 1964): 252-55.

Senatra, P. T. "Role Conflict, Role Ambiguity, and Organizational Climate in a Public Accounting Firm." *The Accounting Review* (October 1980): 594-603.

Smith, K. J., and M. S. Katzman. "Stress and Internal Auditors." *Accountants' Journal* 1 (1983): 27-32.

Sorensen, J. E. "Professional and Bureaucratic Organization In Public Accounting Firms." *The Accounting Review* (July 1967): 553-65.

Sorensen, J. E., J. G. Rhode, and E. E. Lawler. "The Generation Gap in Public Accounting." *Journal of Accountancy* 3 (1973): 42-50.

Sorensen, J. E., and T. L. Sorensen. "The Conflict of Professionals in Bureaucratic Organizations." *Administrative Science Quarterly* (March 1974): 98-106.

Steers, R. N. "Antecedents and Outcomes of Organizational Commitment." *Administrative Science Quarterly* (March 1977): 45-56.

Strawser, R. H., J. M. Ivanevich, and H. L. Lyon. "A Note on the Job Satisfaction of Accountants in Large and Small CPA Firms." *Journal of Accounting Research* (Autumn 1969): 339-45.

Stawser, R. H., and J. P. Kelly, and R. Wise. "What Causes Stress for Management Accountants?" *Management Accounting* (March 1982): 32-35.

Thielen, W., Jr. "Recruits for Accounting: How the Class of 1961 Entered the Profession." Unpublished report, American Institute of Certified Public Accountants, 1966.

Turner, A. N., and P. R. Lawrence. *Industrial Jobs and the Workers.* Boston: Harvard University Graduate School of Business Administration, 1965.

Turney, J. R. "Activity Outcome Expectancies and Intrinsic Activity Values as Predictors of Several Motivation Indexes for Technical-Professionals." *Organizational Behavior and Human Performance* (February 1974): 65-82.

Vroom, V. H. *Work and Motivation.* New York: John Wiley & Sons, 1964.

Wager, L. W. "Leadership Style, Influence and Supervisory Role Obligations." *Administrative Science Quarterly* 9 (1965): 391-420.

Watson, David J. H. "The Structure of Project Teams Facing Differentiated Environments: An Exploratory Study in Public Accounting Firms." *The Accounting Review* (April 1975): 259-73.

Weick, K. E. "Stress in Accounting Systems." *The Accounting Review* (April 1983): 350-69.

Wright, A. "Performance Appraisal of Staff Auditors." *CPA Journal* (November 1980): 37-43.

___. "Performance Evaluation of Staff Auditors: A Behaviorally Anchored Rating Scale." *Auditing: A Journal of Practice and Theory* (Spring 1986): 227-39.

Zweig, J. "Individualisms- A Recruiting Aid for Local Practitioners." *Journal of Accountancy* 2 (1969): 80.

THE PROBLEMATICS OF THE PRODUCTION OF KNOWLEDGE IN ACCOUNTING
6

In its first stage accounting knowledge as formal pure knowledge is essentially the product of academic research and thinking. In the second stage it is transformed by the accounting profession into an accounting working knowledge. In both stages the production of accounting knowledge suffers from problems inherent in a contamination of the research process at the hands of the profession. Both problems are the core of a crisis in the production and dissemination of accounting knowledge.

ACCOUNTING KNOWLEDGE IN THE HANDS OF ACADEMICS
Formal Accounting Knowledge: The Issues of Power and Scholarship

Accounting plays a crucial role in shaping the conduct of business and the management of institutions. The accounting profession and accounting itself as sources of knowledge are assumed to have power. Accounting knowledge gains its power from assumed attributes like financial influence, monopoly of discourse, and social control. But as in all other types of knowledge, the actual accounting knowledge that is used in practice to influence the conduct of business and the management of all types of enterprises is different from the formal knowledge that is the core of the activity of academics and researchers. Actual accounting knowledge is basically the formal accounting knowledge as it gets transformed, adapted, and sometimes misapplied in practice. As it gets applied and hence institutionalized, accounting knowledge gets power from the transformation of formal knowledge to practical means and ends. The professional accountants are the mere agents or carriers of working accounting knowledge, while researchers remain the agents and carriers of formal accounting knowledge, and there lies the conflict separating researcher from practice.

Actual knowledge may be available to all members of the accounting profession as the certification and continuing education programs force the members to be abreast of general accounting developments. Specialized accounts knowledge, however, is available only to some, creating another schism- a professional schism. It is the social division of labor in the exercise of accounting tasks that give rise to the diverse bodies of specialized knowledge and to another form of power within the profession itself. The acquisition of specialized knowledge creates a new power through the expertise label and the acquired special monopoly of discourse.

It is, however, the formal accounting knowledge as practiced and researched by academics and researchers that can be characterized as rational, elite knowledge, aimed at fulfilling the end of functional efficiency. The situation calls for the use of reason and consciousness. It can, however, be perceived as a tool used by academics and researchers to control and dominate the imperative functions of accounting as practiced, sometimes shaping them to meet the demands of special interest groups or even for meeting the specific purposes of the state. As such it may restrict choice, facilitate the control of people and their behavior, and even produce the methods of interpreting and disposing of a diverse group of human behaviors. As Foucault sees these techniques, they "define how one may have a hold over others' bodies, not only so that they may do what one wishes, but so that they may operate as one wishes, with the techniques, the speed and the efficiency that one determines. Thus, discipline produces subjected and practiced bodies."[1]

The power of formal knowledge becomes a control tool, "working to incite, reinforce, control, monitor, optimize and organize the forces under it: a power bent on generating forces, making them grow, and ordering them, rather than one dedicated to impeding them, making them submit, or destroying them."[2] That power expresses itself by a presentation of techniques as solutions rather than submitting the choice to political debate and democratic participation.

The formal accounting knowledge is a tangible good, as it is measureable in the number of accounting books and articles that are proliferating as a result of the works of the agents of such knowledge- the accounting intelligentsia or accounting intellectuals to be more precise. These intellectuals are not interested solely in the practical concerns of the accountants. As Coser, speaking of intellectuals in general, puts it, "intellectuals feel the need to go beyond the immediate concrete task and to penetrate a more general realm of meaning and value."[3] Shumpeter characterized them as those "whose interest is to work up and organize resentment, to nurse it, to voice it and to lead it."[4]

The "intellectuality" of the academic accountant is commendable. It is, however, a way of making a living, and there lies a dilemma. Economic support is needed for the accounting formal knowledge to progress. That support must come from either the practical world of the market or the state. There lies again the risk for a market for excuses. One solution is for the academics to devote their time to a scholarly research, the type that does not generate sufficient market value, and it intended to address other intellectuals rather than the general public or special interest groups. Economic support in that case is limited to university teaching. Accounting researchers have generally opted for the provision of excuses, losing scholarship ground for the sake of increased power.

Scientific Establishments in Accounting: Self-made Prisons

Scientific establishments in accounting are bound by their legitimation of adopted paradigms. Researchers in the particular paradigms play a key role in the development of scientific or formal accounting knowledge. They interact, and through a constant process of consensus, discussions, and power struggles determine which findings should be legitimated as advances in accounting research and part of the formal accounting knowledge. Abuses in these processes can happen, blocking for a while worthwhile discoveries that are judged threatening to a favorite accounting paradigm.

The presence of these conflicting paradigms in accounting is equivalent to a division of labor that is necessary to investigate the various facets and complexities presented by the production and use of accounting phenomena. The division of labor does not, however, produce the desired benefits, as each scientific establishment in accounting starts acting as a sovereign state rather than as a member of a cooperating team. Power considerations as well as insecurity may motivate the member of an accounting paradigm to shy away from cooperation and hide behind the alleged superiority of its views. Other considerations that may contribute to the distancing between members of different scientific establishments result from the unplanned dynamics of the social organization of scientific work in the academic form. Elias views the situation as follows:

Two of its most significant features are, firstly, an unplanned long-term trend towards increasing specialization and, secondly, unplanned power- and status-differentials between the various specialized disciplines. A third connected with these two, is the tendency of scientific establishments to develop professional ideologies, a kind of scientific folklore as for instance, an intra-disciplinary ancestor worship, special benefits about selected "great men and women" belonging to this discipline and to no other, or beliefs about the unique value of one's own field of work, compared with that of others- a folklore which, though perhaps of little cognitive value, does add to the sense of belongingness, to the pride in their own work of members of a discipline which, within reason, people may need. However, all too often these professional ideologies of scientific establishments disguise as theories, thus becoming responsible for the sterility of research efforts. Even cases of deliberate falsification of research results for the greater glory of one's discipline or, maybe, of one's own theory, one's own value scheme and, thus, of oneself, are not unkown.[5]

Those unplanned dynamics characterize the accounting scientific establishments through increasing specialization, power and status differentials among the specialized disciplines, and professional ideologies of "grandeur." All this is contributing to friction among the establishments with the prospects of decreasing interdisciplinary relationships and a decline in the production of useful formal accounting knowledge. In the process the scientific establishments in accounting may have created for themselves a self-made prison. And they would resist any appeal to escape from their man-made trap because it runs counter to organized beliefs and values. As Elias explains:

What is demanded of them is the re-framing of their problem and its solution in terms which, in their eyes, have a lower cognitive status than their own. All that, they may feel, is too high a price to pay for an escape from an intellectual impasse so they prefer to stay in the homely trap of their insoluble problem and to carry along from generation to generation the flag of a tradition which, through it has little intrinsic cognitive value has, as one can well understand, a high value for their representatives.[6]

They rather control and engage in the production of their brand of accounting formal knowledge. Their monopoly of that brand of knowledge allows them to exclude others and/or to admit selectively only those they can reproduce. In the process their brand of accounting knowledge suffers a professional deformation because it is merely used to preserve their and status, control entry into their field, and counteract other paradigms aiming for primacy in the field. The concerns of these accounting academic elites are protection, discipline, and punishment. To rely on Foucault's terms,[7] the production of accounting knowledge is never separate from the exercise of power. One result of this situation is the constraining ideological influence on the production of accounting knowledge. As expressed by Arrington and Francis:

Thus accounting research is less expensive and less intellectually rigorous than it could be because of the disciplining forces of a hegemonic academic elite. The theories proposed by this elite also reflect an extremely conservative political perspective on the role of accounting in producing the social order.[8]

The De-institutionalization and Politicization of Formal Knowledge in Accounting

With the emergence of scientific establishments in accounting came a new power elite in control of the paradigms and journals. This elite got its power from the monopolitization of a specific brand of accounting knowledge methodologies, results, and excuses. The situation has allowed some of these groups to gain strong advisory roles in politics and policymaking. For example, market research-based knowledge, through its specific free market ideology, has gained some political power just because its contents are easily integrated in the definition of political social, and economic problems. But to gain this political power these scientific establishments had to alter the characteristics of the accounting knowledge produced from one identified with academic science to one identifiable with special interests and ideologies. In the process the formal accounting knowledge has been de-institutionalized to be identifiable with policies and ideologies rather than with universities and academic settings. This phenomenon has been also observed for other scientific establishments. Witness the following comment:

Their involvement in politics which has been interpreted as a "scientification" of politics, turns out to be the "politicization" of science at the same time. The professional status of science at the same time. The professional status of science with its sharp dileneation from other social institutions, its self-governance with respect to quality standards, criteria of relevance and a code of ethics becomes subject to political conflicts. Alliances and fractions emerge which run along the lines of political conflicts. Alliances and fractions emerge which run along the lines of political convictions rather than of systems of knowledge.[9]

But to effectively influence policymaking these accounting establishments had to combine their efforts with "experts" from the nonacademic field to include representatives of professional associations or standard selling bodies. In the process they created a "hybrid community" of accounting experts feeding on one another's legitimacy. Hybrid communities

represent the institutional expression of the increased communication pressures between the differentiated systems of politics, science and the economy. Their function is to help define policy problems in terms of systematic knowledge, to translate (operationalize) them into technical goals, to turn them into research, strategies, development programs and correlate policy measures, all of which feed back into the perception an definition of the policy problems themselves. The significance of the "hybrid communities," therefore, lies in their cognitive functions as brokers of even knowledge and political values.[10]

Hybrid communities in accounting include experts coming from different settings to shape the definition of accounting problems in political rather than scientific terms. In the process the academics lose the "power of problem definition" crucial to the resolution of the accounting problems within the framework of the formal accounting knowledge.

Competitive Grazing for Research Topics or Law of Perpetual Inquiring

Certain scientific hierarchies and established scientific paradigm in accounting guide the choice of research topics. The final choice of topics is guided by considerations of competition and rich potentiality. This view of the choice of topics has been labeled the "competitive grazing" model.

The specialty is pictured as a bounded meadow into which individual scientists, competitors for recognition and priority, allocate themselves. Areas of heavy over-grazing become less attractive, virgin pasture is sought out, and the overall territory represented by the available research is uniformly exploited.[11]

Overgrazing includes, for example, the whole question of LIFO/FIFO choice, and market price reactions to FASB pronouncements. Other examples abound in the field of accounting, and differences of opinion may exist on which areas are overexploited. It seems that the topic choice in accounting research is heavily determined by what is considered part of "virgin pasture," given that it is generally better rewarded with recognition. The real fact is that the choice of topics to be researched depends on a complex set of organizational, cultural, political, and intellectual factors. Researchers, as a result of early institutional affiliation and a choice of a dissertation topic for the Ph.D. degree, find themselves working in a given research trail rather than in others. That is what has been termed the "law of perpetual inquiry," with its consequence of some topics being overresearched and others being underresearched.[12] As expressed by Chubin and Connolly:

This assumption, we will suggest, leads directly to an important and unfortunate set of implications for the development of specialties: that there exist important pressures which lead to undue persistence of individuals in some research trails rather than others; that the social processes associated with the development of these trails tend toward conservative pressures for intellectual continuity on new entrants; and that the aggregate result of these processes is that, far from a wide dispersion of research effort around the boundary problem of a specialty, there will be unproductive over-concentration on some far problems, while high potential areas go underdeveloped.[13]

This does not stop new specialties from arising. Examples include cognition research in behavioral accounting, experimental economics, and social accounting. These specialties are first relativized by a definition and then reified through their own scientific establishments, journals, and publications. Using this law of perpetual inquiry, one may describe the research trail of the typical accounting researchers as first, a decision to initiate and complete a given research project identifiable with his own institution or scientific establishment, which may be characterized as a form of local tinkering, and second, to persist on the same research trail or along a new specialty within the same research trail as long as the benefit exceeds the cost. The benefits of persisting in a given accounting research trail rests on the degree of legitimacy of the paradigm researched, the degree of access to resources in the institution, and the training capacity of the institution.[14] Because of this law of perpetual inquiry, one would expect accounting to stagnate in spite of the creations of new specialties within the overresearched topics. The fact is that accounting research is far from stagnating, thanks to a heavy dose of continuous innovations from other disciplines, attracting migrant researchers from other fields and exporting its own researchers to the same fields. This cross-fertilization may have saved accounting from the "law of perpetual inquiry," so dear to those attracted to market-based research, for example. With this migration of researchers in and out of the discipline, accounting will eventually appear as a "scientific specialty" with extra local intellectual linkages among an aggregate of researchers, coming from such fields as finance, economics, management, psychology, and sociology, to name only a few.

ACCOUNTING KNOWLEDGE IN THE HANDS OF THE PROFESSION
The Subjugation of Formal Accounting Knowledge to Economic Interests

The formal accounting knowledge as formulated by researchers and intellectuals finds itself radically transformed by the accounting professionals when they try to meet various and specific demands of their clients. When the formal accounting knowledge is perceived as not suitable- too abstract, too academic for their taste-

the accounting profession has started to fund the types of research that produce what it considers "working knowledge." The accounting profession does so because it assumes that the formal accounting knowledge produced by academics is inbred by a concern for the ideal and the abstract rather than the practical. Even when the accounting profession attempts to apply some of the formal knowledge it does so with a concern for the "primacy of experience over theoretical knowledge, a phenomenon also observed in the field of engineering."[15] It is then a systematic selection and transformation of formal accounting knowledge that finds its use by the accounting profession in the provision of services.[16] If the clients belong to the mass of unorganized small businesses, the accounting profession is more apt to use the transformed formal knowledge to exercise control over its clients. If the clients are large and powerful, the accounting profession finds itself advancing the clients' conception of how formal knowledge should be transformed and applied.[17] As Friedson states:

Those in position to exercise the greatest amount of power over both public and corporate policy and over administration, the specification of public needs and problems by legislation and standard setting, and the allocation of resources to the manufacture of the material world are the profession's administrative members. By virtue of their commitment to private capital they select from and develop formal knowledge in ways that advance the interest of capital, as do accounting and law firms that serve corporations.[18]

The selection and use of formal accounting knowledge is, therefore, dependent on the power, interests, and knowledge of the powerful clients of certified public accounting firms. What happens is that the power the accounting profession has is no longer the special power of formal accounting knowledge, but the vested power of economic interests.

Myth Versus Technology in the Accounting Profession

The formal accounting knowledge is transformed and institutionalized by the accounting profession to gain a situation of privilege in society because that is that applied working knowledge that separates it from nonprofessionals and paraprofessionals.[19-21]

The mastering of this knowledge, what Parsons referred to as the primacy of the values of cognitive rationality,[22] links the profession to its privileges and rewards. This relation between professionals knowledge and professional privilege in accounting is in fact subject to two possible interpretations.

One interpretation is derived from Johnson's "service to capital" model[23] and the other, from Larson's "cognitive exclusiveness" model.[24]

The first interpretation attributes the power of the professions to the uncertainty inherent to professional knowledge. The uncertainty was modeled by Jamous and Peliolle,[25] who suggested that all occupations can be characterized by the ratio of indeterminacy to technicality in their knowledge. Indeterminacy refers to the professional knowledge that cannot be codified; technicality refers to the codified mass of the knowledge. A high ratio of indeterminacy over technicality coupled with legitimation of the organization of knowledge is necessary for reaching professional status. Johnson[26] applied the model to accounting, but argued that the profession's privileges rest on the use of indetermination by a limited segment of the profession to create surplus value.

Johnson's "service to capital" model was challenged by Larson,[27] who argued that indeterminacy holds for the early stages of professionalization, but thereafter the codification of the knowledge and the "production of producers" guarantee the professional status, especially if the profession relies on universities to codify the knowledge based on "scientific" criteria of validity.
The key to professional status within Larson's framework is, thus, not the discretion available in professional knowledge but the ability of the profession to control that knowledge. It may be noted that the control of knowledge is regarded as an independent variable rather than a dimension of professional privilege as in the model developed by Jamous and Peliolle and Johnson. The professions' power is created at an institutional level and not through the power afforded to individual practitioners through the discretion inherent in professional knowledge.[28]

In fact, Richardson tested the two models of the relation between the structure of professional knowledge and the professions' access to social rewards, finding support for Larson's "cognitive exclusiveness theory."[29] In other words, his findings suggest that the accounting profession gain rewards by standardizing its knowledge and institutionalizing the training of practitioners within universities, while simultaneously maintaining autonomy in practice.

Bonald, in fact, argued for a mixed position whereby the knowledge base of accounting represents a mix of technology (codified knowledge) and myth (uncertainty), emerging to manage the profession's legitimacy in the face of competing institutional demands.[30] The interplay of myth and technology does not, however, work in favor of the profession, as it inhibits reform. Boland explains:

The myth of principles, the technology of standard setting and the myth of adequacy that served as vehicles for the profession now encapsulate it in an immobilizing self-justification.

Stripped to its essential, the auditing profession has nothing to offer without public confidence and trust. Just as public confidence in the beneficence of science and technology has deteriorated, the accounting profession may find its public confidence dissipating. Perhaps, only if the profession can transcend its myth and technology and adopt the more romantic ideal of deserving public trust, will the profession avoid the need for disaster to generate reform.[31]

This is difficult knowing the professions' long history of jealousy guarding the right to define their mistakes and failures and misapplying the whole concept of peer review.

Accounting Working Knowledge: A Misplaced Instrument of Power

Formal accounting knowledge, after being transformed into working knowledge, is used by professional accountants for defining accounting behavior and for establishing and enforcing social sanctions over any deviations from accounting standards. It is a responsibility given to them as an occupational group in what Hughes has called "the *moral division of labor*."[32] Accounting professionals use the working knowledge to define the technique of accounting for financial affairs. In so doing they place themselves in the position of those who do not suffer the consequences of ignorance, mistakes, self-deceptions, and biases, or what Mills has termed *"organized irresponsibility."*[33]

The basis of their power is not the monopoly on accounting working knowledge, but the control of such knowledge. In some cases they use it to further the interests of dominant classes in society or the state. In most cases they present the accounting knowledge as a necessary commodity. Two problems present themselves:

First, mere logic indicates that what is presented generally as "accounting services" does not represent the accounting "care" the client desires. The transformation of formal accounting knowledge into working accounting knowledge has stripped it of those services aimed at helping to promote social welfare. Examples include the cases of social accounting and human resource accounting.

Second, given the monopolization of the working accounting language through the process of licensure, the private market does not offer other choices for the consumer but to secure the services of the CPA. In addition, the principle of caveat emptor, part of the social contract between consumer and producer in a free market economy, does not apply in the case of the accounting profession, as the client does not get to see in advance the type of working accounting knowledge he is buying.[34]

CONCLUSIONS

Accounting knowledge is heading toward a crisis as a result of the problems affecting its production by academic accountants and its use by the accounting profession.

At the hands of academic the formal accounting knowledge is produced along well-specified paradigms governed and controlled by well-established scientific establishments. It is used, however, by the same academics as a tool to punish and dominate, with scholarship losing ground to the need for power. In defending their particular paradigms and persisting in the defense of their restrictive views, the same academics are at risk of creating self-made prisons that may hinder the production of quality accounting knowledge. At the same time in allying themselves with political power and policymaking they risk accelerating the deinstitutionalization and politicization of formal accounting knowledge. Caught in these scientific establishments and self-made prisons, accounting researchers may find themselves working on the same research path, contributing to a perpetual inquiry of the same issues without hope for closure.

At the hands of the profession, the formal accounting knowledge is radically transformed and trivialized to serve the economic interests of clients. the profession finds itself asserting its privilege by providing a mix of technology and myth, which may inhibit reforms. And the profession is interested only in keeping control of the accounting knowledge, and minimizes the consequences of its organized irresponsibility in the provision of accounting services.

NOTES

1. M. Foucault, *Discipline and Punish: The Birth of the Prison* (New York: Vintage Books, 1979), 138.

2. M. Foucault, *The History of Sexuality, Vol. 1: An Introduction* (New York: Vintage Books, 1980).

3. L. A. Coser, *Men of Ideas: A Sociologist's View* (New York: Free Press, 1970), viii.

4. J. A. Shumpeter, *Capitalism, Socialism and Democracy*, 3rd ed. (New York: Harper & Row, Torchbooks, 1950).

5. Norbert Elias, "Scientific Establishments," in *Scientific Establishments and Hierarchies*, ed. N. Elias and H. Martins (Dordrecht, Holland: North-Holland, 1982), 76.

6. Ibid., 31.

7. M. Foucault, *Power/Knowledge: Selected Interview and Other Writings 1972-1977*, ed. C. Gordon (New York: Random House, 1977).

8. C. Edward Arrington and Jere R. Francis, "Letting the Cat Out of the Bag: Deconstruction, Privilege and Accounting Research," *Accounting, Organizations and Society* (January 1989): 1-28.

9. Peter Weingart, "The Scientific Power Elite- The Re-Institutionalization and Politicization of Science," in *Scientific Establishments and Hierarchies*, ed. Elias and Martins, 73.

10. Ibid., 78.

11. D. E. Chubin and T. Connolly, "Research Trails and Science Policies: Local and Extra-local Negotiation of Scientific Work," in *Scientific Establishments and Hierarchies*, ed. Elias and Martins, 293.

12. Ibid., 307.

13. Ibid., 294.

14. Ibid., 303.

15. R. Zussman, *Mechanics of the Middle-Class: Work and Politics Among American Engineers* (Berkeley: University of California Press, 1985).

16. T. J. Johnson, *Professions and Power* (London: Macmillan, 1972).

17. P. D. Montagna, "The Public Accounting Profession: Organization, Ideology, and Social Power," in *The Professions and Their Prospects*, ed. E. Friedson (Beverly Hills, Calif.: Sage, 1973), 135-51.

18. E. Friedson, *Professional Powers* (Chicago: University of Chicago Press, 1986), 222.

19. G. Millerson, *The Qualifying Associations* (London: Routledge & Kegan Paul, 1964).

20. W. E. Moore, *The Professions: Roles and Rules* (London: Macmillan, 1970), 233-44.

21. P. Elliot, *The Sociology of the Professions* (London: Macmillan, 1972), 126-30.

22. T. Parsons, "Professions," in *International Encyclopedia of the Social Sciences* (New York: Macmillan, 1968), 62-71.

23. T. Johnson, "Professions and the Class Structure," in *Industrial Society: Class, Cleavage, and Control* R. Scase, ed. (New York: St. Martin's Press, 1979).

24. M. S. Larson, *The Rise of Professionalism* (Berkeley: University of California Press, 1977).

25. H. Jamous and B. Peliolle, "Changes in the French University Hospital System," in *Professions and Professionalization*, ed. J. A. Jackson (Cambridge: Cambridge University Press, 1970), 63-78.

26. Johnson, "Profession and the Class Structure," 10.

27. Larson, *Rise of Professionalism*, 20.

28. Alan T. Richardson, "Accounting Knowledge and Professional Privilege," *Accounting, Organizational and Society*, June 1988, 381-96.

29. Ibid.

30. Richard J. Boland, Jr., "Myth and Technology in the American Accounting Profession," *Journal of Management Studies*, 919:1 (1982): 105-27.

31. Ibid., 126.

32. F. C. Hughes, *Men and Their Work* (Glencoe, Ill.: Free Press, 1958).

33. C. W. Mills, *Commitment to Welfare* (New York: Pantheon Books, 1968).

34. T. H. Marshall, "The Recent History of Professionalism in Relation to Social Policy," *Canadian Journal of Economics and Political Science*, August 1939, v. 325-34.

REFERENCES

Belkaoui, A. *Public Policy and the Practice and Problems of Accounting*. Westport, Conn.: Greenwood Press, Quorum Books, 1985.

Boland, Richard J., Jr. "Myth and Technology in the American Accounting Profession." *Journal of Management Studies* 19:1 (1982): 105-27.

Chubin, D., and T. Connolly. "Research Trails and Science Policies: Local and Extralocal Negotiation of Scientific Work." In *Scientific Establishments and Hierarchies*, edited by N. Elias and H. Martins. Dordrecht, Holland: North-Holland, 1982.

Coser, L. A. *Men of Ideas: A Sociologist's View* New York: Free Press, 1970.

Elias, Norbert. "Scientific Establishments." In *Scientific Establishments and Hierarchies*, edited by N. Elias and H. Martins. Dordrecht, Holland: North-Holland, 1982, 7-70.

Foucault, M. *The History of Sexuality, Vol. 1: An Introduction*. New York: Vintage Books, 1980.

Friedson, E. *Professional Powers*. Chicago: University of Chicago Press, 1958.

Jamous, H., and B. Peliolle. "Changes in the French University Hospital System." In *Profession and Professionalization*, edited by J. A. Jackson. Cambridge: Cambridge University Press, 1970.

Johnson, T. "Professions and the Class Structure." In *Industrial Society: Class, Cleavage and Control*, edited by R. Scase, New York; St. Martin's Press, 1979.

Johnson, T. J. *Professions and Power*. London: Macmillan, 1972.

Larson, M. S. *The Rise of Professionalism*. Berkeley: University of California Press, 1977.

Marshall, T. H. "The Recent History of Professionalism in Relation to Social Policy." *Canadian Journal of Economics and Political Science* (August 1939): 325-34.

Millerson, G. *The Qualifying Associations*. London: Routledge & Kegan Paul, 1964.

Mills, C. W. *Commitment to Welfare*. New York: Pantheon Books, 1968.

Montagna, P. D. "The Public Accounting Profession: Organization, Ideology, and Social Power." In *The Professions and Their Prospects*, edited by E. Friedson. (Beverly Hills, Calif.: Sage, 1973): 135-51.

Moore, W. W. *The Professions: Roles and Rules*. London: Macmillan, 1970.

Richardson, Alan T. "Accounting Knowledge and Professional Privilege." *Accounting, Organizations and Society* (June 1988): 381-96.

Shumpeter, J. A. *Capitalism, Socialism and Democracy*. 3rd ed. New York: Harper & Row, Torchbooks, 1950.

Watts, R. L., and J. L. Zimmerman. "Towards a Positive Theory of the Determination of Accounting Standards." *The Accounting Review*, (January 1978): 112-34.

___. "The Demand for and Supply of Accounting Theories: The Market for Excuses." *The Accounting Review*, (April 1979): 273-305.

Weingart, P. "The Scientific Power Elite-A Chimera; The Reinstitutionalization and Politicization of Science." In *Scientific Establishments and Hierarchies*, edited by N. Elias and H. Martins. Dordrecht, Holland: North-Holland, 1982, 71-88.

Zussman, R. *Mechanics of the Middle-Class: Work and Politics Among American Engineers*. Berkeley: University of California Press, 1985.

www.ingramcontent.com/pod-product-compliance
Lightning Source LLC
Chambersburg PA
CBHW071257220526
45468CB00001B/172